Contents

Figures and Tables

Figures

Tables

Preface

This was not an easy book to write. It is difficult chronicling the many deficiencies of something you love, and I cannot escape the fact that I do love my country, even though it often frustrates, angers, and disappoints me. I grew up in McLean, Virginia, right outside Washington, D.C., in the years after World War II when the United States was shaping the era into the "American Century." My father and most of our neighbors worked for the federal government in one capacity or another. Our neighborhood, in those days consisting of modest bungalows and Cape Cods, was quintessential patriotic small-town Americana, even though we were only twenty minutes from the Washington Monument.

We celebrated the Fourth of July with a parade down Springvale Avenue with a fire engine leading the way followed by the neighborhood kids riding streamer-festooned bicycles and distinguished civil servants wearing funny hats. The neighbors put loudspeakers in their yards and played Sousa marches. We ended up in the neighborhood "park" for a picnic, speeches by public officials and politicians, and a reading of the preamble to the Declaration of Independence. When I turned thirteen, I was asked to take over the honor of delivering that reading. I can still recite the words from memory, almost a half century later. "We hold these truths to be self-evident, that all men are created equal, that they are endowed by their creator with certain unalienable rights, that among these are life, liberty and the pursuit of happiness. That to secure these rights, governments are instituted among men, deriving their just powers from the consent of the governed." I learned later that the ideas behind this stirring language, composed by Jefferson, were borrowed from the English philosopher John Locke, who in the late seventeenth century elucidated the ideas of natural rights, social responsibility, and popular sovereignty.

Since those days in McLean, I have protested much about our government and its policies, including the wars in Vietnam, Iraq, and elsewhere; the proliferation of nuclear weapons; the destruction of the environment; the neglect of our schools; and the treatment of minorities. But I never gave up on the United States and its ideals, as articulated by Locke and Jefferson and their idealistic successors like Franklin Roosevelt and Martin Luther King Jr. The United States and its democratic system always seemed to present the possibility, at least, of fixing problems, redressing grievances, and making a better world. Over the past decade, however, the United States seemed to have lost ground in almost every conceivable area—political, economic, social, and international—and, even worse, seemed to have lost its bearing in terms of values and principles. Arrogance, belligerence, individualism, materialism, and violence were trumping the values of human rights, equality, participation, community, charity, and cooperation. Unlike before, all this seemed be happening at once and together, as America became weaker internally and less admired and influential on the global scene. A broken political system, barely representative of the population and awash in money, no longer functioned to correct the problems and indeed often made them worse. Lots of prominent people were talking about America as the greatest power in the history of the world, dominating the globe as the sole remaining superpower. But to me and from all the evidence, it seemed America was sinking fast. Most people I talked to, academic colleagues or not, seemed to feel the same—that something was seriously amiss with the country. All around us, from the school and the workplace to the federal government and the global environment, things were falling apart.

Teaching and studying comparative and international politics naturally led me to look at the United States in comparison with other countries and to explore the ways in which other countries and peoples saw us. Through most of the Cold War era, the United States was pretty unbeatable: it had the biggest economy, the most prosperous citizens, the most freedom, the broadest equality, and the most successful and admired political system. It led the world in science, technology, and education. But now, in comparing the United States with other developed countries, we do not look so good. Our reputation around the world, because of both our own failings and our international behavior, has plummeted.

Looming Poverty and Decline

This burden is likely to be substantial because of the very real possibility of large-scale poverty among the retired baby-boomer generation. Even assuming that Social Security will continue to be viable (a risky assumption, as discussed previously), Social Security will not help most people to a comfortable retirement. The average annual Social Security benefit for retired workers is less than $12,000, which is roughly the same as the official poverty line for a two-person household. This figure of $12,000 is less than a third of the median household income in the United States and a third of the average annual earnings of full-time workers. So on average, people moving from full-time jobs into a retirement based only on Social Security will suffer a threefold drop in their standard of living.

To be optimistic, one might expect that most workers would have other retirement savings that would supplement the meager Social Security benefits. But the facts here do not merit much optimism. Half of all workers and a third of baby boomers have zero retirement savings. A survey by the Federal Reserve Board in 2001 found that a typical worker fifty-five to sixty-four years old had only $42,000 in his or her 401(k) and individual retirement accounts, about enough for an annuity payment of $200 a month.[24] This mind-bogglingly small nest egg, combined with Social Security, would together provide an annual income of less than $15,000—still perilously close to the poverty line. Most experts estimate that about a third of the workforce is putting aside enough for a comfortable retirement. That means that two-thirds are not. Probably between a third and a half of baby boomers will experience a severe reduction in their standard of living with retirement, and many will dip below the poverty line. As we will see in a later chapter, the overall poverty rate in the United States is already alarmingly high and has grown sharply in recent years. The problems of financing the huge number of baby boomers in retirement will inflate the overall poverty rate even faster.

The lack of savings is particularly worrisome for those who are about to retire, but the problem in the United States is much more widespread than simply the baby boomers. The household savings rate in the United States has been declining for two decades, is the lowest among all developed countries, and in 2005 reached zero for the first time ever. Americans have never been very good savers, and the household savings rate (defined as the amount saved as a percentage of total disposable income) in the United States has always been considerably lower than that in Europe and Japan. In the early 1990s, for example, the U.S. savings ratio was about 9 percent, compared to about 14 percent in Europe. But at least in those years, there was some household savings. The U.S. rate has dropped steadily since then, falling to 1.8 percent in 2004—the lowest annual rate since 1934 (in the midst of the Depression)—and into negative territory in 2005 and 2006.[25] Instead of savings, Americans are borrowing at record rates. Household debt as a percentage of disposable income is at the highest level in two decades.

Peter Peterson refers to the lack of personal savings as the third, or "triple," deficit along with the budget and trade deficits. This lack of savings is risky and dangerous in personal terms, affecting the future standard of living of profligate citizens, but also problematic in terms of long-term economic health of the country. It is savings that provides the pool of money for investments, and it is investments that generate economic growth and productivity increases.

Compounding the problem of personal debt is the uncertain status of the assets of Americans. For most Americans—and especially older ones—their largest financial asset is their home. But this can be a shaky financial reed, particularly if people have taken out mortgages larger than they can manage or at variable interest rates that can suddenly increase their mortgage payments. Indeed, as became apparent in the summer of 2007, there were millions of people in such a situation as a result of "subprime" lending to home buyers with inadequate assets or incomes. A surge of mortgage defaults that year threatened both the home ownership of the borrowers and the solvency of the banks and mortgage firms that extended the loans. Bankruptcies in the United States were already at record-high levels before the subprime mortgage crisis (more than 1.6 million filed in 2004) and were likely to accelerate in its aftermath. The number of housing foreclosures rose 42 percent from 2005 to 2006, to 1.2 million, and most analysts expected another 1 million to 2 million people to be at risk of losing their homes from the subprime loan crisis.[26] This would only intensify the problems of poverty or near poverty for the baby-boomer generation as it neared and entered retirement.

The lack of savings by Americans is partly caused by the very *encouragement* of debt by those who make money off of lending, which has become an increasingly large piece of the U.S. economy. A shrinking manufacturing sector now accounts for only about 10 percent of total corporate profits, compared to 44 percent of such profits from the financial sector. Author Kevin Phillips refers to this as the "financialization" of the U.S. economy. Banks, mortgage companies, loan agencies, and credit card companies make their money by making loans, and they are constantly seeking new customers and encouraging existing ones to borrow more. This is why American mailboxes are full of credit card offers and why so many Americans carry thousands of dollars in credit card debt at highly inflated interest rates. It also explains why mortgage companies and banks were so willing to extend new credit to customers with shaky credit histories and minimal resources—the subprime mortgage crisis. So the normal inclination of Americans to consume and spend is reinforced by enticing offers of unlimited credit and free spending. Phillips, like Paul Kennedy, sees the debt problem as a harbinger of economic decline. "Historically, top world economic powers have found 'financialization' a sign of late-stage debilitation, marked by excessive debt, great disparity between rich and poor, and unfolding economic decline."[27]

In the Red? Increase Spending and Cut Taxes

Perhaps the most astounding aspect of all this is the lack of concern for and attention to these problems by our policymakers and elected officials and especially our president. Instead of addressing the problem of unprecedented budget deficits, trade deficits, and national and personal debt, Washington simply makes the problem worse by cutting taxes (and thereby federal revenue) and increasing spending. The solution, as almost all economists agree, is the exact opposite on both counts: to cut spending and raise taxes to help reverse the growing tide of deficit spending. It is obvious by now that no remedy will come during the Bush administration, which has become a major source of the problem. The worry is that the hole being dug now is so large that even more cognizant and responsible successors to the presidency will not be able to get the nation out of it.

In the past few years, the major source of increased federal spending has been defense and homeland security. American military spending had declined steadily after the collapse of communism and the end of the Cold War in 1989–1991 until the beginning of the George W. Bush presidency. It accelerated sharply after September 11, jumping from $288 billion in 2000 to $439 billion in 2006, and that figure did not even include supplemental appropriations of at least $50 billion a year for the wars in Iraq and Afghanistan. By that time, U.S. military spending constituted almost half of the world's total military spending. American defense spending was six times larger than that of Russia, which was number two in the world in military spending, and seven times larger than China, which was number three. Russia, China, and the seven "rogue" states (including North Korea and Iran) spend less than one-third of the U.S. total combined.

One could debate about the needs for such extravagant defense spending when there were no significant military powers in a position to confront the United States. But leaving that debate aside, the fact remains that military spending, by far the largest "discretionary" component of the U.S. budget, is a huge strain on the U.S. economy and the primary contributor to the large budget deficits and the growing federal debt. And it brings into sharp relief the observation of Kennedy in *The Rise and Fall of the Great Powers* that great powers in decline "respond by spending more on 'security,' and thereby divert potential resources from 'investment' and compound their long-term dilemma."[28]

Spending more on military security has also meant spending less on virtually all other federal programs, including welfare, education, and transportation—all of which were scheduled for cutbacks in the president's proposed budget for 2006. Yet, broadly considered, these areas are also components of America's national security, and the problems associated with them—poverty, inequality, illiteracy, infrastructure, and the environment—were also in dire need of attention and resources. But the single-minded focus on military security in the aftermath of September 11 marginalized these issues, and they continued to deteriorate.

These issues of societal deterioration became grimly apparent in 2005 with the federal government's virtual impotence in the face of the Hurricane Katrina disaster in Louisiana and Mississippi. Washington pledged hundreds of billions of dollars to help rebuild the coastal cities. But the federal government was already broke, so any such funds would simply entail more debt and more borrowing (much of it from abroad). Katrina had laid bare the huge scale of poverty and inequality in just one city, though the problem was much more widespread than that. And despite government promises, the task of restoring order, health, and stability to New Orleans seemed beyond the reach of a weak and ineffectual government.

The collapse of the levees in New Orleans, at a cost of more than a thousand lives, called attention to an even more widespread problem across the United States: the aging of its infrastructure. A 2005 report by the American Society of Civil Engineers (ASCE) estimated that some 74,000 bridges in the country were "structurally deficient." This report was largely ignored until one of them, a highly traveled forty-year-old highway bridge in Minneapolis, collapsed in August 2007, dropping fifty cars into the abyss and killing thirteen people. The engineers estimated that it would require $9.4 billion a year for twenty years to fix all the deficient bridges. Congress authorized $1 billion—once. Other reports came to light, including an ASCE grade of D on U.S. dams, with more than 3,500 rated as "unsafe."[29] American's aging roads and sewers, many built just after World War II, were also falling apart. Overall, the ASCE estimated that the government would have to spend $1.6 trillion over five years to repair infrastructure. But there was little chance that anything near this would be forthcoming. As one expert opined on the pages of the *New York Times*, "Americans are easily persuaded to spend hundreds of billions of dollars combating debatable terrorist threats from outside the United States, while failing to notice that inside the country, the infrastructure is crumbling. True, outside forces from time to time topple established regimes, but usually not before their insides have started to rot."[30]

Most economists suggest and common sense would dictate that the solution to these huge annual budget deficits and the pressing needs presented by September 11, Katrina, and Social Security would be an increase in federal revenue and that the only real source for such revenue is personal and corporate taxes. As we saw earlier, the staff of the IMF recommended in 2004 a substantial, immediate, and permanent hike in the federal income tax. Pete Peterson says flatly that the deficits are so large that "Americans cannot tax their way out of" them, figuring that payroll taxes would have to increase by 50 percent by 2020 and 200 to 350 percent by 2040.[31]

Such sizable tax increases are surely politically impossible. But rather than moving to ameliorate these problems with even modest tax increases, the George W. Bush administration has gone in precisely the opposite direction, with some of the largest tax cuts in American history. Tax cuts passed by Congress in 2001 and 2003 would cost about $1.7 trillion over ten years (2001–2010), and that is assuming that the "sunset" provisions on some of them remain in place. President Bush and the Republican leaders of Congress, however, have been lobbying hard to eliminate those sunsets so that the tax cuts remain permanent. If that is the case—and also adding in the interest payments on the new debt from these lost revenues—the ten-year cost of the tax cuts exceeds $2.6 trillion.[32]

Virtually all of this amount will simply be added to the already ballooning federal debt. The politicians who defend these tax cuts argue that the cost will be made up for by increased consumer spending and economic growth, which will in turn generate more tax revenue. But there is virtually no historical or economic analysis that supports this assumption. The last major tax cuts, during the Reagan administration, may have contributed some to economic growth, but those years also saw a tripling of the national debt due mostly (like under the present Bush administration) to increased defense spending combined with reduced tax revenue. A recent study by the Congressional Budget Office (headed up by a conservative economist who had worked in the Bush White House) estimated that cuts in personal taxes would generate enough economic growth to replace only between 22 and 32 percent of the lost revenue even under the most optimistic assumptions. Under less favorable conditions, none of the losses would be recouped through economic growth.[33] Even Federal Reserve Chairman Ben Bernanke admits that tax cuts "usually do not pay for themselves."[34] As Peterson puts it, the Bush tax cuts "were an obligation driven by faith, not a policy guided by evidence."[35]

Binge Spending and Economic Decline

These problems of overspending and undersaving—essentially of national bankruptcy—closely fit Kennedy's model of the decline of great powers, although the scale of national indebtedness in the United States far surpasses that of any previous great power in decline. It is tempting to place the blame for these problems on the doorstep of the Bush White House, and indeed the Bush administration has contributed more to the problem than any in history. But the problems are more long standing, more widespread, and more deep seated than that. Both the American government and American citizens have been overspending—living beyond their means—for most of the past twenty-five years.

Most of this spending has been for short-term advantage or simply for consumer goods that would be considered luxuries almost everywhere else in the world: houses, cars, televisions, appliances, and so on. Perhaps such consumption, per se, would not be a problem except that Americans have not been producing enough to merit such expenditures—thus the high levels of debt in all its manifestations. At the government level, spending is increasingly devoted to defense, which also may have short-term benefit but does little to promote domestic economic or social health and stability. The U.S. military may be the strongest in the world, but by almost any measure of social, economic, or cultural health, the United States has become weaker and weaker and less and less competitive internationally.

For most of the postwar period, the "American Century," the United States was a world leader and widely admired throughout the world on almost every count. The U.S. model of democratic institutions and processes was emulated or envied almost everywhere. The American economic system and standard of living were also coveted, and the country was a magnet for people desiring a better life from all corners of the globe. America was the land of opportunity and a melting pot of disparate peoples and cultures. But most of those assets and much of that reputation have eroded, especially since the turn of the new century. American influence in the world is now mostly material and military. Where the United States once drove the world economy through economic growth, invention, and productivity, now it is doing so almost entirely by consumption but at levels it cannot pay for. And where before the military was seen by some as an instrument to protect and spread democracy, now it is widely viewed as a threat to world peace and stability. Americans often do not understand why foreigners dislike them, but their image of Americans as materialistic, arrogant, and violent is difficult to rebut.

Increasingly, foreigners have been subsidizing the American binge, but that certainly cannot continue, just as large-scale deficit spending cannot continue forever. The ballooning national debt, the increasing burden of interest payments on that debt, and the widening trade deficit will soon lead to rising interest rates, a declining stock market, a weakening dollar, and a slowing economy. This will discourage foreigners (both banks and governments) from further investments in the U.S. dollar, the U.S. debt, and the U.S. economy, which will be another body blow to economic health. Indeed, this trend is already evident, with foreign investors dumping dollars, the U.S. currency hitting a record low against the euro (in late 2007), and foreign banks and governments beginning to shift their currency holdings out of the greenback. A Chinese central bank official declared that the dollar was "losing its status as the world currency."[36]

A serious recession, perhaps even a depression, is the probable outcome. Such a recession will actually be necessary, however, for the long-term viability of the American economy. It will cause unemployment in the short run and declining wages and incomes in the long run, but this is inevitable if balance is to be restored. The U.S. economy will shrink, as will the country's standard of living. This will simply reflect the actual economic situation in the United States, which for so many years has been obscured by mortgaging the future with deficits and debt. The United States will no longer be the dominant economic power in the world, and with economic decline will come military, diplomatic, and political decline. As has become evident since September 11 and the Iraq War, this process is already well under way.

Notes

1. Paul Kennedy, *The Rise and Fall of the Great Powers* (New York: Random House, 1987), xvi.

2. The concept of "soft power" is developed by Joseph Nye Jr. in *The Paradox of American Power* (New York: Oxford University Press, 2002).

3. Kennedy, *The Rise and Fall of the Great Powers*, xvi and xxiii.

4. Kennedy, *The Rise and Fall of the Great Powers*, 515.

5. Kennedy, *The Rise and Fall of the Great Powers*, 526 (italics in original).

6. Joseph S. Nye, *Soft Power: The Means to Success in World Politics* (New York: Public Affairs, 2004), and *Bound to Lead: The Changing Nature of American Power* (New York: Basic Books, 1990).

7. Kennedy, *The Rise and Fall of the Great Powers*, 527.

8. Cited in Peter Peterson, *Running on Empty* (New York: Picador, 2005), xliii.

9. Peterson, *Running on Empty*, 30.

10. Peterson, *Running on Empty*, 31.

11. Kevin Yao and Benjamin Kang Lim, "Senior China Official Urges Cut in US Debt Holding," Reuters, April 4, 2006.

12. Martin Muhleisen and Christopher Towe, eds., *U.S. Fiscal Policies and Priorities for Long-Run Sustainability*, International Monetary Fund, 2004, http://www.imf .org.

13. Ben Stein, "Note to the New Treasury Secretary: It's Time to Raise Taxes," *New York Times*, June 25, 2006, B3.

14. *New York Times*, October 18, 2007, C3.

15. The trade deficit, the difference between what is exported and what is imported, is the largest component of the "current account deficit," which also includes the balance of international financial transactions.

16. U.S. Census Bureau data at http://www.census.gov/foreign-trade/balance.

17. *Indianapolis Star*, April 10, 2006, A8.

18. Edmund Andrews, "Trade Deficit Hits Record, Threatening U.S. Growth," *New York Times*, December 15, 2005, C3.

19. Cited by Lee Hamilton in the *Indianapolis Star*.

20. Much of this discussion and these data are drawn from Peter Peterson's sensible and clear description of the problem in his *Running on Empty*, esp. 31–35. The "Financial Report of the United States Government" for 2006 estimates that the shortfall for Social Security, Medicare, and other benefit programs will be more like $45 trillion. Associated Press story in *Indianapolis Star*, December 18, 2007.

21. Cited in Peterson, *Running on Empty*, 33.

22. Peterson sees the only real solution to the problem as cutting some of the eligibility and benefits of the Social Security and Medicare programs, but this is a very hard sell politically. And in this respect, as in so many others, the United States has been moving in the opposite direction, with the recent congressional approval of the Medicare drug benefits program, which is also largely unfunded.

23. "$45 Trillion Shortfall in Benefits Projected," Associated Press story in *Indianapolis Star*, December 18, 2007.

24. Eduardo Porter, "Step by Step," *New York Times*, April 12, 2005, E1. A 2007 study of all baby boomers showed that their average savings and investments were about $50,000.

25. "Personal Savings Drop to 74-Year Low," Associated Press story on MSNBC .com, February 1, 2007.

26. Bob Ivry, "Foreclosures May Hit 1.5 Million in U.S. Housing Bust," March 12, 2007, http://www.bloomberg.com.

27. Kevin Phillips, *American Theocracy: The Peril and Politics of Radical Religion, Oil and Borrowed Money in the 21st Century* (New York: Viking, 2006), 268.

28. Kennedy, *The Rise and Fall of the Great Powers*, xxiii.

29. Jacques Leslie, "Before the Flood," *New York Times*, January 22, 2007, A23.

30. Jacques Leslie (author of *Deep Water: The Epic Struggle over Dams, Displaced People and the Environment*), "Before the Flood," *New York Times*, January 22, 2007, A23.

31. Peterson, *Running on Empty*, xxxiv.

32. See the model of the Institute for Taxation and Monetary Policy at http://www.ctj.org/pdf/gwbdata.pdf.

33. Sebastian Mallaby, "Tax Cuts Don't Raise Revenue," *Hartford Courant*, June 21, 2006.

34. "Fed Chief Warns That Entitlement Growth Could Harm Economy," *New York Times*, November 9, 2007, C1.

35. Peterson, *Running on Empty*, xlii.

36. "Markets and Dollar Sink as U.S. Slowdown Grows," *New York Times*, November 8, 2007, A26.

~

CHAPTER TWO

The End of Affluence and Equality

I see one-third of a nation ill-housed, ill-clad, and ill-nourished. The test of our progress is not whether we add more to the abundance of those who have much; it is whether we provide enough for those who have too little.

—Franklin Delano Roosevelt, 1937

At the beginning of the "American Century" in 1941, the United States was committed to both a domestic and a world order based on freedom from want and fear. These principles appear in Henry Luce's "American Century" article as well as important declarations by President Franklin Roosevelt in the same year, and they were restated and articulated by every postwar president. The American commitment to freedom, equality, and prosperity, even more than the country's achievements in those areas, was a principal component of America's appeal across the globe and its unparalleled power and influence in the twentieth century. But by the beginning of the twenty-first century, U.S. rhetoric was no longer matched by reality either at home or abroad. Rising levels of both poverty and inequality in the United States put the country in an unfavorable light in comparison with other developed countries and even in comparison with some Third World countries. The failure of the United States to provide for its own people undermined both its efforts and its reputation for addressing these problems globally and further eroded the country's global image.

Spreading the U.S. Dream

Luce's February 1941 essay was an appeal for American engagement in the war and the world and could be criticized for being both arrogant and imperialist. But central to the piece was an altruism that called for the United States to become "the Good Samaritan of the entire world" and to produce and dispatch "to the four quarters of the globe" enough food for every hungry person. The essay is also chock full of references to America's ideals, including freedom, equality of opportunity, cooperation, justice, and charity.

Luce's essay was influential, but of course he did not set the course of American foreign and domestic policy. The same year as "The American Century" appeared in *Life*, however, President Roosevelt (whom, incidentally, Luce detested) enunciated many of the same ideas in two important documents: the "Four Freedoms" speech and the Atlantic Charter. In a January 1941 address to Congress (a month before the appearance of Luce's essay), in what was mainly an appeal for aid to Britain and faster production of armaments, Roosevelt envisioned "a world founded on four essential human freedoms": freedom of speech, freedom of religion, freedom from want, and freedom from fear. All of these, he argued, should be accorded to people "everywhere in the world." In this speech, Roosevelt did not lay out any specific programs or policies to accomplish these goals, but he did address what he believed were "the basic things expected by our people of their political and economic systems." These are, he said, "simple":

- Equality of opportunity for youth and for others
- Jobs for those who can work
- Security for those who need it
- The ending of special privilege for the few
- The preservation of civil liberties for all
- The enjoyment of the fruits of scientific progress in a wider and constantly rising standard of living

This was an ambitious list and constituted the essence of Roosevelt's New Deal, which had helped bring the country out of the Great Depression and along the way brought Social Security, protection for workers and labor unions, public assistance for the poor and unemployed, and a vastly increased role for the federal government.

The summer following his Four Freedoms speech, President Roosevelt met for the first time with Britain's Prime Minister Winston Churchill off the coast of Newfoundland. Their joint declaration, dubbed the Atlantic Charter, laid out the goals of the war against fascism. It also reflected Roosevelt's four freedoms, calling for peace, self-determination, and freedom from fear and want, which should be facilitated by economic collaboration among governments to secure, "for all, improved labor standards, economic advancement and social security." These were noble and lofty ambitions, much as Roosevelt's domestic program was. They helped distinguish U.S. global objectives as different from normal great power politics in that they were not based entirely on self-interest. These aspirations, in combination with the evident wealth and might of the United States at the conclusion of the world war, set the country on course to dominate the world in the second half of the twentieth century.

The End of the American Dream

For most of the postwar period, the United States was an economic powerhouse, with steady growth, rising productivity, and a steadily increasing standard of living for most Americans. But much of that began to change in the last decade of the American Century and, given the structural economic problems discussed in chapter 1, seems likely to deteriorate even further in the first decades of the twenty-first century. The problems have affected virtually all Americans (except for the very rich) but have hit the poor especially hard.

While the average American and the average American household experienced almost continuous increases in real wages and incomes ("real" meaning adjusted for inflation) from the 1950s forward, incomes stagnated or declined in the first five years of the new century. According to U.S. Census Bureau data, for example, median "real" household incomes actually declined steadily from 1999 to 2004. They picked up slightly in the next two years, but by 2006, median incomes were still below the 1999 levels.[1] Per capita income in the United States—a broad indicator of a country's standard of living—also declined each year after 2000. By some measures, the erosion in the standard of living for average workers has been much longer. Real wages for nonfarm workers (the vast majority of Americans), for example, reached a peak in 1972, declined steadily for a decade after that, and have stagnated since the mid-1980s.[2]

It could be that the declines of the past five years are simply short-term blips. Indeed, in the face of long-term increases in wages, incomes, and the standard of living, there have been other short-term reversals in American history. But never before in the postwar period has a continuous decline in real incomes or per capita income lasted more than two or three years. After

2000, the decline persisted for at least four years. And given the unprece-dented scale of government, trade, and personal debt in the United States—far surpassing that of previous recessions in the country—it seems likely that the decline will continue for many more years. The steadily rising tide of American prosperity has already begun to ebb.

For the poor in the United States, the problems are much more long standing. Even using the official definition of poverty (used by the U.S. Census Bureau), there were more than 36 million people living below the poverty level in 2006. This is an astonishingly high number—comparable to the population of a medium-sized country—for one of the most affluent countries in the world, but the percentage of poor people in the United States (12.3 percent of the total population in 2006) has barely changed since the late 1960s. As one might expect from the decline in the overall standard of living in the years since 2000, both the number and the percentage of the poor have also increased in those years.[3]

These census figures conceal the true extent of poverty in the United States in several telling respects. The official poverty line (about $15,000 for a family of three) significantly understates the amount of money needed to maintain a minimally sufficient standard of living. As one disillusioned U.S. immigrant points out (in his book *Discovering America As It Is*), "as too many people in America know too well, you can't pay for food, shelter and other basic necessities here for a family of three on $13,650 a year" (the official poverty line at the time).[4] Academic studies confirm this sentiment. Both estimates of low-income family budgets and public opinion surveys suggest that a family needs an income of about 150 percent of the official poverty line just to buy minimally sufficient goods (e.g., food and housing) and services (e.g., education and health care) and to pay taxes. Using that baseline for poverty, the number of full-time workers who live in poverty is actually two times higher than the official estimates of the Census Bureau.[5]

At least part of the increase in poverty is due to the stagnation in the minimum wage, which until 2007 had remained at $5.15 an hour for a decade. A person working full time at the minimum wage earned only $10,700 a year, well below the poverty line. In 1968, when the minimum wage was its highest in real terms, the annual wages in today's dollars was about $18,000. In 2006, the minimum wage was only a third of the average hourly wage (for all workers), the lowest such percentage since 1949.[6] This translated into real day-to-day problems for minimum-wage workers. Barbara Ehrenreich, a writer and reporter who tried to work and live on minimum-wage jobs, documented in *Nickel and Dimed* that she (and her coworkers) could simply not make ends meet on such a wage. And the *New York Times* recently reported that for the first time, a full-time minimum-wage worker cannot afford a one-bedroom apartment anywhere in America.[7] A lot of people are trying to manage on the minimum wage—an estimated 7.3 million people, constituting almost 6 percent of the workforce.

Poverty in the United States becomes even more glaring and egregious when considered in comparison to other countries. Among the nineteen rich industrialized countries that belong to the Organization for Economic Cooperation and Development (OECD), the United States has, by far, the highest overall poverty rate. And even among a broader group of twenty-five countries, the only country with a higher poverty rate than the United States is Mexico. The U.S. poverty rate (at 17 percent of the workforce) is about twice that of the OECD average.[8] Furthermore, the incidence of poverty in the United States is both deeper and more persistent than in other countries. Among OECD countries, the United States had a much higher share than any other country of people who were poor continuously over three years. The United States also had the highest rate (14.5 percent) of "permanent poverty" of all OECD countries.[9] So despite the enduring myth of Horatio Alger, the possibilities of moving out of poverty are more limited in the United States than in any of the other rich and developed countries in the world.

Despite many complaints in the United States about government spending on the poor (leading to a virtual abandonment of the federal welfare programs in 1996), government in the United States has been much less effective than other developed countries in reducing the ranks of the poor. A comparative study in the 1990s found that overall poverty rates in the United States "*before* government programs" was actually about the average of fifteen other developed countries. But the poverty rate "*after* government programs" (e.g., cash transfers, food stamps, housing allowances, and so on) was far higher in the United States (19 percent in 1994) than in any other country and more than twice the overall average for all sixteen countries. The United States was able to achieve only a 28 percent reduction in poverty with government programs; the other countries averaged a greater than 63 percent reduction in poverty with such programs.[10]

Perhaps the most disturbing and disgraceful aspect of poverty in the United States is the extent to which it affects children. At least one in five American children live in poverty and about half of those in "extreme" poverty—in households earning less than $8,000 a year. A UNICEF study published in 2005 found that the United States had by far the highest child poverty rate (22 percent) among rich countries and was second only to Mexico among all OECD countries.[11] The lowest child poverty rates were in the

Scandinavian countries, where only about 3 percent of children were poor. As with overall poverty, childhood poverty was more persistent and enduring in the United States than elsewhere. In an earlier version of its report card on childhood poverty, UNICEF concluded that "American children are less likely to move out of the bottom of the income distribution than children elsewhere, something which challenges common perceptions about mobility and opportunity in the US."[12] As we will see in later chapters, childhood poverty contributes to a host of other problems in the United States, including illiteracy, poor health, and violence.

Fundamentally, though, the depth and persistence of overall poverty and childhood poverty in the United States belies the goals and ideology of the United States, expressed by people as different in their political views as Henry Luce and Franklin Roosevelt. Far from being a model of wealth and development in the world, the United States falls far behind other developed countries in providing a decent standard of living for its people. The country's image and reputation as the "beacon on the hill" and a refuge for the dispossessed can no longer be deserved in the face of its own poor record. If a nation can be judged by the same standards as individuals, in caring for "the least among us," then the United States must be judged as a failure.

The Rich–Poor Chasm

The growth in poverty in the United States has been accompanied by even sharper growth in the wealth of the very rich, causing huge increases in income and wealth inequality, to the highest levels in more than sixty years. As with poverty levels, economic inequality in the United States is far higher than in other developed countries. Again, for a country committed to equality (or at least equality of opportunity), fairness, and justice, it is difficult to see how the United States could any longer be considered exemplary in this respect, and it contributes to the deteriorating reputation of the United States around the globe.

There are many ways to measure financial inequality in a population, and the statistic one uses depends in part on what groups one is comparing. Probably the most intuitive method, though, is to compare the average incomes of the poorest segment of the population with the average incomes of the richest segment. The ratio of these two numbers provides an index of the "gap" between rich and poor. Figure 2.1 shows such data, calculated by the U.S. Census Bureau, for average household incomes received by each fifth of the population, from the poorest ("lowest") fifth to the richest ("highest") and also including the highest 5 percent.

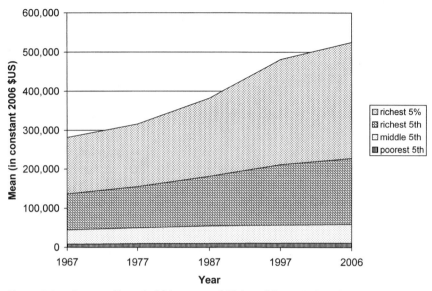

Figure 2.1.   Average Household Incomes of Rich and Poor, 1967–2006
Source: U.S. Census Bureau data at http://www.census.gov/hhes/www/income/histinc/h06ar.html.

The first thing to notice about this figure is the flatness of the bottom segment—the average inflation-adjusted incomes of the poorest fifth of the population. The real incomes of this group have actually declined since 1999 and are barely higher now than in 1978. So over that quarter century, there was virtually no gain in the incomes and standard of living of the poorest fifth of the population. Compare this to the progress of the richest fifth of the population and the richest 5 percent. Since 1990, the average real incomes of the top fifth has grown from about $130,00 to more than $168,000—an increase of almost 30 percent at a time when the poorest segment actually lost ground and even middle-income households (the middle fifth) grew hardly at all. The wealthiest 5 percent made even more rapid gains during this period. It is these opposite patterns—declining incomes for the poor and increasing incomes for the wealthy—that have contributed to the sharp increase in income inequality in the past fifteen years and especially in the past five years.

From 1967 to 2006, the ratio of the top fifth to the bottom fifth has grown from 11.1 to 14.8 (meaning that, in 2006, the richest fifth on average earned almost fifteen times what the poorest fifth earned). The ratio of the top 5 percent to the lowest fifth rose from 17.6 to 26.2. These growing disparities have raised concerns even on the business pages of major newspapers. Anna Bernasek of the *New York Times* observes that "inequality has always been part of the American economy, but the gap between the rich and the poor has recently been widening at an alarming rate. Today, more than 40 percent of total income is going to the wealthiest 10 percent, their biggest share of the nation's pie in at least 65 years."[13] Her article addresses not the social and political repercussions of these changes, which are widely discussed and debated elsewhere, but rather the economic effects, which have received little attention. She points to research, for example, that shows inequality leading to health problems, corruption, and lower productivity. But the bigger problems, of course, are the human, social, and moral dimensions of American inequality, and this too has hurt America's reputation and standing in the world.

Another measure of income inequality is the Gini index, which, unlike the ratios of top to bottom that we used earlier, takes into account inequality throughout the income distribution. It is therefore a broader measure of inequality and as a single number is also useful to describe trends over time and to compare different countries. The Gini index ranges from 0 to 1, with 0 meaning complete equality—everyone has the same income—and 1 representing complete inequality—all income would belong to one individual. In the United States, the Gini index of income inequality for families stood at about .37 in the 1940s, dipped down to about .35 in the early 1970s, and began a steady rise after that, reaching new record highs in the 1980s and topping out at .44 in 2004—representing the greatest income inequality since World War II.[14] As one might expect, the United States compares unfavorably with other developed countries in terms of inequality. The United States has the highest Gini index—the greatest inequality—of any advanced industrialized country, and when compared to twenty-seven countries in the OECD, only Mexico, Turkey, and Poland have Gini indexes higher than that of the United States (see figure 2.2).

The growth of inequality in the United States is particularly evident at the extremes and particularly at the top: the very rich have gotten richer at a much faster rate than everyone else. This is evident from figure 2.1, which shows incomes of the richest 5 percent of the population growing the fastest of any other group in recent years. But this phenomenon is even more true among the "superrich" and in particular of corporate chief executive officers (CEOs). In the 1950s, big-company CEOs earned about fifty times the pay of an average worker. Even then, that ratio was very high compared to other countries. But since then, CEO pay in the United States has skyrocketed in comparison to average salaries. By 1990, average CEO pay was about 100 times the average worker's salary, and by 2000, it was more than 500 times that of the average worker.[15] Former Chrysler CEO Lee Iacocca once said

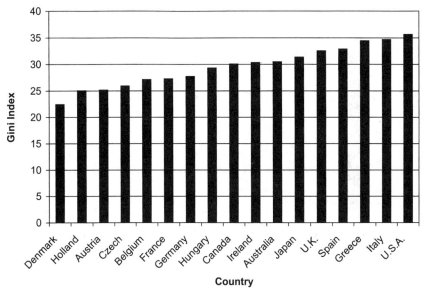

Figure 2.2. Income Inequality in OECD Countries

Note: Coefficients multiplied by 100. Most recent year is 2000 for most countries.

Source: Michael Forster and Marco Mira d'Ercole, *Income Distribution and Poverty in OECD Countries in the Second Half of the 1990s,* OECD Working Paper no. 22, online at http://www.oecd.org/dataoecd/48/9/34483698.pdf.

that no executive was worth $1 million.[16] But in 2006, the average compensation for CEOs at 150 "big public companies" was more than $12 million. Occidental Petroleum's Ray Irani topped the list with an annual take of $52 million.[17]

Americans seem to have accepted as legitimate these grossly inflated benefit packages for corporate executives, but they are far out of line with those in other developed capitalist countries. In 2004, the *New York Times* reported comparative ratios of CEO pay to employee averages. In Japan, CEOs earned about ten times that of the average employee. In Germany the ratio was 11 to 1, in the United Kingdom 25 to 1, and in the United States 531 to 1 (see figure 2.3).[18] It is difficult to see how American companies can justify these huge executive compensations when these other countries, with much smaller CEO pay, have generally managed faster economic growth, greater productivity increases, and greater gains in their stock markets.

In this book, we are more interested in the *consequences* of poverty and inequality than the *causes*, but even so it is worth considering what has accounted for the dramatic rise in both poverty and inequality in the United States in recent years. As we have seen, by international standards, the

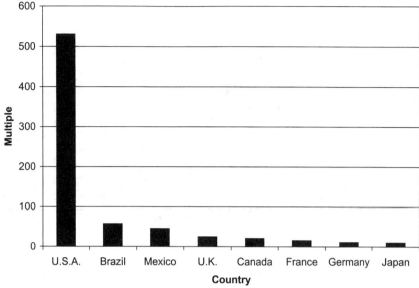

Figure 2.3.   CEO Pay as Multiple of Average Worker Pay
Source: *New York Times*, November 25, 2004.

United States has had high levels of both poverty and inequality for at least the past two decades. But in the past decade, both have soared to unprecedented levels, both in comparison to past U.S. history and in comparison to other wealthy countries.

The rapid rise in the ranks of the poor is due to a number of factors, including globalization and the outsourcing of American jobs, the elimination of the federal welfare system, and the stagnation of the federal minimum wage. The biggest transformation of the American economy in the past generation has been from manufacturing to service industries. Jobs in manufacturing, which are generally well paid, declined from 28 percent of all jobs in 1970 to only 12 percent of all jobs in 2001. Some of this decline was due to automation—replacing workers with machines—but much of it was due to the increased competitiveness of foreign manufacturing (e.g., in automobiles), driving American companies out of business or to reduced operations. The declining number of high-paid workers in manufacturing was accompanied by increased employment in the low-paid service sector, contributing both to the overall stagnation of real wages and to an increase in the number of people below the poverty line. In more recent years, the downward pressure on wages has begun to affect even the service sector, as high-tech U.S. companies have shifted operations (e.g., telephone call centers) to countries (like India) with much lower wages. The corporation has become increasingly flexible, mobile, and multinational, enabling it to follow cheap labor, while the people who make up "labor" have remained country bound and the losers in globalization. These processes have affected all workers in the United States, including the middle class, but the biggest impact has been on the already marginal workers who have increasingly been driven into unemployment or poverty.

In the face of these global and economic forces appeared a major legislative reform that made the plight of the poor even more precarious: the Personal Responsibility and Work Opportunity Act, approved by a Republican Congress and signed into law by a Democratic president, Bill Clinton, in 1996. This bill, which was meant to "end welfare as we know it," essentially ended the federal government's role in providing public assistance to the poor. Instead, the federal government would provide "block grants" to the states (under a program called Temporary Assistance for Needy Families [TANF]) that would then administer antipoverty programs according to their own criteria. But federal guidelines limited state welfare payments to a maximum of five years for any recipient and required recipients to work after two years of assistance.

It should be kept in mind that federal welfare programs were already insubstantial and largely ineffective even before the 1996 welfare reform. In the early 1990s, for example, federal spending on assistance for the poor totaled about $50 billion a year,[19] which was less than 5 percent of the federal budget and less than 7 percent of all federal spending on "entitlements."[20] The average welfare grant in 1993 was less than $5,000 a year, which was only about a third of the federal poverty level for a family of three. Even with food stamps added in, a family receiving benefits under Aid to Families with Dependent Children received benefits that were less than half the poverty line. And the combination of welfare, food stamps, and housing subsidies was able to raise above the poverty line only about one in five welfare families.[21] In comparison with other developed countries, the United States spent far less and achieved much less success in reducing poverty. Government spending helped reduce overall poverty by only 29 percent in the United States compared to an average of 63 percent in other OECD countries.[22]

The impact of the 1996 welfare reform on poverty is hard to measure and uncertain, but it seems clear that the huge decreases in federal welfare spending have not been matched by corresponding reductions in poverty. As one recent study found, "monumental reductions in the rate of public assistance to households have been matched by only incremental improvements in rates of poverty . . . and child well being."[23] The national poverty rate declined a bit until 2000 but then increased steadily in the years after that. In the early years of the welfare reform program, up to half of all families leaving welfare were not able to find jobs. Many of those who did find jobs were part time or minimum wage and earning less than they received on public assistance. Under the new TANF program, many states required those receiving public assistance to work in "workfare" jobs that often paid much less than the minimum wage. In New York City, for example, at the same time that the city was laying off full-time employees, it was hiring workfare workers (sometimes into the very same jobs) at a fraction of the pay of city employees and without benefits.[24] Another consequence of the reduction in welfare rolls nationally was that about a million people would be added to the ranks of job seekers, mostly at the bottom of the pay scale, putting downward pressure on wages. This also increased the competition for minimum-wage jobs, making it easier for federal lawmakers to delay increases in the federal minimum wage.

It is reasonable to wonder why it is that falling wages, declines in living standards, increasing poverty, and growing inequality have not generated more political protest in the United States or at least more political debate. In 1995, the economist Lester Thurow speculated that there could eventually be serious political problems. "No one has ever tried survival-of-the-fittest capitalism for any extended period in a modern democracy," he wrote in the *New York Times Magazine*, "so we don't know how far rising inequality and falling real wages can go before something snaps."[25] Thurow offers an answer to his own question in "the extreme American belief in individuality."[26] When things are going well, Americans attribute it to their own personal achievements, and when things are going badly, they assume that they themselves (or the other victims) are to blame. Americans tend not to blame the system. Of course, American individualism is a central element of the national self-image and a source of much national pride. It also sets the United States off, for better or worse, from most other countries and has become a component of American "exceptionalism." Cross-national public opinion surveys show that Americans are much more likely than people in other countries to believe that poverty and wealth are due more to individual achievements or shortcomings than to problems with the system. And they are much less likely than people in other countries to favor the government guaranteeing a minimum standard of living or a job for everyone who wants one.[27]

But there is a less benevolent side to this American worldview: it can appear to be, and take the form of, coldheartedness. Americans seem less concerned about poverty and inequality than people in other rich countries and are less inclined to take action to rectify those problems. Indeed, in international surveys on such issues, American attitudes are wildly different from those in other countries. In a 1991 survey of thirteen countries, when respondents were asked whether "the government should guarantee everyone a minimum standard of living," 56 percent of Americans strongly or somewhat agreed. But in every other country in the study, at least 75 percent agreed, and in some countries almost everyone did.[28] Another study by Gallup in the same year found 50 to 60 percent of Europeans agreeing that the government should "take care of very poor people who can't take care of themselves." Less than a quarter of Americans agreed with that statement. These American attitudes help explain a lot of things about poverty and inequality: why it exists in the first place, why there is neither protest nor political action to redress them, and why people in other countries take a dim view of the American profession to value fairness, compassion, and justice.

Converging on Insolvency

It is possible, of course, that these problems of poverty, inequality, and stagnant living standards could ameliorate over time either by government action or by a rising tide of affluence. After all, most of the economic problems we have addressed both in this chapter and in the previous one have been faced by the United States before and have been overcome. Debt, incomes, poverty, and inequality all rise and fall over time, so perhaps they will improve over time. At the beginning of the twenty-first century, though, the nexus of these problems is bigger and less tractable than ever before. The federal debt, the budget deficits, the trade deficits, the poverty rates, and the level of inequality are all simultaneously at or near record levels in U.S. history. The federal government is bankrupt so is hardly in a position to make the large investments necessary to alleviate poverty. The national debt (and the interest on that debt) is a ticking time bomb that will increasingly eviscerate the national economy. And the incipient retirement of the baby boomers, without their own savings and depending on the "unfunded liabilities" of Social Security and Medicare, is likely to swell the ranks of the poor. It does not seem that America's economic and social problems can be solved.

Despite the American commitment to and reputation for affluence, fairness, and opportunity, the United States is hardly a role model on these dimensions any longer. The standard of living for most Americans has stagnated in the past generation, while levels of both poverty and inequality have increased sharply. In comparison to both the American past and other developed countries, the contemporary United States fares badly. Many other countries have higher standards of living, lower levels of poverty, and less egregious inequality. And some of these, especially if you consider the amalgam of countries in the European Union, are also surpassing the United States even in overall economic success, size, and clout. So both in terms of its domestic fiber and its economic prestige and influence worldwide, the United States is already on the decline as the world's most important great power.

Some influential writers take for granted America's global primacy but believe that the country risks losing influence because of its hubris and unilateralism. Harvard's Stephen Walt, for example, in his book *Taming American Power*, puts it this way: "If we want the rest of the world to welcome U.S. primacy, therefore, we must convince them that American power is not something to be tamed, but rather something that will be used judiciously and for the broader benefit of mankind."[29] This language and sentiment is much the same as that of Henry Luce in a different era. But Walt's assertion betrays the very attitude that is part of the American problem and reflects a fundamental misunderstanding of the U.S. situation and the way the country is perceived in the rest of the world. First of all (as Walt himself reveals in his chapter on the "roots of resentment"), few people in the rest of the world "welcome U.S. primacy." People in other countries increasingly resent the United States precisely because this country is viewed as being motivated primarily by narrow (and largely material) self-interest in its foreign policy. And it is easy to see why foreigners are skeptical of the American commitment to the "broader benefit of mankind" when it evades that responsibility even at home on the one hand and flouts international law and multilateral institutions on the other. These issues are addressed in subsequent chapters.

Notes

1. http://www.census.gov/hhes/www/income/histinc/h06ar.html.

2. U.S. Bureau of Labor Statistics data reported by the Institute for Labor Research at http://www.laborresearch.org.

3. U.S. Census Bureau, "Historical Poverty Tables," at http://www.census.gov/hhes/www/poverty/histpov/hstpov2.html.

4. Valdas Anelauskas, *Discovering America As It Is* (Atlanta: Clarity, 1999), 63.

5. See, for example, John E. Schwarz and Thomas J. Volgy, *The Forgotten Americans* (New York: Norton, 1992), 33–41, 61–63.

6. Some of these figures are drawn from the Economic Policy Institute at http://www.epi.org/content.cfm/issueguides_minwage_minwagefacts.

7. Cited in *The Nation*, May 1, 2006, 5.

8. The poverty rate used in these OECD calculations is the percentage of the workforce earning less than half the median income. See data at http://www.oecd.org/dataoecd/12/4/35445297.xls.

9. From the international comparisons chapter of *The State of Working America 2004/2005* published by the Economic Policy Institute and summarized at http://www.epinet.org.

10. Timothy M. Smeeding, *Financial Poverty in Developed Countries: The Evidence from LIS*, Working Paper no. 155, Final Report to the UNDP, April 1997, 34, http://www.lisproject.org.

11. *Child Poverty in Rich Countries in 2005*, available at the UNICEF website at http://www.unicef.org/brazil/repcard6e.pdf.

12. *Child Poverty in Rich Nations* (Florence: UNICEF, 2000), 18, http://www.unicef-icdc.org/publications/pdf/repcard1e.pdf.

13. "Income Inequality, and Its Cost," *New York Times*, June 25, 2006, B4.

14. U.S. Census Bureau, *Current Population Survey, Annual Social and Economic Supplements*, http://www.census.gov/hhes/www/income/histinc/f04.html.

15. Eric Dash, "Off to the Races Again, Leaving Many Behind," *New York Times*, April 9, 2006, sec. 3, p. 1; *New York Times Magazine*, April 16, 2006, 11.

16. Cited in Roger Lowenstein, "The Inequality Conundrum," *New York Times Magazine*, June 10, 2007, 12.

17. "Executive Pay," *New York Times*, April 8, 2007, Business section, 10.

18. *New York Times*, November 25, 2004.

19. Including welfare and family support (the largest of which was Aid to Families with Dependent Children), food stamps, and Supplemental Security Income for the poor elderly and disabled.

20. "Taxpayers Are Angry. They're Expensive, Too," *New York Times*, November 20, 1994.

21. Sharon Parrott, *How Much Do We Spend on "Welfare"?* (Washington, D.C.: Center on Budget and Policy Priorities, March 1995), 10, cited in Anelauskas, *Discovering America As It Is*, 330–31.

22. Smeeding, *Financial Poverty in Developed Countries*, 34.

23. Dennis Andrulis, Lisa Duchon, and Hailey Reid, *Before and after Welfare Reform* (Brooklyn, New York: SUNY Downstate Medical Center, 2003).

24. Steven Greenhouse, "Many Participants in Workfare Take the Place of City Workers," *New York Times*, April 13, 1998, A1.

25. "The Rich: Why Their World Might Crumble," *New York Times*, November 19, 1995.

26. Lester Thurow, "Geared for Slow Growth," *Minneapolis Star Tribune*, April 21, 1996, A27.

27. Data from the International Social Justice Project survey of thirteen countries in 1991, reported in Duane Alwin, ed., *ISJP Codebook* (Ann Arbor, Mich.: Institute for Social Research, 1991).

28. Alwin, *ISJP Codebook*, 115.

29. Stephen M. Walt, *Taming American Power: The Global Response to U.S. Primacy* (New York: Norton, 2005), 26.

CHAPTER THREE

~

Torn Social Fabric
Inadequate Health Care and Violent Crime

The United States has less than 5 percent of the world's population [and] a quarter of the world's prisoners.

—*New York Times*, April 23, 2008

The idea of the "American Century"—that the United States would guide, succor, and lead the rest of the world—was based on the assumption that the United States itself would be a dynamic, healthy, productive, and prosperous country. Even in 1941, when Henry Luce coined the phrase, it seemed like a pretty safe assumption. The most developed countries in the world were either under the control of dictators like Hitler, Hirohito, and Mussolini or under siege by those militarized regimes. The industrial and economic development of the United States during and after World War II confirmed its position as the world's most affluent and stable great power.

As we have seen in the previous chapters, the economic health of the United States is now in serious jeopardy, mostly because of the unprecedented and mounting deficits and debts and the looming burdens of retirement of the baby-boomer generation. These problems are compounded by and will also contribute to the growth in poverty and inequality in the United States, which are already near record levels and far worse than any other industrial democracy in the world. Poverty and inequality are, in turn, closely related to a whole host of other serious social problems in the United States, including inadequate health care, rampant crime, and collapsed public education. In all these areas, the United States has deteriorated and compares unfavorably with other developed countries. It can no longer be said that this country is a model in providing for the health, education, and safety of its citizens. And in these regards as well, the rest of the world has a far different view of the United States than its citizens have of themselves.

The Withering of American Health Care

One of the most surprising and sobering aspects of societal decline in the United States is the poor record of health care in the country. It is surprising because the United States indeed does have available the best medical care in the world and spends more on health care than any other country. The problem, as with so much else in the United States, is the inequitable nature of health care delivery. For people who can afford it, there is no place better than the United States to fall ill and be hospitalized. But the United States is the only major industrialized country that does not provide free (or basically free) health care to its citizens. Those who are poor—and even many middle-class working people—are simply unable to afford health insurance and are therefore often reluctant to seek medical care when they do get sick. Because there are so many poor people in the Untied States and so many people without access to health care, the *average* level of health and medical care in the United States is among the worst in the developed world.

Data from the U.S. Census Bureau show that the number of uninsured Americans reached 47 million in 2006. This was a record-high number, reflecting an increase of 7 million people since 2000.[1] Almost 16 percent of the U.S. population was without health insurance and therefore without access to adequate health care. As one might expect, lack of health insurance coverage is especially prevalent among the poor and among minorities, but the vast majority—four-fifths—of the uninsured are actually employed. Their numbers have also been on the increase, as many employers find that they can no longer afford health plans. On average, an employer has to pay a premium of about $11,500 for a health plan for a family of four and $4,200 for a single employee. Since 2000, there has been a steady decline in private employment-based health insurance coverage, and the problem is likely to continue and worsen. Health care costs and spending are rising at the fastest rate in American history. In 2005, total national health expenditures rose by almost 7 percent over the previous year, twice the rate of inflation. Total health expenditures were $2 trillion, constituting 16 percent of the nation's gross domestic product (GDP) and averaging $6,700 per person; they were expected to grow within a decade to $4 trillion and 20 percent of GDP.[2] The combination of the high cost of medical care and the lack of insurance is what keeps many people from seeking medical care when they should. Thus, this problem is not just an economic one; when the health of the nation's citizens is at jeopardy, it is a social and moral issue as well.

Forty-seven million people without health insurance is an astounding number but is almost taken for granted now in the United States. In the 1990s, there was a substantial outcry when that number was far lower, and the issue sparked one of the major political debates of the decade over the proposal for a system of national health insurance. In no other industrialized country do so many people (or such a large percentage of the population) lack access to medical care. Indeed, the number of people without health insurance in this country could populate a medium-sized country all their own.

The Worst Health Care among Wealthy Countries

The consequence of this lack of access to basic medical care is that, on average, the United States has the worst record of health care of any industrialized country. In the late 1990s, the World Health Organization ranked the United States at thirty-seventh in the world in overall performance of the health system—the lowest ranking of any country in the Organization for Economic Cooperation and Development (OECD). This is despite the fact that the United States spends far more on health care than any other industrialized country and two to three times more on a per capita basis than most other OECD countries. The United States has lower life expectancy and far higher infant mortality rates than most high-income countries (see figure 3.1). And public opinion surveys show that Americans are much less satisfied with their health care system compared to people in other rich countries.[3] Comparisons of the health systems in Australia, Canada, Germany, New Zealand, the United Kingdom, and the United States, conducted by the highly regarded Commonwealth Fund, ranked the U.S. health care system in last place and found that Americans were the most negative about their health care system among the five countries. A third of Americans called for rebuilding the entire system, compared to only 13 percent who felt that way in Britain and 14 percent in Canada.[4]

All other developed countries besides the United States have either a government-supported universal health insurance plan (as in Canada) or a government-run health system (as in Britain) or some combination of the two. Critics of such systems assert that such government programs are both expensive and bureaucratic. But over the past two decades, the American system of health care, with its mixture of private providers, private insurance, and government programs (like Medicare and Medicaid), has grown both

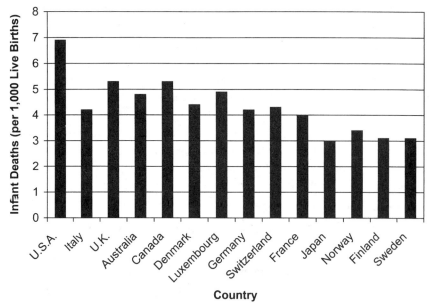

Figure 3.1. Infant Mortality Rates in Wealthy Countries, 2003
Source: OECD Health Data 2006, online at http://www.oecd.org.

more expensive and more bureaucratic than those in other wealthy countries. Health expenditures in the United States are higher than other OECD countries both on a per capita basis and as a percentage of GDP (see figure 3.2).

The reasons for the especially high health care costs in the United States are numerous and include the pervasiveness of expensive medical technology, the high salaries of doctors (in comparison with other countries), and the high cost of prescription drugs. An even more important factor—and a more surprising one—is administrative costs. Many Americans assume that the largely private medical care in the United States is more efficient, less bureaucratic, and less costly than the government-run programs in other countries. In fact, administrative costs in the United States are higher in for-profit hospitals than in public ones, and overall administrative costs are higher in the United States than in countries with government-run programs. Even in the 1990s, according to a study reported in the *New England Journal of Medicine*, administrative costs for profit-making hospitals absorbed 34 percent of total expenditures, compared to 25 percent for private non-profit hospitals and 23 percent for public hospitals.[5] In cross-national comparisons, the United States also comes up high on administrative costs in health care. A 2003 study in the *New England Journal of Medicine* estimated that administrative costs absorbed 31 cents of every health care dollar in the

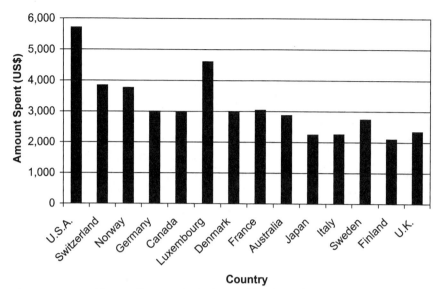

Figure 3.2.   Health Spending per Capita in Wealthy Countries, 2003
Source: OECD Health Data 2006, online at http://www.oecd.org.

United States, compared to only 17 cents in Canada, which has a universal health insurance plan paid for by the government.[6] It may seem counterintuitive that a largely private health care system could be more expensive than a government-administered one given what we know about government red tape. But the U.S. health care system is a jumble of private, non-profit, and government programs, with the insurance industry added in, all with their own bureaucracies. Furthermore, in the private sector and in the insurance business, there are not the restrictions on salaries and profits that governments can impose. Consider the following example, cited by a physicians' group: "When U.S. Healthcare merged with Aetna in 1996, the $967 million received by CEO Leonard Abramson could have provided health insurance to every uninsured child in the state of Massachusetts until they reached puberty."[7]

Poor Health Care Hurts the Poor and Children

The high costs of medical care affect everyone, but the real burden of costly health care falls especially hard on the poor. And for many of them, it is not just a matter of money but one of life and death itself. Those without health insurance coverage are less likely to seek medical care when they need it. A study by the Harvard School of Public Health found that almost half of uninsured Americans were unable to obtain medical care when needed.[8] The consequence is that the poor are far more likely to get sick, to have serious illnesses, and to die early. The National Center for Health Statistics reported that in 1986, people with annual family incomes of less than $9,000 had a death rate three to seven times greater than those with family incomes over $25,000 and that this rich–poor death gap had widened considerably since 1960.[9]

This inequity is even more tragic when it affects children. A study by the National Academy of Sciences titled *America's Children: Health Insurance and Access to Care* found that uninsured children "are more likely to be sick as newborns, less likely to be immunized as preschoolers, less likely to receive medical treatment when they are injured, and less likely to receive treatment for illnesses such as acute or recurrent ear infections, asthma and tooth decay."[10] Another study from the National Center for Health Statistics reported that poor children were 3.6 times more likely to have poor health than children from affluent families.[11] The United States is the only developed country in the world where children suffer poor health and die simply because their parents are poor or unemployed. But the problem of inadequate and inequitable health care goes beyond even the issues of fairness, compassion, and morality. When children suffer from ill health or malnutrition (another health consequence of poverty), it affects their abilities to perform well in school and to interact with others, and this has societal consequences that affect everyone. The National Academy of Sciences report titled *America's Children* has this to say in its executive summary:

> Access to health care can influence children's physical and emotional growth, development, and overall health and well-being. Untreated illnesses and injuries can have long-term—even lifelong—consequences. For example, untreated ear infections can lead to hearing loss or deafness. Children who are unable to hear well can have trouble performing well in school and trouble interacting normally with their families and friends. Language or other developmental delays due to untreated neurological problems also can frustrate normal development and social interactions.[12]

A 1994 study by a blue-ribbon panel commissioned by the Carnegie Corporation referred to the situation of America's youngest children as "a quiet crisis." It found that millions of children in the United States were suffering from the effects of poverty, poor health care, and the absence of parents and pointed out that stress from such factors could affect the very brain development of young children: "An adverse environment can compromise a young child's brain function and overall development, placing him or her at greater risk of developing a variety of cognitive, behavioral, and physical difficulties. In some cases these effects may be irreversible."[13] Thus, the social and economic problems of poverty can create a biological problem that itself reinforces the preexisting social one.

The 1994 Carnegie Commission recommended a series of initiatives on all fronts, including government initiatives to provide better schools and education, reduce childhood poverty, and improve health care for children and young families. But there has been almost no action in any of those areas. As we have already seen, the ranks of the poor and of children living in poverty have continued to grow since the turn of the millennium. And this has simply fed the problems of deteriorating education and accelerating crime, as we will see later in this chapter.

American Exceptionalism Gone Awry

In its treatment of children, even more so than in the prevalence of poverty and inequality, the United States is out of step with most of the rest of the world. As seen previously, international statistics on child health, health care, and poverty show the United States to be among the worst of all developed countries. In terms of the rights of children, though, the United States stands completely alone in the world. In 1989, the United Nations adopted the United Nations Convention on the Rights of the Child, which laid out the civil, economic, political, social, and cultural rights of children. Among these, in article 24, is "the right of the child to the enjoyment of the highest attainable standard of health and to facilities for the treatment of illness and rehabilitation of health." One hundred and ninety-two countries have ratified the Convention on the Rights of the Child. Only two countries have failed to do so: Somalia, which has no working government, and the United States. Opposition to the treaty in the United States has come mostly from conservatives in Congress but, since 2000, even more decisively and forcefully from President Bush. In 2001, the Bush administration rejected the convention, contending that

> the Convention on the Rights of the Child may be a positive tool in promoting child welfare for those countries that have adopted it. But we believe the text goes too far when it asserts entitlements based on the economic, social and cultural rights contained in the Convention and other instruments. The human rights-based approach, while laudable in its objectives, poses significant problems as used in this text.[14]

This is yet another example of "American exceptionalism" gone awry. But it is part of several patterns increasingly setting the United States apart from the rest of the world: its reluctance to provide for its own population, its rejection of international conventions and international law, and its increasing willingness to go it alone in the world despite what other countries think. As we will see later in this chapter, one of the main reasons the United States was unwilling to sign the Convention on the Rights of the Child was that the United States was one of the only countries in the world that then still allowed capital punishment for children—which is also banned by the convention (and by many other international conventions).

The poor state of health care in the United States and the problem of affordable coverage have become increasingly prominent political issues, particularly so with the escalating costs of health insurance and health care. As Americans age, as employers cut back on coverage, and as out-of-pocket expenses increase, more people are looking to Washington for a solution. A bipartisan Citizens' Health Care Working Group set up by Congress recently fielded a large-scale opinion survey that found that more than 90 percent of respondents believed "it should be public policy that all Americans have affordable coverage."[15] Rarely does one see an opinion on any political subject that shows such universal agreement. But it seems unlikely that there will be much movement to improve the health care situation in the United States. When a limited but comprehensive health care reform plan was put forward by the Clinton administration in the 1990s, it was shot down by special interests that used a media campaign to frighten people into thinking that the quality of care would decline and that expenses would increase (even though the United States already fared poorly on both measures). In any case, even if a government-sponsored plan would, in the long run, lead to lower overall health care costs, it is unlikely that in the short run a bankrupt federal government could leverage the funds to pay for a national health care plan.

The Most Violent Country

The United States is the most violent country in the industrialized world. According to reports by the Federal Bureau of Investigation (FBI), in 2004 there were 1,367,009 violent crimes in this country. Of these, more than 16,000 were homicides. In that year, there was one violent crime every twenty-three seconds and one murder every thirty-three minutes.[16] Americans seem to take this phenomenon for granted and shrug it off as an inevitable consequence of modern urban society. But these violent crime rates are far higher than earlier in American history and many times higher than in other industrialized countries. Since the mid-1970s, more than 500,000 Americans have been murdered—more than all the American battle casualties of World War I, World War II, the Korean War, and the Vietnam War combined. The murder rate in the United States particularly affects young people. This homegrown slaughter is far beyond the experiences of people in other industrialized countries. In the late 1990s, the youth homicide rate in the United States was five to ten times that of other industrialized countries (see figure 3.3). Since the 1990s, when these comparative data were collected by the World Health Organization, the overall U.S. homicide rate has declined somewhat, to about six per 100,000 for the whole population. But this number is still high by U.S. historical standards and still many times higher than the rates in other developed countries.

Much of the violence in the United States happens among people who know each other, especially within the home. The Justice Department reports more than 500,000 incidents of "intimate partner" violence every year—most of this against women. About 1,200 women are killed every year by husbands or boyfriends, and on average eight children are killed each day, often by members of the family.[17] As one Indiana advocate against domestic violence observes, "If foreign terrorists were killing more than 12 Americans a day or nearly 4,500 a year, this country would be in a very *real* state of emergency."[18]

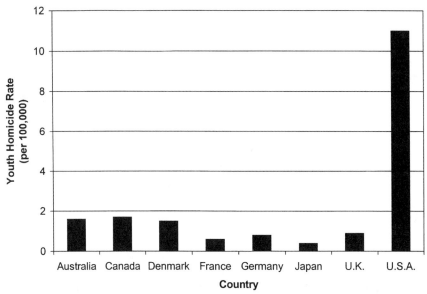

Figure 3.3.   Youth (ages 10–29) Homicide Rates in Industrialized Countries, Late 1990s
Source: World Health Organization, *World Report on Violence and Health* (Geneva: World Health Organization, 2002).

Two thousand years ago, the Roman emperor Marcus Aurelius asserted that "poverty is the mother of crime," and modern social science affirms this sentiment. In cross-national studies of violence and crime, the most persuasive evidence points to poverty and inequality as the main culprits both within countries and among them.[19] Populations with high incidence of income inequality and of poverty suffer far more violence and murder than others. Societal violence is also more common in countries that have weak social and economic safety nets to help the poor, the disadvantaged, or the marginalized. As we have seen, the United States fares poorly on all these dimensions. Compared to other developed countries, the United States has high rates of poverty and inequality and weak social welfare systems, including poor health care services for the poor. In such environments, people are more likely to feel desperate, hopeless, frustrated, and alienated, and those feelings provide a potent ferment that can lead to violence.

While poverty, inequality, and hopelessness may be the major contributing factors to crime and violence in the United States, it is almost certainly the prevalence of guns that makes violence so deadly and that so inflates the homicide rate. About two-thirds of all murders are committed with firearms, and about three-quarters of those are handguns.[20] There are almost 200 million privately owned firearms in the United States—almost as many guns as there are people—including some 65 million handguns. Every year, about 30,000 Americans die from firearm injuries; about 40 percent of these are homicides, and most of the rest are suicides. Firearm homicides are the leading cause of death of young African American males and the second leading cause of injury death for all young people, after only automobile accidents. As noted previously, the death toll from gun violence in the United States is more intense and more sustained than from most of the full-scale wars that the country has been involved in. And many doctors and physicians' organizations are now treating firearm violence as a medical epidemic: the number of annual deaths from gun violence far exceeds those from polio in the 1950s or AIDS in more recent years.

Despite the scale and tragedy of the homicide and gun violence epidemic in the United States, there is curiously little public outrage or political action on the problem. Public opinion polls show overwhelming popular support for a broad range of measures to make guns less accessible and less dangerous, including licensing firearms in much the same way that automobiles are.[21] Even most gun owners favor such legislation. But under pressure from the National Rifle Association (NRA), one of the most powerful lobbies in Washington, neither Congress nor most state legislatures have been willing to take action on these issues. Indeed, since the inauguration of George W.

Bush, the most progun president in a century, both Congress and the states have been rolling back some of the limited gun control laws that were already in place.

The seeming indifference of the American public to the problems of homicide and gun violence may be due, in part, to the continued racism in the United States. The costs of gun violence are disproportionately born by African Americans, who are about half of all homicide victims but make up only about 13 percent of the total population. A young black male is nine times more likely to be murdered than a young white male. Yet whites are more likely to own guns than blacks, and the NRA membership is overwhelmingly white. In one of his early movies, the black filmmaker Spike Lee pointed out that the people who manufacture and sell guns are mostly white and that the people who die from guns are mostly black. Lee believed then—and still believes—that "racism is woven into the very fabric of America" and that violence in the African American community is a function of that.[22] Perhaps it is going too far to assert that the white community intends for blacks to suffer the consequences of gun violence. But it seems pretty evident that the lack of concern about homicides in the United States is partly due to the relatively small direct impact it has on white middle-class Americans.

The proliferation of guns in America and the apparent national obsession with them is based mostly on fear, but it also reflects a decline in the sense of community and public spiritedness that helped define and shape the country. People who buy guns do so mostly for self-protection and out of fear of crime and criminals. This attitude reflects a lack of confidence in the ability of the police and the courts to protect them and ultimately a lack of faith in the community. Using a gun to defend one's house and family becomes an extreme form of individualism. In recent years, this has been given legal sanction by a raft of state laws that allow crime victims to use deadly force to defend home, vehicles, and property. As a *New York Times* editorial has pointed out, these laws confer a right to lethal force that is not even granted to the police.[23]

The willingness to actually kill an intruder or an assailant essentially confers on the gun owner the powers of judge, jury, and executioner. In most societies, these are powers conferred and exercised by the community or the government of that community and are carefully circumscribed. Individual gun ownership erodes that power of the community and the sense of community in the name of individual justice. Few countries in the world and no other developed countries permit such easy individual access to guns and especially handguns.

For a minority of gun owners, the main reason for owning a gun is a far more thoroughgoing distrust of the community and the government. For those people, who include some of the leaders of the NRA and most of the so-called militias in the United States, gun ownership provides an extra check on government itself. They see the Second Amendment to the Constitution as an implicit right of armed Americans to forcibly overthrow the federal government if they view it as tyrannical. It is hard to imagine any constitutional document, especially one with so many democratic checks and balances built into it, providing for its own violent overthrow. But many Americans seem to believe this—yet another reason why the United States is increasingly seen around the world as swimming against the tide of modern civilization.

Why are Americans so fearful? In part the fear is justified simply because there is indeed so much violent crime in the United States. But the fearfulness may also be part of the "mean-world syndrome," a phrase coined by the media researcher George Gerbner to describe the outlook of people who watch a great deal of television and are therefore more likely to view the world as an unforgiving and frightening place.[24] American television and movies are particularly violent—more so than in most countries—and Americans watch an extraordinary amount of television. The average American young person watches about twenty-eight hours of television each week and some 1,500 hours over the course of a year compared to only about 900 hours spent in school. The average American will witness 16,000 murders and 200,000 other violent acts on television by the time he or she is eighteen.[25] There is much evidence that links this television exposure to the attitudes and behavior of young people, and this carries over into adulthood. Viewing violence and aggression leads to more aggressive behavior and, as Gerbner found, to a more fearful outlook as part of the mean-world syndrome. In 1981, he testified before Congress that "fearful people are more dependent, more easily manipulated and controlled, more susceptible to deceptively simple, strong, tough measures and hard-line postures. . . . They may accept and even welcome repression if it promises to relieve their insecurities. That is the deeper problem of violence-laden television."[26] A quarter century since that testimony, Americans watch even more television, television is even more violent, and the level of real violence has escalated sharply. Americans are more fearful, so they purchase more guns, and the violence increases in a vicious circle. And if Gerbner is right about fearful people being easily manipulated, this may contribute to the political problems as well—another topic for a later chapter.

For people in other countries and especially for people in other developed countries, the levels of violence and the prevalence of guns in the United States provide a source of both amazement and horror. But it also fits in with the widespread stereotype of the United States as a violent and aggressive country. Global opinion surveys conducted by the Pew Research Center found that the two most common negative characterizations of Americans by foreigners are "greedy" and "violent."[27] Interestingly in this poll, almost half of all Americans also saw themselves as violent, but this view was far more prevalent in other countries and especially in Middle Eastern and Islamic ones. In Turkey, for example, a member of the North Atlantic Treaty Organization and one of the Middle Eastern countries more friendly to the United States, 70 percent of the population view Americans as violent, the most common characterization of Americans among Turks. Compared to this, only 61 percent of Turks see Americans as hardworking, 54 percent as inventive, and a mere 16 percent as honest. As we will see in a later chapter, these negative attitudes among foreigners toward America and Americans are widespread and growing; certainly one of the reasons for this is the view of the United States being violent both in its foreign policy and inside its own borders.

The incidence of violence is particularly high in the United States, which is also especially harsh and violent in the way it punishes criminals. The United States has the largest prison population in the world, with more than 2 million people in federal, state, and local jails. This is almost a quarter of all the world's prisoner population. The 2 million U.S. prisoners constitute a rate of 714 per 100,000, which is the highest incarceration rate in the world and far higher than any other industrialized democracy. Three-fifths of the countries in the world have a prison population rate of under 150 per 100,000, and almost all of western Europe and Japan are under 100 per 100,000.[28] Something is deeply wrong with a country that has so many of its citizens in jail. The proportion of the population in prison in the United States (714 per 100,000) is far higher even than in countries the United States considers authoritarian or politically repressive, including Cuba (487), Libya (207), Iran (194), Zimbabwe (155), China (118), and Syria (93). Furthermore, the United States is widening the gap: the U.S. prison population has been growing at 3.4 percent annually since 1995[29]—much faster than the overall population growth of about 1 percent a year. The American prison population is disproportionately African American: 12 percent of all African American males are in prison or jail.

The United States is also one of the few developed countries in the world that still employ capital punishment. In the words of *Newsweek* columnist

Anna Quindlen, "Americans still live in one of the few countries that kill people to make clear what a terrible thing killing people is."[30] In 2005, according to Amnesty International, 94 percent of all known executions worldwide occurred in just four countries: China, Iran, Saudi Arabia, and the United States. This is not good company. The favored method in Saudi Arabia is beheading. Iran uses stoning and hanging. The United States employs electrocution and, along with China, the supposedly more humane method of lethal injection. Eighty-seven countries worldwide, including every other industrial democracy, have abolished the death penalty. The European Convention on Human Rights, which applies to all twenty-seven members of the European Union, bans capital punishment totally. The continued use of the death penalty in the United States has hindered the struggle against global terrorism because other countries are reluctant to or prohibited by national law from turning over suspects to countries that employ the death penalty.

International law and global sentiment is even more emphatic about banning the execution of children, but here too the United States has until recently stood apart from the rest of the world. The International Covenant on Civil and Political Rights, adopted by the United Nations in 1966 and ratified by the United States in 1992, prohibits the death penalty for those under eighteen years of age. The Convention on the Rights of the Child also prohibits the death penalty for children, though as we saw previously, the United States is one of two countries that have not ratified that treaty. A UN commission has ruled that the execution of those under eighteen at the time of the crime is "contrary to customary international law."[31] Yet until 2005, the United States was one of the few countries in the world that allowed the practice, along with China, the Democratic Republic of the Congo, Iran, and Pakistan. Between 1995 and 2005, the United States executed more people who were juveniles at the time of their offense than all of those other countries combined, and most of those were in Texas.

The United States finally aligned itself with the rest of the world only because of a five-to-four Supreme Court decision in 2005 (*Roper v. Simmons*) that ruled it "cruel and unusual punishment"—and therefore unconstitutional—to sentence anyone to death for a crime committed when they were younger than eighteen. Justice Anthony Kennedy, who wrote the opinion for the court, acknowledged that their decision found confirmation "in the stark reality that the United States is the only country in the world that continues to give official sanction to the juvenile death penalty." The decision saved the lives of seventy-two people on death row who were juveniles when they committed their crimes, including twenty-nine in Texas and fourteen in Alabama. No other state had more than five.[32]

The United States claims a special position in the world, and our leaders believe that we have the goals and accomplishments that suit us to world leadership—and the right and responsibility to help bring the American model to other countries. This has been part of the American self-image and the American dream almost from the beginning of the Republic, and especially since Henry Luce's essay defining and prescribing the American Century sixty-five years ago.

But the United States no longer lives up to this image even within its own borders. The country has failed to deliver even the basics of modern civilization—including health care and personal security—to a large and growing proportion of its citizenry. The injustice of this is magnified in that most of those who do not have access to health care or who are victims of crime are the poor, the minorities, and the children. The United States is one of the most violent and fearful in the industrialized world, imprisons more of its people, and uses legal instruments of the state to kill its own citizens. In all these respects, it is the African American minority that disproportionately suffers from all of this. This is hardly a record of fairness, benevolence, and civility that other countries would want to imitate. Increasingly, most do not.

Notes

1. U.S. Census Bureau, *Income, Poverty and Health Insurance Coverage in the United States: 2006* (Washington, D.C.: U.S. Government Printing Office, 2007), http://www.census.gov.

2. Data from the National Coalition on Health Care available at http://www.nchc.org/facts/cost.shtml.

3. Many of these data from table 1 of "The U.S. Health Care System: Best in the World, or Just the Most Expensive?" prepared by the Bureau of Labor Education, University of Maine, 2001, available at http://dll.umaine.edu/ble/U.S.%20HCweb.pdf.

4. "World's Best Medical Care?" *New York Times*, August 12, 2007 (op-ed); Karen Davis et al., *Mirror, Mirror on the Wall: An International Update on the Comparative Performance of American Health Care*, 2007, http://www.commonwealthfund.org/usr_doc/1027_Davis_mirror_mirror_international_update_final.pdf?section=4039.

5. Steffie Woolhandler and David Himmelstein, "Costs of Care and Administration at For-Profit and Other Hospitals in the United States," *New England Journal of Medicine* 336 (1997): 769–74, cited in "The U.S. Health Care System," 2.

6. Paul Krugman, "The Medical Money Pit," *New York Times*, April 15, 2005, A19.

7. From Physicians for a National Health Plan, cited in "The U.S. Health Care System," 2.

8. Karen Donelan et al., "Whatever Happened to the Health Insurance Crisis in the United States?" *Journal of the American Medical Association* 276, no. 16 (1996): 1348.

9. Oliver Fein, "The Influence of Social Class on Health Status," *Journal of General Internal Medicine* 10, no. 10 (1995): 582.

10. National Academy of Sciences, Institute of Medicine, *America's Children: Health Insurance and Access to Care* (Washington, D.C.: National Academy Press, 1998), executive summary available at http://darwin.nap.edu/execsumm_pdf/6168.pdf.

11. Cited in Valdas Anelauskas, *Discovering America As It Is* (Atlanta: Clarity, 1999), 122.

12. National Academy of Sciences, *America's Children*, 4.

13. *Starting Points: Meeting the Needs of Our Youngest Children*, report of the Carnegie Task Force on Meeting the Needs of Young Children (New York: Carnegie Corporation, 1994), 2, 4, abridged version available at http://www.carnegie.org/starting_points/index.html.

14. Statement by Ambassador E. Michael Southwick, deputy assistant secretary of state for international organization affairs, in the Preparatory Committee for the General Assembly Special Session on the Children's World Summit, February 1, 2001, available at http://www.un.int/usa/01_015.htm.

15. Cited in Patricia Barry, "Coverage for All," *AARP Bulletin*, July–August 2006, 8.

16. FBI, *Crime in the United States 2004: Uniform Crime Reports* (Washington, D.C.: U.S. Government Printing Office, 2005), http://www.fbi.gov/ucr/cius_04/documents/CIUS2004.pdf.

17. U.S. Department of Justice, Bureau of Justice Statistics, "Intimate Partner Violence in the United States," 2007, http://www.ojp.usdoj.gov/bjs/pub/pdf/ipvus.pdf.

18. Kerry Blomquist, "Help Them Live without Fear," *Indianapolis Star*, December 30, 2007.

19. World Health Organization, *World Report on Violence and Health* (Geneva: World Health Organization, 2002).

20. FBI, *Crime in the United States 2004*, 19.

21. See, for example, the survey results of the National Opinion Research Center reported in Tom Smith, *Public Attitudes towards the Regulation of Firearms*, March 2007, http://www-news.uchicago.edu/releases/07/pdf/070410.guns.norc.pdf.

22. Interview at Bowdoin College, as reported in the *Portland Phoenix*, May 10–17, 2001, at http://www.portlandphoenix.com/archive/features/01/05/11/tji/scene.html.

23. "Shoot First—No Questions Asked," *New York Times*, August 14, 2006, A24 (editorial).

24. An obituary for George Gerbner appears in the *New York Times*, January 3, 2006, A17.

25. U.S. Senate Judiciary Committee, *Children, Violence and the Media*, September 1999, http://judiciary.senate.gov/oldsite/mediavio.htm. Other statistics on television

viewing, complete with source citations, are reported in Anelauskas, *Discovering America As It Is*, 260–61.

26. Quoted in his obituary in the *New York Times*.

27. Andrew Kohut and Bruce Stokes, *America against the World: How We Are Different and Why We Are Disliked* (New York: Times Books, 2006), 33.

28. Roy Walmsley (from London's International Centre for Prison Studies), *World Prison Population List*, 6th ed., http://www.kcl.ac.uk/depsta/rel/icps/world-prison-population-list-2005.pdf.

29. U.S. Department of Justice, "Prison Statistics," December 2006, http://www.ojp.usdoj.gov/bjs/prisons.htm.

30. "The Failed Experiment," *Newsweek*, June 26, 2006, 64.

31. Cited by Amnesty International at its website on the death penalty at http://www.amnestyusa.org/abolish/juveniles.html.

32. Charles Lane, "5-4 Supreme Court Abolishes Juvenile Executions," *Washington Post*, March 2, 2005, A1.

~

CHAPTER FOUR

The Dimming of America

Education, Science, and Fundamentalism

If an unfriendly foreign power had attempted to impose on America the mediocre educational performance that exists today, we might well have viewed it as an act of war.

—National Commission on Excellence in Education, 1983

Poverty and inequality in the United States are closely tied to educational attainment. The rise of poverty and inequality since the 1970s is both a cause of and a consequence of the deterioration of literacy, education, and schools in this country. So the problems of one accentuate and reinforce the problems of the other. And as education declines in the United States, so does U.S. competitiveness and respect in the world community and its standing among other nations. As Americans become less educated and less literate, they are increasingly ignorant of science or even resistant to its explanations and messages. They also become more susceptible to the blandishments of fundamentalism, whether it is preached from the pulpit or the rostrum. In a world threatened by global warming and global epidemics, this is a dangerous trend.

One-third of Americans Are Functionally Illiterate

The extent of adult illiteracy in the United States surprises most people because one is used to the notion that literacy is practically universal in the United States as in other developed countries. Statistics from the United

Nations show the United States with a literacy rate of 99.9 percent along with twenty other countries. But the criteria used for literacy in these measures vary from country to country and are usually based on a minimal skill of simply being able to read and write (in some cases, in any language).

A more useful measure, though, is "functional" literacy, which reflects the ability to use language to get along in society. The data on functional literacy in the United States are quite startling. In his pathbreaking 1985 book *Illiterate America*, Jonathan Kozol titled his first chapter "A Third of the Nation Cannot Read These Words." He asserts there that

> twenty-five million American adults cannot read the poison warnings on a can of pesticide, a letter from their child's teacher, or the front page of a daily paper. An additional 35 million read only at a level which is less than equal to the full survival needs of our society.[1]

These 60 million people at that time constituted more than a third of the entire adult population of the United States. As one might expect, the problem was particularly dire for minorities: 44 percent of African Americans and 56 percent of Hispanic citizens were functional or marginal illiterates. National studies of adult literacy in the two decades since Kozol's book have shown no improvement in functional literacy and even a slight decline by most measures.[2] Even college education does not do much to solve the problem. Only 31 percent of college graduates and 41 percent of graduate students are "proficient in reading prose" according to surveys of the U.S. Department of Education. Those figures, from 2003, show a substantial decline from a decade earlier.[3]

This stasis was in spite of the considerable academic and political attention to the problem of illiteracy: the publication in 1983 of *A Nation at Risk*, calling attention to the failures of American public education; a 1990 resolution of the National Governors Association, calling for all Americans to be fully and functionally literate by 2000; and Congress's passage in 1991 of the National Literacy Act. None of these had much impact on the problem, nor did President Bush's more recent No Child Left Behind initiative.

Functional illiteracy is only one aspect of a broader decline in the quality of American education and American schools, at almost every level, and a decline in the number of people graduating from high school. This is a recent and novel phenomenon in American history. America has been justifiably proud of its educational system and its educational attainment, and few countries in the world have so quickly educated such a large proportion of their population. In his "American Century" essay in 1941, Henry Luce offered to "send throughout the world" its teachers and educators. Public education was a high priority after World War II, and the GI Bill enabled millions of returning soldiers to enter college. The country's high school graduation rate, which was only about 30 percent in 1930, grew to 60 percent in 1950 and to almost 80 percent by 1970. This was a remarkable achievement, fueled in large part by the widespread conviction that democracy depended on an informed citizenry—articulated by Thomas Jefferson in the eighteenth century and reemphasized by John Dewey in the twentieth.

But these gains came to an end in the 1970s, at about the same time that we begin to see the rapid rise in poverty and inequality in the United States. High school graduation rates stagnated after 1965 and then began to decline. By the 2002–2003 school year, the high school graduation rate reported by the U.S. Department of Education was 74 percent, though some other recent studies suggest that the figure is closer to 70 percent—in either case a substantial decline since 1970.[4] More than a third of dropouts never get beyond ninth grade. A disproportionate number of dropouts are minorities.

The high dropout rate has contributed to the low levels of literacy, functional and otherwise, but that is not the only source of the problem. Even when children (and young adults) stay in school, they are not learning very much, and the quality of education delivered, from primary schools through universities, is also declining. Americans at all age levels know less than their counterparts in other industrialized countries. The problem begins at the youngest ages and is closely connected to the consequences of poverty, addressed in chapter 2. A Carnegie Corporation Task Force Report in the 1990s found that about a third of all kindergarten-age children arrive at school unprepared to learn. One teacher cited in this report said that "children come to school who don't know where they live, can't identify colors, and are unable to recite their full and proper name." Many children had emotional problems or were simply too hungry, interfering with their ability to concentrate or learn.[5] High student-to-teacher ratios and large class sizes in most American schools make it difficult for teachers to address such issues or to provide individual attention to troubled children.

The seminal 1983 study *A Nation at Risk* warned that "the educational foundations of our society are being eroded by a rising tide of mediocrity that threatens our very future as a nation and a people,"[6] and the situation in the schools has not improved and has even deteriorated since that time. Periodic surveys by the National Assessment of Educational Progress (NAEP), attached to the U.S. Department of Education, reveal dismal (and mostly declining) academic standards at all levels of elementary and high school.[7] In 2005, 36 percent of fourth graders were below the "basic" level in reading, with no significant improvement since 1992. (The "basic" level is the lowest level in the scale, denoting "partial mastery of the knowledge and skills fundamental for proficient work at each grade.") In 2005, 31 percent of eighth graders were below basic levels in math, and 46 percent of twelfth graders were below basic in science. In science and math, in particular, the problem gets worse as students progress through the grade levels.

If anything, the level of knowledge is even worse in the social sciences, especially in history and geography. Earlier NAEP studies revealed that a third of seventeen-year-olds did not know when Columbus reached America and could not identify Abraham Lincoln. Those "below basic" in the NAEP history tests increase as they move through grade levels, from 33 percent in grade 4 to 57 percent in grade 12. A recent study by the National Geographic Society showed that a third of young adults estimated the population of the United States to be between 1 billion and 2 billion. Young adults in nine other countries were better able to estimate the U.S. population than young Americans.[8] In November 2002, on the eve of the Iraq War, only 13 percent of Americans aged eighteen to twenty-four, the prime age for military service, could find Iraq on a map. Eleven percent could not find the United States on a map. Four years later and three years into the war, 63 percent of young Americans still could not find Iraq on a map.[9]

Part of the problem may be the limited amount of time that students spend doing homework—two-thirds of high school students spend less than six hours per week doing so. This is less than a third of the time that most students spend watching television.

Given these results, it is not surprising that America does not do well in international comparisons of educational achievement, especially in math and science. A 2003 study of the "mathematical literacy" of fifteen-year-olds by the Program for International Student Assessment found the United States ranking twenty-fourth in the world, well below the average of countries in the Organization for Economic Cooperation and Development (OECD) and behind almost every European country.[10] Even the best students in the United States generally know less math and science than the average student in these other countries. These poor results are compounded by a good deal of self-deception: in one international math test in 1989, the United States had the highest percentage of students saying, "I am good at mathematics," but they ranked dead last in actual math performance.[11] American students also do poorly in comparison to other developed countries on tests in other areas, including history and geography, where they typically score near the bottom among other wealthy countries. This problem is not just a moral and social one within the United States; it also affects, ultimately, the country's international economic competitiveness as well as its standing in the world. As former Labor Secretary William Brock admitted, "We have public education at the elementary and secondary level that ranks below every industrial competitor we have in the world."[12]

Standards and educational achievement at the primary and secondary school levels have declined so dramatically over the past several decades that it is no surprise that these problems have also transferred into the university level. High school seniors are increasingly less prepared for college both academically and emotionally. The average SAT scores (based on the standardized college admissions test) for college-bound seniors declined steadily in math and precipitously in verbal from the 1960s to the 1980s. Since about 1990, there has been a small improvement in both verbal and math scores, though verbal scores still remain far below the 1967 level.[13]

According to scores on the 2006 ACT college entrance exam, only 21 percent of applicants to four-year institutions were ready for college-level work in all four areas tested: reading, writing, math, and biology.[14] The reduced abilities of incoming college students have meant that universities and college professors expect and demand less. Many formerly standard requirements have disappeared from the university curriculum. A 1993 survey of colleges and universities by the National Association of Scholars found that about a third of the institutions did not require a history or a science course, almost half did not require a literature course, and about three-quarters required no foreign language for graduation.[15] Many colleges and universities have almost no admission requirements, and most colleges accept at least three-quarters of all applicants. So students know that they can get into some college no matter how poorly they do in high school. A quarter of college students do not make it to the sophomore year, and half of those who start do not graduate.

Even in college, most students do not put a great deal of effort into the academic side of things. Two-thirds of college students spend fifteen hours or less per week in class preparation time, including reading for classes. About one-fifth spend only one to five hours per week studying. Most college students spend as much time watching television as studying.[16] Time devoted to study is made even more difficult for those students who have to work while they are in school. A fifth of college students work full time during the school year, and more than two-thirds work at least fifteen hours a week. One reason for this is the increasing gap between the costs of tuition and the amount of student aid available, increasing the out-of-pocket expenses for college students and their families. In 1972, for example, federal Pell Grants (assisting students with financial need) covered 95 percent of the tuition at a public university. Now they cover less than half of tuition. Thus, more students are having to work part time, and most students are going into debt to pay for their college education.[17] The average college graduate has some $17,000 in loans. (This, of course, simply contributes to the growing problems of private and public debt referred to in chapter 1.)

The result of all of this has been an across-the-board decline in the knowledge and competencies of college graduates. A 1993 survey by the National Center for Education Statistics showed that about half of all American college graduates could not read and understand a simple bus schedule, identify an argument in a newspaper article, or calculate Social Security benefits from a pamphlet on eligibility.[18] A 2002 survey of college seniors conducted by the National Association of Scholars came to the grim conclusion that in terms of "general knowledge," today's graduating college students know about as much as high school graduates from fifty years ago. And "by almost every measure of cultural knowledge" in their survey, today's college seniors appear to rank far below the college graduates of mid-century.[19] Other surveys have shown that the average college graduate in the United States knows about as much as the average high school graduate from schools in Europe and Japan. And increasingly, the best students in American high schools, colleges, and graduate schools are not native-born Americans but people born in other countries. Even students in graduate school are showing alarming tendencies of illiteracy. A federal study in 2003 found that only 41 percent of graduate students were considered "proficient" in prose—reading and understanding information in short texts; this was down ten percentage points from 1992.[20]

Some people claim that this picture of American education is misleading, pointing to the huge increases in numbers and diversity of students at all levels. Between 1947 and 1995, for example, the number of high school graduates entering college rose from 2.3 million to 14.3 million, a rate of growth almost three times that of the growth in population.[21] At the same time, the percentage of minorities in the schools as well as in the general population has increased substantially. So, the argument goes, the task of education is far more difficult now than it was in the 1950s or than it is today in most other developed countries because of both the numbers and the heterogeneity of the student population.[22] This may well be the case, but it does not take away from the blunt fact that the United States is no longer a world leader in education as it once was. Furthermore, that argument simply highlights the much broader problems of poverty, inequality, and racism that continue to afflict the country and that are reflected in the dismal showings of its schools. It is precisely because there are so many poor, such inequality, and so many racial inequities that the nation's schools and children suffer. As with the discussion of many of the other domestic maladies of the United States addressed in this book, our purpose is not so much to explain them as to show their consequences for the United States and its position in the world. Even in the 1980s, the commission that produced *A Nation at Risk* put this issue in stark terms:

> The educational foundations of our society are presently being eroded by a rising tide of mediocrity that threatens our very future as a Nation and a people. . . . If an unfriendly foreign power had attempted to impose on America the mediocre educational performance that exists today, we might well have viewed it as an act of war. As it stands, we have allowed this to happen to ourselves. . . . We have, in effect, been committing an act of unthinking, unilateral educational disarmament.[23]

Since that report was written, the educational situation in the United States has deteriorated even further, and the country has fallen further behind many other countries. The rate of college completion in the United States is lower than in most developed countries, and the abilities of its graduates are also less. The 2006 *National Report Card on Higher Education* published by the National Center for Public Policy and Higher Education concluded that higher education in the United States is falling behind that of other countries. While other countries have significantly improved and expanded their educational systems, the United States has stalled since the 1990s. Patrick Callan, the president of the center, observed that the problem particularly affects the younger generations: "The strength of America is in the population that's closest to retirement, while the strength of many [other] countries is in their younger population. . . . For the first time in our history, the next generation will be less educated."[24]

These failings in the U.S. educational system mean that it can hardly be said anymore that the United States is a global model for education. They are also a major factor in the United States becoming increasingly less competitive in the global marketplace.

Science Illiteracy Hurts Public Policy

The increasingly poor education in the United States—and especially the low achievement levels in science education—has contributed to a startling lack of knowledge and understanding of some basic scientific principles, such as those of evolution and global warming. Even worse, it contributes to a deep and widespread skepticism and even hostility toward science, empiricism (knowledge based on experience), and even facts. This might not be such a problem in many countries—after all, many societies have survived and even prospered with a population that was mostly illiterate or uninformed. But in the United States, it is a special problem for a number of reasons: the huge impact that America (and American science) has on the rest of the world, the importance of an informed electorate for a democratic political system, and the large role that religion plays in American public life.

Doubting Evolution

The most obvious example of this is the knowledge and beliefs among Americans about the scientific theory of evolution. This theory, first advanced by Charles Darwin in his 1859 book *The Origin of Species*, was quickly adopted by most scientists and has now become the central organizing principle of the biological sciences. It is difficult to find a single professional biologist who does not accept the theory, and only a handful of other professional scientists (not biologists) contest it. Yet a stunning 54 percent of Americans do not believe that humans evolved from an earlier species, and fully 45 percent accept the proposition that "God created human beings pretty much in their present form at one time within the last 10,000 years or so."[25] This last part of the statement, limiting the span of human existence to ten millennia, also runs up against basic facts from archaeology, anthropology, and history, quite apart from biology. The prevalence of such beliefs in the United States, in combination with a revival of religious fundamentalism, has led to a systematic assault on the teaching of evolution in the schools or at least an effort to introduce creationism or "intelligent design" as alternative explanations for the development of human beings.

This has had negative consequences in this country in several ways. First, it has undermined the teaching of science and the already weak grasp of science by American students. In areas of the country where religious conservatives hold sway, science teachers are often reluctant to teach evolution or even to teach about the long span of the earth's history or current theories about the origins of the universe. In those school districts where creationism or intelligent design is given equal billing with the theory of evolution, religion intrudes into science and politics. Students may be led to believe that both faith and science can explain the same phenomena and that science, with its dependence on experiment, evidence, and replication, offers no special advantage over religion. In the process, the underpinnings of modern society, derived from Enlightenment principles of reason and evidence, are undermined.

A second negative consequence of this fundamentalist challenge to science is the way that it is perceived in much of the rest of the world. The

United States stands virtually alone among developed countries in the majority's rejection of the theory of evolution. When Darwin's theory was first put forward in the mid-nineteenth century, it ran up against religious fundamentalism among both the clergy and the populations all over Europe. But over time, most churches and theologians on the Continent came to terms with evolution, agreeing that faith and science were separate spheres and not necessarily incompatible ones. By the mid-twentieth century, acceptance of evolution was almost universal in Europe (with some exceptions, such as the overwhelmingly Roman Catholic Poland). A 2001 "Eurobarometer" poll found that only 17 percent of Europeans do not believe in evolution, compared to the 54 percent of Americans who do not.[26]

There are many explanations for this huge difference in evolution beliefs between the United States and Europe. One of them is the difference in the educational systems, which as we have seen are much weaker in the United States, and the consequent differences in scientific competence and literacy levels between the two continents. But an even more important factor is the different levels of religiosity between the United States and Europe, which has also become one of the major sources of distrust and tension between the peoples and governments on each side of the Atlantic. Americans are far more likely than Europeans to express a belief in God (94 percent compared to half of Germans), to regularly attend religious services (40 percent compared to 20 percent of British), and to say that religion is a very important part of their lives (59 percent compared to 11 percent of French). A large majority of Americans think it is necessary to believe in God in order to be moral, whereas only small minorities of western Europeans feel that way. A majority of Americans think America is not religious enough; Europeans are more likely to think we are too religious.[27] These differences have exacerbated the political divide between the United States and Europe. Europeans are uncomfortable with the interjection of religion into politics in the United States (both in the domestic arena and in foreign policy), and they see Americans as more likely to think politically in terms of good and evil and black and white. After September 11, most European citizens and leaders were disturbed by President Bush's frequent invocation of morality and religion in discussing the "war on terror." His decision to attack Iraq in 2003 (and his initial reference to a "crusade") seemed more a matter of missionary zeal than hard evidence of weapons of mass destruction or Iraqi links to terrorism. All these were factors in the declining trust and confidence in the United States from other countries. As Andrew Kohut, the director of polls conducted by the Pew Research Center, has put it, American religiosity has "generated fear of a faith-driven U.S. foreign policy that risks endangering

American alliances." Such perceptions, he worries, "could feed the level of anti-Americanism that is already high as a result of cultural differences with both secular Europe and the more religious Muslim world."[28]

Ignoring Global Warming

On the issue of climate change and global warming, Americans are not as scientifically ill informed as they are on evolution, but they are poorly informed enough to allow politicians to give the issue short shrift. It is true that the issue of climate change and its connection to human activity has only been systematically investigated by scientists in the past several decades. But by the turn of the millennium, the evidence had become sufficiently overwhelming that almost all climate scientists and scientific organizations had come to accept the reality: global temperatures were increasing, and most of the change was due to human activity, in particular from carbon emissions generated by the use of fossil fuels. In 2001, the Intergovernmental Panel on Climate Change, created in 1988 by the World Meteorological Organization and the UN Environmental Program to evaluate the state of climate science, stated unequivocally that this was the consensus of scientific opinion. Since then, the National Academy of Sciences, the American Meteorological Society, the American Geophysical Union, and the American Association for the Advancement of Science have all issued statements agreeing that there is compelling evidence that human activity has caused climate change. A review of 928 peer-reviewed scientific papers on the subject published from 1993 to 2003 found that, "remarkably, none of the papers disagreed with the consensus position."[29] So the agreement among physical scientists on the reality and causes of global warming is nearly as universal as the consensus among biologists on the theory of evolution. There is not so much agreement on what to do about climate change, but many scientists are pointing to this as an increasingly urgent problem with potentially catastrophic consequences. The Intergovernmental Panel on Climate Change predicted that continued carbon dioxide emissions would increase global temperatures by 1.4 to 5.8 degrees centigrade by the end of the twenty-first century.[30] The Natural Resources Defense Council points out the far-reaching effects of such changes: "Sea levels will rise, flooding coastal areas. Heat waves will be more frequent and more intense. Droughts and wildfires will occur more often. Disease-carrying mosquitoes will expand their range. And species will be pushed to extinction . . . many of these changes have already begun."[31] A temperature change of a few degrees centigrade may not seem like much until one considers that during the last Ice Age 15,000 years ago, the planet was only about five degrees colder.

This is the way that science works: theories based on evidence gradually become accepted by most scientists and so become "fact" for all intents and purposes (until a new theory comes along to challenge the previous one). Yet despite the overwhelming scientific evidence and consensus for global warming, most Americans are still "not highly concerned" about the problem, according to a recent Gallup poll. Almost two-thirds of Americans think there is "a lot" of scientific disagreement on climate change, and only a third think global warming is "mainly caused by things people do." By contrast, most people in Europe and Japan recognize the scientific consensus about global warming and the human role in it.[32] Only a third of Americans think that global warming will pose a serious threat in their lifetime, and it is at or near the bottom of a list of ten environmental concerns (including air and water pollution).[33] So, while Americans are somewhat more informed about the science of this issue than they are about evolution, the issue is not very important or urgent for most Americans. And a significant minority—perhaps a third of the population—continues to doubt that it is a problem at all or that human activity affects global climate.

The combination of public ignorance and public indifference to global warming, an issue that many scientists see as the single major threat to the globe, has allowed U.S. politicians and political leaders to sidestep the issue. An international treaty addressing the issue of climate change, called the Kyoto Protocol, was signed by President Clinton but never submitted to the Senate after that body voted ninety-five to zero to oppose any such treaty that could hurt the American economy. President Bush expressed strong opposition to the Kyoto treaty and has declared emphatically that he will not seek U.S. ratification of the treaty. Meanwhile, almost every other country in the world has signed and ratified the treaty—more than 160 countries as of early 2006. But progress on reducing global warming will be difficult without the United States being involved because the country is the largest contributor to global warming. In 2003, the United States alone accounted for almost a quarter of the world's emissions of carbon dioxide—the major factor in "greenhouse gases." By contrast, the whole of the European Union and the People's Republic of China, the next two biggest contributors, contributed only about 15 percent of carbon emissions (see figure 4.1).

The Kyoto Protocol—and the whole issue of global warming—has become highly politicized in the United States and is one of the many examples of President Bush's unilateralist approach to international politics, to be discussed in more detail in chapter 6. So it is not surprising that there are huge differences between Democrats and Republicans on the issue of global warming. A large part of this difference can be attributed to the president's

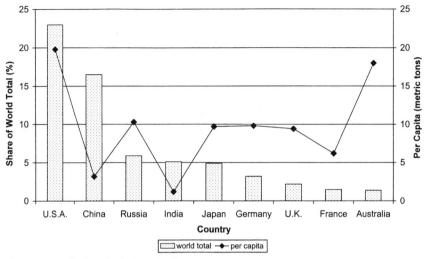

Figure 4.1. Carbon Emissions by Country, 2003
Source: United Nations Development Program, *Human Development Report* 2006 (New York: United Nations, 2006).

very public and vocal stance on global warming and the Kyoto treaty. From the last year of Bill Clinton's presidency to the first year of George Bush's administration, the Gallup poll found no changes in the attitudes of Democrats on global warming but a fourteen-point drop in concern among Republicans. In 2000, there was only a fourteen-point difference in concern about global warming between Democrats and Republicans; by 2006, the gap had widened to a thirty-two-point difference—77 percent to 45 percent.[34] On this issue, science is being trumped by politics as well as by science illiteracy. It has been easy for the Bush administration to convince the public that global warming is not a problem because they know and care so little about it. And Americans, who are increasingly inclined to disregard science and empirical evidence in the first place, are receptive to the distortions emanating from their political leadership. This is causing problems both in terms of U.S. efforts to address an increasingly urgent need and in the country's relationship with the rest of the global community, where the issue of climate change is taken much more seriously.

Gullible on Weapons of Mass Destruction

An even more flagrant example of the government distorting, hiding, or inventing evidence for political purposes was on the issue of so-called weapons of mass destruction (WMD) in Saddam Hussein's Iraq on the eve of the U.S.

invasion in March 2003. In the lead-up to that attack, the president linked Hussein's Iraq to the September 11 terrorist attacks, even though there was no evidence of such a connection, and warned that Saddam "possesses the most deadly arms of our age," even though all the evidence suggested exactly the opposite. There is no doubt that in the early 1990s, Iraq had some biological and chemical weapons and probably was working on a nuclear weapons program. But under the terms of the UN resolutions following the Gulf War of 1990–1991, the Iraqi government was required to dismantle all WMD programs under UN supervision. By the reports of both the United Nations and Iraqi insiders, all of those weapons had been dismantled or destroyed by 1995. Scott Ritter, the chief UN weapons inspector for Iraq, testified repeatedly in 2002 and 2003 that the UN teams had eliminated all WMD in Iraq. Saddam Hussein's son-in-law, Hussein Kamel, who was in charge of Iraq's nuclear, chemical, biological, and missile programs and defected from Iraq in 1995, testified bluntly at the time that "all weapons— biological, chemical, missile, nuclear—were destroyed."[35] But this testimony had been withheld from the public, and, in fact, in 2002 both President Bush and Secretary of State Powell cited Kamel as a source for the existence of such weapons. Despite this evidence, the United States insisted on reinserting the UN weapons inspections teams into Iraq in September 2002. After the new UN inspection teams had combed the country for five months, both Hans Blix, the chief UN weapons inspector, and Mohammed El Baradei, the head of the International Atomic Energy Agency, were able to testify in numerous televised reports to the UN Security Council that they had found no evidence of any nuclear, chemical, or biological weapons in Iraq. And, of course, after the defeat and occupation of Iraq by several hundred thousand U.S. troops, no WMD of any kind were found.

Despite all this expert testimony and documented evidence, the American public blindly went along with the president's drumbeat of assertions that Saddam possessed or was assembling a whole arsenal of chemical, biological, and nuclear weapons and was prepared to use them against the United States and its allies.[36] Americans of all stripes overwhelmingly believed that Iraq had WMD and believed that was the main reason that the United States had to invade and occupy the country. A Gallup poll conducted in February 2003, on the eve of the American invasion, found that 55 percent were "certain" that Iraq had "facilities to create weapons of mass destruction," and another 38 percent thought it was "likely" but not certain.[37] Thus, fully 93 percent of Americans believed the assertions of the president in spite of the evidence to the contrary. One almost never sees 90 percent of

Americans agreeing on anything in public opinion polls, so this number is especially disturbing.

What is even more startling is that in 2006, half of all Americans still believed that Iraq had WMD at the time of the U.S. invasion in 2003. This faith in WMD claims persists even after a sixteen-month $900 million investigation by the U.S. weapons hunters, known as the Iraq Survey Group, declared in 2004 that Iraq had dismantled its chemical, biological, and nuclear arms programs in 1991 under UN supervision. This report confirmed the work and reports of the UN inspection teams from 2002 to 2003 (mentioned previously) as well as the reports from the inspection teams of the 1990s headed up by Scott Ritter. Commenting on the Harris poll released in July 2006 showing that the percentage who believed that Iraq had such weapons had actually grown from 36 percent in 2005 to 50 percent in 2006, opinion analyst Steven Kull concluded that people tend to become "independent of reality."[38]

The problem here is threefold: Americans' lack of ability at critically evaluating information, their disinclination to insist on and use evidence, and their susceptibility to propaganda and dogma, which is itself fueled by fearfulness. All three problems can be traced back, ultimately, to the failure of the education system. The consequences are wide ranging. Americans are increasingly out of touch with the rest of the modern world and increasingly less competitive globally. Americans can easily be led astray by demagogic politicians or radio and television personalities who prey on fear to preach hate or violence. In the process, the very foundations of democracy are jeopardized.

The Erosion of Science

The decline of science literacy in the schools and the general population has been accompanied by or has helped cause both an erosion of the role of science within the United States and a decline in America's scientific and technological predominance worldwide. As with many of the other problems addressed in this book, the decline in science has been particularly dramatic and worrisome in the years of the Bush presidency, but in many cases the damage done since 2000 is irreversible, and in other cases it simply reflects deeper and more long-term problems.

The shorter-term and more acute problems are related to the debasement and politicization of science by the Bush administration. This was apparent from the examples mentioned previously (evolution, global warming, and WMD) but has extended into virtually all areas of science and science policy. Numerous prominent scientists and professional scientific organizations have complained about the ways in which the Bush administration has misrepresented or suppressed scientific information. In 2004, a group of sixty leading scientists and former government officials, including twenty Nobel laureates, signed a statement castigating the Bush administration for "misrepresenting and suppressing scientific knowledge for political purposes" and "the distortion of scientific knowledge for partisan political ends."[39] The report cited numerous examples but pointed especially to the administration's pressure on the Environmental Protection Agency to alter its findings on air pollution and climate change:

> Thus in June 2003, the White House demanded extensive changes in the treatment of climate change in a major report by the Environmental Protection Agency (EPA). To avoid issuing a scientifically indefensible report, EPA officials eviscerated the discussion of climate change and its consequences.

The statement also alluded to the distortion of scientific evidence about WMD in the run-up to the Iraq War:

> In making the invalid claim that Iraq had sought to acquire aluminum tubes for uranium enrichment centrifuges, the administration disregarded the contrary assessment by experts at Livermore, Los Alamos and Oak Ridge National Laboratories.

The signatories warned that this political interference with science would have serious effects both on the development of science in the United States and on "human health, public safety, and community well-being." More than 9,000 scientists and researchers eventually signed on to the document, including forty-nine Nobel laureates, sixty-three recipients of the National Medal of Science, and 171 members of the National Academy of Sciences.[40]

Concern about the misuse and abuse of science has come from many quarters, including professionals in many executive agencies of the government, congressional Democrats, and even, most recently, journalists. Chris Mooney has revealed the breadth and depth of the problem in his book *The Republican War on Science*, which documents the role of the White House in distorting, misrepresenting, or undermining science in almost every area of science and public policy, including acid rain, global warming, stem cell research, endangered species, the links between condom use and prevention of sexually transmitted diseases, the links between smoking and cancer, the impact on health of dietary sugar and fat, and the efficacy of abstinence-only sex education programs. This had come to affect almost every agency of the federal government, including especially the Department of the Interior, the National Cancer Institute, the Centers for Disease Control, the Food and Drug Administration, and the Environmental Protection Agency. Recently, even the National Aeronautics and Space Administration (NASA) has had to trim its scientific mission under political pressure. The agency's mission statement had previously included the phrase "to understand and protect our home planet," but this phrase was eliminated, under political pressure, because of the administration's concern that NASA scientists were using this as an umbrella to advance research on greenhouse gas emissions and global warming.[41]

Even the surgeon general's office encountered political pressure to suppress scientific studies. Former Surgeon General Richard Carmona testified before Congress that top Bush administration officials repeatedly tried to suppress or weaken important public health reports for political considerations. The administration, he said, would not allow him to speak or issue reports about "stem cells, emergency contraception, sex education, or prison, mental and global health issues."[42]

For the Bush administration, many of these antiscience gambits are due to the president's close ties to private industry or fundamentalist Christian organizations. The systematic nature of this assault on science led Donald Kennedy, the editor in chief of *Science* magazine, to wonder if we are entering the "twilight of the Enlightenment." "When the religious/political convergence leads to managing the nation's research agenda, its foreign assistance programs, or the high-school curriculum," writes Kennedy, "that marks a really important change in our national life."[43]

U.S. Decline in Science, Technology, Engineering, and Competitiveness

The results of all these problems with education and science in the United States are already beginning to show in terms of the country's quickening decline in international competitiveness. A recent report from the American Electronics Association titled *Losing the Competitive Advantage?* sums up the problem by asserting,

> We are slipping. Yes, the United States still leads in nearly every way one can measure, but that does not change the fact that the foundation on which this lead was built is eroding. Our leadership in technology and innovation has benefited from an infrastructure created by 50 years of continual investment, education, and research. We are no longer maintaining this infrastructure.[44]

For much of the postwar period, the United States was the world leader in science, technology, and innovation, with the best scientists, the best universities, and the most advanced research and development programs. But all that has begun to change as other countries and regions have become more advanced and more competitive and increasingly challenge U.S. dominance.

One sees this slippage in many areas of U.S. science, education, and technology. One measure, for example, of innovation and competitiveness in the world of science and technology is the number of patents granted. Before 1990, about two-thirds of all U.S. patents were granted to people of U.S. origin. That percentage dropped steadily over the years, by 2003 dipping to just 52 percent.[45] The United States still led the world in the number of patents granted, but other countries were catching up fast.

Similar trends are evident in the publication of science and engineering articles in academic publications. National Science Foundation data show that between 1988 and 2001, the number of such publications originating in the United States increased by 13 percent. But they increased by 25 percent for India, by 59 percent for western Europe, and by 354 percent for China.[46] In absolute numbers, in 2001, western Europe had more science articles than the United States. In this respect, as in so many others noted in this book, Europe has improved on the United States. In science and technology, India and China are also making rapid gains, fortifying their international economic positions as well.

Certainly one of the reasons that the United States has slipped in patents, inventions, articles, and so on is the declining quality and numbers of science, math, and engineering students in the United States. We have already seen that American elementary school, high school, and college students fare poorly in international comparisons and competitions in science and mathematics. But there is also a decline in the quantity of Americans studying science, math, and especially engineering at all levels of higher and postgraduate education. As figure 4.2 shows, the United States ranks only sixth in the number of bachelor degrees awarded in engineering. China graduates almost four times as many engineers as the United States, and South Korea, with only one-sixth the population of the United States, has almost as many engineering graduates as the United States.

In doctoral degree programs, the United States still leads other countries in the number of such degrees in science and engineering, though the EU-15 as a whole awards more such degrees than the United States. And here too, the U.S. lead is slipping. Between 1989 and 2001, science and engineering doctoral degrees awarded increased by 19 percent in the United States but by 39 percent in Germany and by 81 percent in the United Kingdom.[47]

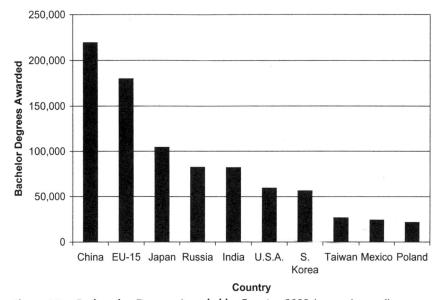

Figure 4.2.   Engineering Degrees Awarded by Country, 2000 (or most recent)

Source: American Electronics Association, *Losing the Competitive Advantage? The Challenge for Science and Technology in the United States* (Washington, D.C.: American Electronics Association, 2005), 7.

The United States is also losing its edge in funding for research and development (R&D), which has fueled much of the technological, scientific, and economic growth of the country since World War II. Federal funding of R&D peaked in dollar terms in 1987 and has not regained that level since then in real terms. As a percentage of gross domestic product (GDP), the decline is even more precipitous, dropping from 1.25 percent of GDP in 1985 to 0.75 percent in 2002. In overall spending on R&D, as a percentage of the economy, the United States trails Sweden, Finland, Japan, Switzerland, Iceland, and South Korea. Looking only at nondefense research as a share of the economy, the United States slips to twenty-second among OECD countries.[48]

The situation does not promise to get much better. In 2004, Congress actually cut the 2005 budget of the National Science Foundation by $105 million, the first actual cut in that agency's budget in sixteen years.[49] The anti-science bias in the Bush administration is not likely to help in the short term, but even in the long term the ballooning federal debt and deficits will make it harder to carve out more money for any federal programs in this area or others.

Losing the Edge

Through much of the twentieth century, the "American Century," the United States led the world in education, science, and technology. The universal and egalitarian system of education and especially American universities were admired throughout the world and mimicked in many other countries. The U.S. spirit of pragmatism, entrepreneurship, rationality, and efficiency were magnets and models for enterprising people all over the world. And the close relationship between science, technology, R&D, and industry helped fuel U.S. economic growth and international economic competitiveness.

All these advantages are being lost, though, as the country's growing poverty and inequality have weakened the educational system, generated increased illiteracy, and eroded U.S. efficiency, competence, and competitiveness. American students and graduates fare poorly in comparison with their counterparts in other industrialized countries. The deteriorating educational system has impaired critical thinking, science, and science literacy, making Americans more susceptible to fundamentalist religious and political doctrines that appeal to people's emotions and fears instead of reason and evidence. All this has contributed to the decline of America's image abroad. The very things that made the country great have now become the main sources of its weaknesses. What is even more disturbing, perhaps, is the effect this has had on internal American politics and on democracy itself. This is the subject of the following chapter.

Notes

1. Jonathan Kozol, *Illiterate America* (New York: Doubleday, 1985), 4.

2. See the results of the National Assessment of Adult Literacy (conducted in 1992 and 2003 by the National Center for Education Statistics) at http://nces.ed .gov/NAAL/PDF/2006470.PDF.

3. National Endowment for the Arts, *To Read or Not to Read*, Research Report no. 47, November 2007, http://www.nea.gov/research/ToRead.pdf.

4. The magazine *Education Week*, June 22, 2006, devoted its cover story "Diplomas Count" to the issue of graduation rates, available at http://edweek.org/ew/ toc/2006/06/22/index.html.

5. Carnegie Task Force on Meeting the Needs of Young Children, *Starting Points: Meeting the Needs of Our Youngest Children* (New York: Carnegie Corporation, 1994), cited in Valdas Anelauskas, *Discovering America As It Is* (Atlanta: Clarity, 1999), 163.

6. National Commission on Excellence in Education, *A Nation at Risk: The Imperative for Educational Reform* (Washington, D.C.: National Commission on Excellence in Education, 1983), 8.

7. The website for NAEP has much data and even allows users to analyze the data on their own, selecting variables and years: http://nces.ed.gov/nationsreportcard/nde. The site also includes many of their periodic "report cards" on science, reading, mathematics, and so on.

8. National Geographic Education Foundation, *National Geographic—Roper 2002 Global Geographic Literacy Survey*, November 2002, http://www.nationalgeographic.com.

9. National Geographic Education Foundation, *National Geographic—Roper Public Affairs 2006 Geographic Literacy Study*, May 2006, http://www.nationalgeographic.com.

10. See results at http://nces.ed.gov/surveys/pisa/PISA2003HighlightsFigures.asp?Quest=1&Figure=9.

11. Cited in Anelauskas, *Discovering America As It Is*, 168.

12. In an interview in *Time*, July 23, 1990, 12.

13. SAT data available from the College Board at http://www.collegeboard.com/prod_downloads/about/news_info/cbsenior/yr2005/table2-mean-SAT-scores.pdf.

14. Diana Schemo, "At 2-Year Colleges, Students Eager but Unready," *New York Times*, September 2, 2006, A1.

15. Stephen H. Balch and Rita Zurcher, "The Dissolution of General Higher Education: 1914–1993," report from the National Association of Scholars, available at http://www.nas.org/reports/disogened/disogened_full.pdf.

16. Jeffrey Young, "Homework, What Homework?" *Chronicle of Higher Education*, December 6, 2002, A35.

17. Many of these issues are documented in a PBS documentary *Declining by Degrees: Higher Education at Risk* (PBS Home Video, 2005), which concludes with the observation that "while American higher education is declining, much of the industrialized world is moving up, fast."

18. Paul Barton and Archie LaPointe, *Learning by Degrees* (Princeton, N.J.: Educational Testing Service, 1995), 7.

19. *Today's College Students and Yesteryear's High School Grads: A Comparison of General Cultural Knowledge*, 2002, http://www.nas.org/reports.html.

20. Lois Romano, "Literacy of College Graduates Is on Decline" (on the study by the National Center for Education Statistics), *Washington Post*, December 25, 2005, A12.

21. *Today's College Students and Yesteryear's High School Grads.*

22. It is no longer true, however, that the United States has far more young people in college than other developed countries. In 2003, the United States had 35 percent of eighteen- to twenty-four-year-olds enrolled in higher education. Most European countries have between a quarter and a third of that age-group in higher education, and some, like Belgium and Finland (37 percent) and Greece (43 percent), have more. In Korea, almost half the age-group is enrolled. OECD data from

National Center for Public Policy and Higher Education, *Measuring Up 2006: The National Report Card on Higher Education*, 2006, http://measuringup.highereducation.org/_docs/2006/NationalReport_2006.pdf, 8.

23. *A Nation at Risk: The Imperative for Educational Reform*, 5.

24. *Measuring Up 2006*; Tamar Lewin, "Report Finds U.S. Students Lagging in Finishing College," *New York Times*, September 7, 2006, A24.

25. Frank Newport, "Third of Americans Say Evidence Has Supported Darwin's Evolution Theory," Gallup Poll News Service, November 2004, http://poll.gallup.com/content/default.aspx?ci=14107.

26. Allan Mazur, "Believers and Disbelievers in Evolution," *Politics and the Life Sciences* 23, no. 2 (2005): 55.

27. Data from the Pew Research Center, reported in Andrew Kohut and Bruce Stokes, *America against the World: How We Are Different and Why We Are Disliked* (New York: Times Books, 2006), 102–4.

28. Kohut and Stokes, *America against the World*, 119.

29. Naomi Oreskes, "The Scientific Consensus on Climate Change," *Science* 306, no. 5702 (2004): 1686.

30. 2001 Report of the Intergovernmental Panel on Climate Change, referenced in United Nations Environmental Program, *Planet in Peril* (Arendal, Norway: United Nations Environmental Program, 2006).

31. "Consequences of Global Warming," http://www.nrdc.org/globalWarming/fcons.asp.

32. Polls cited in *Newsweek*, August 13, 2007, 22.

33. Lydia Saad, "Americans Still Not Highly Concerned about Global Warming," Gallup Poll News Service, April 7, 2006, http://poll.gallup.com.

34. Saad, "Americans Still Not Highly Concerned about Global Warming."

35. Cited in Chalmers Johnson, *The Sorrows of Empire: Militarism, Secrecy and the End of the Republic* (New York: Henry Holt, 2004), 303.

36. The president was especially emphatic and detailed about this in his State of the Union Address in January 2003, http://www.whitehouse.gov/news/releases/2003/01/20030128-19.html.

37. Frank Newport, "Americans Still Think Iraq Had Weapons of Mass Destruction before War," Gallup News Service, June 16, 2003, http://poll.gallup.com.

38. "Poll: Faith in WMD Claims Endures," *Indianapolis Star*, August 7, 2006, A6.

39. The statement, "Restoring Scientific Integrity in Policymaking," is available at http://www.ucsusa.org/scientific_integrity/interference/scientists-signon-statement.html.

40. Chris Mooney, *The Republican War on Science* (New York: Basic Books, 2005), 239.

41. "NASA's Goals Delete Mention of Home Planet," *New York Times*, July 22, 2006, A1.

42. "Surgeon General Says He Endured Political Stress," *New York Times*, July 11, 2007, A1.

43. "Twilight for the Enlightenment?" *Science* 308 (2005): 165.

44. American Electronics Association, *Losing the Competitive Advantage? The Challenge for Science and Technology in the United States* (Washington, D.C.: American Electronics Association, 2005), http://www.aeanet.org.

45. National Science Foundation, "Science and Technology Indicators 2006," http://www.nsf.gov/statistics/seind06/pdf_v2.htm#c2.

46. American Electronics Association, *Losing the Completive Advantage?* 11.

47. American Electronics Association, *Losing the Completive Advantage?* 8.

48. Anna Bernasek, "The State of Research Isn't All That Grand," *New York Times*, September 3, 2006, Business section, 3.

49. American Electronics Association, *Losing the Completive Advantage?* 15.

CHAPTER FIVE

~

Ailing American Democracy

Progress toward realizing American ideals of democracy may have
stalled, and in some areas reversed.

—Task Force of the American Political Science Association

During the "American Century," the worldwide appeal of the United Sates
was based on its democratic model and principles as much as its economic or
military strength. The United States had built the most successful, resilient,
and durable democracy in world history while at the same time providing for
a highly diverse population, consisting largely of immigrants and their de-
scendants. The American democracy was a work in progress, of course, rather
than an accomplished fact. At the formation of the republic in the eighteenth century, only a small percentage of the population was even eligible
to vote, with women, African Americans, and most poor people excluded
from the franchise. But over the centuries, visionary leaders like Abraham
Lincoln, Franklin Roosevelt, Elizabeth Cady Stanton, and Martin Luther
King and movements and organizations for the rights of workers, minorities,
and women helped create a political system as broadly democratic, representative, and egalitarian as any in the world. In the 1940s, the United States
was in an excellent position to promote its form of democracy abroad, and
Americans as far apart ideologically as Henry Luce and Franklin Roosevelt
proclaimed the country's intent to foster and "incite" (Luce's term) democratic principles "throughout the world." In many countries, political leaders
and citizens alike professed admiration for the American model of democracy

and welcomed U.S. efforts to promote it. There was, indeed, an amazing movement toward democracy and free governments in the years after World War II. In the 1950s, only a few dozen countries worldwide could be counted as genuinely democratic. By the 1970s, that number had almost doubled and by the turn of the millennium had doubled once more.

American democracy was in some ways a victim of its own success. It had helped inspire a world of other democracies and in the process lost its monopoly on democracy promotion and lost its cachet as the world's most successful and emulated democratic political system. With the collapse of communist governments in Russia and Eastern Europe, for example, most people in those countries professed a wish to model their new political systems on European democracies (like Germany or Sweden) rather than on the United States. Within the United States itself, there seemed to be some backtracking in progress toward the democratic ideal, with declining rates of political participation, growing inequality in political representation, seemingly uncontrollable growth in the role of money in politics, and, especially after September 11, worrisome restrictions on both civil rights and freedom of the press. As the democratic world became more heterogeneous and the United States became seemingly less democratic, the country was no longer seen as the world's beacon of freedom and democracy.

Inequality Undermines Democracy

In chapter 2, we discussed the startling growth in inequality in the United States, especially since the early 1980s, and the effects this has had on the standard of living in the country and on the health, education, and welfare of Americans. The effects of inequality are broad and pervasive, however, and have also reached into the American political system. Compared to the affluent, poor people are far less likely to vote or participate politically in other ways. Only about half of people earning under $15,000 are voters, for example, compared to almost 90 percent of those earning more than $75,000 yearly. Figure 5.1 displays similar rich–poor differences for other forms of political participation, from a prestigious study conducted in 1990. Campaign contributors are particularly unrepresentative of the citizenry as a whole. A report of the American Political Science Association found that households with incomes over $100,000 in 2000 made up only 12 percent of households but contributed a whopping 95 percent of all campaign contributions.[1]

When people do not vote, lobby, or contribute to political campaigns, they are less likely to be listened to by legislators or policymakers, and their interests are less likely to be taken into account in the political process. In

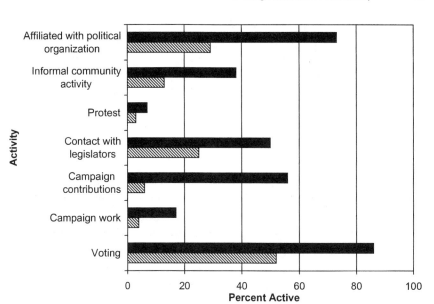

Figure 5.1.   Political Activity by Income Level
Source: American Democracy in an Age of Rising Inequality (Washington, D.C.: American Political Science Association, 2004).

the words of the eminent political scientist Sidney Verba, they lose political "voice."[2] A task force of the American Political Science Association found that members of Congress pay far more attention to wealthy constituents than poor ones, that the votes of legislators correspond more with the policy preferences of rich constituents, and that "government officials disproportionately respond to business, the wealthy, and the organized and vocal when they design America's domestic and foreign policies."[3] Widening political and economic inequalities in the United States are threatening the accomplishments of the "rights revolutions" and jeopardizing the commitment to political equality and civil rights that are at the heart of the American political system and reflected in the country's founding documents.

The American Political Science Association task force points out the paradox of the United States pushing for freedom, equality, and democracy in other countries at a time when many of these principles are eroding in the United States itself:

> Equal political voice and democratically responsive government are widely cherished American ideals. Indeed, the United States is vigorously promoting democracy abroad. Yet, what is happening to democracy at home? Our coun-

try's ideals of equal citizenship and responsive government may be under growing threat in an era of persistent and rising inequalities. Disparities of income, wealth, and access to opportunity are growing more sharply in the United States than in many other nations, and gaps between races and ethnic groups persist. Progress toward realizing American ideals of democracy may have stalled, and in some areas reversed.[4]

Money Buys Influence

The class differences in political participation in the United States are related to the role of money in the country's political campaigns and political processes. Money has always played a role in politics, of course, both in the United States and elsewhere. But there has been a virtual explosion of money and monied influence in politics in the past twenty years.

The costs of election campaigns, for both the presidency and Congress, have escalated sharply in the past two decades. In the 1987–1988 election cycle, House and Senate candidates raised some $365 million in "hard" money (money contributed directly to candidates), which seemed like a lot at the time. By the 2003–2004 cycle, the hard money totaled almost $1.5 billion, and this was after passage of a campaign finance law in 2002 that was meant to restrain such spending.[5] In the 2004 congressional elections, incumbent senators raised $223 million for their races, and incumbent members of the House raised $456 million. This averaged out to $8.6 million for each incumbent senator (compared to $610,000 in 1976) and about $1.1 million for each incumbent representative. The average challenger to an incumbent senator raised only about one-ninth of what the incumbent raised, and the average challenger for the House raised less than one-fifth of the incumbent. It is perhaps not surprising, then, that in that year, 98 percent of House incumbents were reelected, and 96 percent of incumbent senators were reelected. Once elected, a member of Congress has such advantages in fund-raising that he or she can, in effect, serve for life or until retirement. Virtually the only chance for a newcomer to make it into Congress is to run for an "open" seat when an incumbent has died or retired. One of the principal features of a democratic political system—periodic competitive elections—has been much eroded in the American political process. In no other advanced democracy does money play such a prominent role in the electoral process.

The necessity of raising so much money to run for national political office has a number of other deleterious effects on democratic principles and ideals. It tends to produce a Congress made up of representatives who are highly unrepresentative of the U.S. population. Even in the 1980s, Senator Daniel Patrick Moynihan admitted that "at least half the members of the Senate today are millionaires" and mused that "we've become a plutocracy. . . . The Senate was meant to represent the interests of the states; instead it represents the interests of a class."[6] About half of both houses of Congress are lawyers, and there are almost no blue-collar workers or ordinary working people in its membership. Congress is also unrepresentative of minorities and women. African Americans and Latinos together make up about a quarter of the country's population, yet in 2006 there were only thirty-seven African Americans and twenty-three Latinos in the House of Representatives—less than 14 percent of the total. Women are more than half the U.S. population but have only seventy-one of the 435 seats in the House. The United States ranks seventieth in the world in the percentage of women in the national legislature, behind such countries as Bolivia, Uzbekistan, Zimbabwe, Pakistan, and China.[7]

The role of money in politics also raises issues of corruption and special interest influence in the legislative process. While it is often difficult to prove that campaign contributions influence legislation and policymaking, both the public (according to public opinion polls) and members of Congress (based on their periodic efforts to reform campaign finance) recognize that it is a problem. And the huge and growing number of lobbyists in Washington indicates that they also recognize the payback of their activity and their spending. The number of lobbyists registered in Washington doubled from 2000 to 2005 so that they now number some 35,000. As television journalist Bill Moyers wryly points out, that's "sixty-five lobbyists for every member of Congress."[8] He notes that "the total spent per month by special interests wining, dining and seducing federal officials is now nearly $200 million. *Per month.*" Various studies have shown that lawmakers who receive large contributions from particular business interests, such as tobacco companies or defense contractors, are several times more likely to vote for bills favored by those companies than legislators who receive little or no money from those groups.[9]

The recent bribery scandals involving lobbyist Jack Abramoff and California Representative Randy Cunningham highlighted the issue of congressional "earmarks"—the pet projects lawmakers insert into spending bills, often anonymously and with little vetting or oversight. But despite these scandals, the number and cost of such projects have soared in recent years. The Congressional Research Service found that over the past twelve years, the number of earmarks tripled to 16,000, worth $64 billion a year.[10] These earmarks make it relatively easy for members of Congress to target federal funding for special interests or pork-barrel projects in their own districts. But it does not satisfy the requirements of representative democracy for the public good. In this regard, as in so many others, the United States does not fare well in comparison with other democracies. In Transparency International's 2006 annual index of corruption around the world, the United States rates only 7.3 on a ten-point scale and ranks twentieth in the world, with virtually all the other affluent democracies ranked ahead of the United States.[11]

Spectator Democracy

The bottom-line measure for any democracy is the extent to which citizens can—and do—vote in competitive elections. As we have seen previously, poor people and minorities in the United States are far less likely to participate politically than upper-income whites. This is one factor that contributes to an overall lack of interest and participation in politics in the United States and the lowest voter turnout rate of any democratic country in the world. Looking at voter turnout in national elections from 1945 to 1998, in the United States, only 48.3 percent of those eligible voted. The United States ranked 114th in the world on this measure out of only 140 countries in the comparison. In all other wealthy democracies, at least two-thirds of citizens voted.[12] A comparison of the United States to other advanced democracies appears in figure 5.2. The data in this figure reflect voter turnout over almost the whole postwar era, but in fact U.S. voter turnout has been

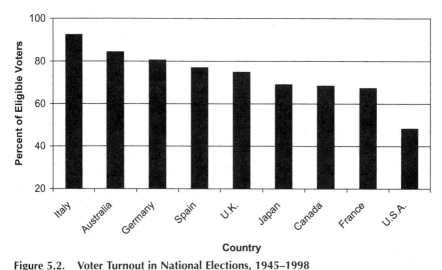

Figure 5.2.   Voter Turnout in National Elections, 1945–1998

Source: International Institute for Democracy and Electoral Assistance; online at http://www.idea.int/vt/
survey/voter_turnout_pop2-2.cfm.

on a steady decline since the 1960s, dropping from about 47 percent of eligible voters in 1962 to 37 percent in 2002.

There are many possible explanations for the low and declining voter turnout in the United States, and many scholarly articles and books have been written on the subject. One important factor, though, is the obvious one: that people increasingly feel that their votes do not really matter or that the government is not responsive to the interests of ordinary (and especially poor) people. Given what we have seen previously about the role of money in politics, it is a pretty logical assumption to make. Periodic public opinion surveys of Americans' attitudes about government show a sharp decline in trust in government beginning in the 1960s. Although there was some upsurge in such trust after 1994 (the nadir of such trust), it still remains very low. In 1964, more than three-quarters of Americans trusted the federal government to do what is right just about always or most of the time; by the early twenty-first century, less than half felt that way (see figure 5.3).

Similarly, when people are asked if the government is run for the benefit of all the people or for a few big interests looking out for themselves, only about 40 percent pick the first option compared to almost two-thirds in the 1960s (see figure 5.4).

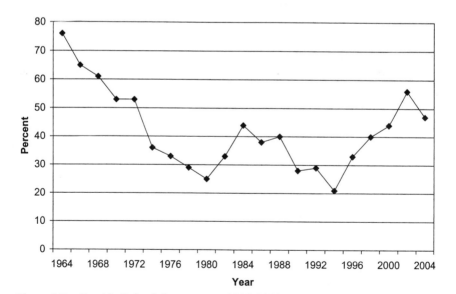

Figure 5.3.   Trust in Federal Government, 1964–2004
Note: Percent answering "most of the time" or "always" to the question, "How much of the time do you think you can trust the government in Washington to do what is right?"
Source: American National Election Studies data at http://www.electionstudies.org/nesguide/toptable/tab5a_1.htm.

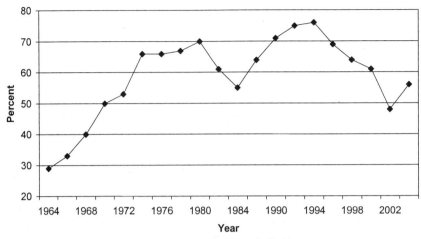

Figure 5.4. Who Does Government Benefit? A Few Big Interests

Note: Percent answering "a few big interests" to the question, "Would you say the government is pretty much run by a few big interests looking out for themselves, or that it is run for the benefit of all the people?"

Source: American National Election Studies data at http://www.electionstudies.org/nesguide/toptable/tab5a_2htm.

In terms of both behavior and attitudes, Americans are not very support-ive of their own political system, so it is not surprising that people in other countries might express reservations about following the U.S. democratic model. It should be noted that people in other democracies often are dis-trustful of government as well, but in most of them there is still overall satis-faction with their own systems. A Eurobarometer survey in the European Union countries in 2004, for example, showed that 54 percent of the Euro-pean population were "very" or "fairly" satisfied with the way democracy works in their countries.[13]

Declining political participation and trust is part of a broader decay in the country's "civic health." The National Conference on Citizenship, a non-profit organization chartered by the U.S. Congress, has constructed "Amer-ica's Civic Health Index," which includes forty indicators of Americans' par-ticipation in politics and other civic activities, understanding of politics, volunteering activities, and levels of trust in other people and institutions. Its 2006 report concluded that "our civic health shows steep declines over the last 30 years" and echoed the concern of the 1998 blue-ribbon National Commission on Civic Renewal that America was turning into a "nation of spectators" rather than the active participants democracy requires. The "key findings" of the 2006 report quotes an earlier report on civic engagement that worried about the future of democracy in America:

Without strong habits of social and political participation, the world's longest and most successful experiment in democracy is at risk of losing the very norms, networks, and institutions of civic life that have made us the most emulated and respected nation in history.[14]

A small but telling example of the way Americans have turned into spectators is that at sporting events, many no longer sing the national anthem but watch someone else sing it.

Political Ignorance and the Failure of the Media

Whether or not Thomas Jefferson said that "an informed citizenry is the bulwark of democracy," this idea has been central to the American conception of democracy and our educational system. Yet Americans are remarkably ignorant and apathetic about politics, and the situation has deteriorated over time. Many American citizens are unaware of even the basic facts of political life in the country. Only about two-thirds can name the current vice president and the governor of their own state. Only two-thirds know that the United States has a trade deficit, and only three-quarters know which political party controls the House of Representatives. Even more disturbing, about a third of Americans believe the president has the power to adjourn Congress, and 49 percent think that he has the power to suspend the Constitution.[15] Knowledge of foreign affairs is even more limited, as one might expect, with only about a third able to name Vladimir Putin as the president of Russia in 2007, for example.[16] The ability to answer such questions has declined sharply from a generation ago and even more so over a longer span. Today's college graduates have about the same level of political knowledge as high school graduates from fifty years ago.[17] This trend in political awareness and knowledge is a piece of the bigger picture of education and knowledge more generally, as discussed in chapter 3, but it carries a special challenge for American politics and the health of democracy. Political knowledge is closely tied to political participation: 90 percent of those with high political knowledge are registered to vote, compared to only 53 percent of those with low political knowledge.[18]

The Pew Center study on which some of these statistics are based raised the question of how political knowledge could deteriorate in the face of "news and information revolutions." After all, Americans, more than any other people in the world, have a huge array of information resources available to them, with broad choices in terms of content, political orientation (left to right), and type of media. Web-based news sources, a proliferation of cable television networks, and satellite radio have supplemented the traditional venues of local and national newspapers and radio and television programs. Despite the booming (or, perhaps, because of the bombardment) of news, Americans are less informed now than their parents or grandparents were. In part, this is due to the type of news media they depend on. Most Americans now rely primarily on local television for their news, and such news broadcasts have minimal coverage of national political news and negligible coverage of international events. Only a slim majority of the population reads a local daily newspaper, and a tiny minority (18 percent in one study[19]) regularly reads a major national one. Newspaper readership has declined precipitously in recent years, leading to the closing down of a number of big-city newspapers. Newspapers, especially national and major city ones, provide the most broad-based and in-depth political and international coverage, but these are increasingly less available and less read. Almost four in ten people regularly use an Internet news source, but such news gathering tends to be selective and relies on headline news, much like television news.

A further problem is the increasing centralization and consolidation of the most important media outlets in the United States. According to political scientist Michael Parenti,

> As of 2006, only six giant conglomerates—Time Warner, General Electric, Viacom, Bertelsmann, Walt Disney, and News Corporation—(down from twenty-three in 1989) owned most of the newspapers, magazines, book publishing houses, movie studios, cable channels, record labels, broadcast networks and channels and radio and television programming in the United States.[20]

Almost all contemporary daily newspapers in the United States have a monopoly in their own cities, in sharp contrast to other industrialized countries, where, for example, London has twelve daily papers, Paris thirty-three, and Tokyo thirty-one.[21]

The concentration and corporate ownership of the news sources to which most Americans are exposed means a narrowing of the range of news and ideas available to most people and, in the view of many media analysts, an increasing tendency to focus on "edutainment" rather than hard news or political news. It can also lead to outright censorship as, for example, when the conservative Clear Channel radio chain, which runs 1,240 radio stations nationwide, stopped playing songs by the Dixie Chicks after the group's lead singer made a remark critical of President Bush and the Iraq War.

Even the rightly vaunted U.S. freedom of the press has lost stature in recent years. In the annual Freedom House rankings of global press freedom, the United States typically ranks about fifteenth in the world, with most of the other rich democracies above the United States. In 2005, the U.S. ranking fell to twenty-fourth, largely because of pressure from the government on reporters concerning their coverage of the war, terrorism, or national security issues.[22] "Reporters without Borders," another group that constructs an annual press freedom index, has the United States falling from seventeenth place in the world in 2002 to fifty-third in 2006. The organization pointed to the "sharp deterioration" in relations between the media and the government "after the president used the pretext of 'national security' to regard as suspicious any journalist who questioned his 'war on terrorism.'"[23]

Even more discouraging than these rankings is the reaction to these trends by American citizens, particularly in the aftermath of September 11 and the beginning of the Iraq War. In 2002, 49 percent of Americans agreed that "the First Amendment goes too far in the rights it guarantees" (up from 28 percent in 1999), and in 2003, 46 percent thought that the press in America "has too much freedom."[24] By 2006, the latter figure had slightly declined to 40 percent. These are disturbingly high figures for a country and a population that prides itself on its respect for freedom and where the freedom of the press has been an important component of maintaining that freedom. They also suggest a worrisome strain of authoritarianism in the American public that could be exploited by demagogic politicians or leaders, particularly in times of crisis.

Apathy, Ignorance, and Propaganda

The alarming weakness of the American educational system, in combination with growing political apathy and political ignorance, is a dangerous trend for democratic politics. An uninformed public is an easy target for demagogues and propagandists. In chapter 3, we saw how relatively easy it has been to mislead Americans on issues such as evolution and global warming, where science has run up against religion and politics. The problem became more serious and more of a potential threat to democracy when the country was led to war on the basis of false premises or misleading information. It is not likely to go away as long as the country is in a state of war without apparent end.

The ease with which the American public and Congress can be bamboozled is nowhere more evident than the run-up to the U.S. invasion of Iraq in

2003. President Bush and members of the administration systematically misled the public on the connections between Saddam Hussein and al-Qaeda and on the presence of weapons of mass destruction (WMD) in Iraq. In some cases, they presented "evidence" for these charges even after they knew the evidence had been disproven or discredited. All three of the most specific sources of evidence for Iraqi WMD cited by the administration were disproven or discredited by either UN weapons inspectors, U.S. intelligence, or both—before the U.S. invasion in March 2003. The first was Secretary of State Colin Powell's assertion before the UN Security Council and later repeated by President Bush of the discovery of mobile biological weapons laboratories in Iraq. Both UN weapons inspectors before the invasion and a U.S. team after the invasion examined these labs and determined that they had nothing to do with biological weapons. But the president continued to refer to them.[25] Continuing to lie was apparently judged to be less damaging politically than to admit having misled the American public.

A second assertion made by Powell to the United Nations and repeated by the president was that Hussein had tried to purchase "high-specification aluminum tubes" for uranium enrichment for nuclear weapons. But the evidence for this was sketchy in the first place—based on a single Iraqi defector (an alcoholic)—and was already disputed both by U.S. intelligence analysts and by UN weapons inspection teams who had determined and announced that the tubes were for conventional rocket artillery casings.

The third piece of dubious evidence was that Iraq was buying uranium from the African country of Niger, an assertion made by President Bush in his State of the Union Address just a few weeks before the Iraqi invasion. It was later revealed that in 2002, a retired U.S. ambassador, Joseph Wilson, had been sent to Niger to investigate the Iraqi uranium link and had reported that the charges were unfounded. Furthermore, the head of the International Atomic Energy Agency, Mohammed El Baradei, reported on this issue to the UN Security Council on March 7, 2003, asserting that the reports of Iraqi purchases of uranium from Niger were "not authentic" and that the allegations were "unfounded."[26] Despite all this, the United States proceeded to war, with the president continuing to assert the presence of WMD in Iraq, even several months into the war with no evidence of such weapons found anywhere in the country. Americans overwhelmingly supported the war, as did Congress, which with large majorities in both houses passed a joint resolution authorizing the war in October 2002 with almost no debate.

The U.S. press, which James Madison described as "one of the great bulwarks of liberty," did almost nothing to investigate, evaluate, or challenge the administration's assertions about WMD. Mostly, they simply relied on press releases from the White House, the State Department, or the Pentagon. A comprehensive study of WMD coverage conducted by the University of Maryland found that too many press stories simply repeated the "official line" and concluded that "the American media did not play the role of checking and balancing the exercise of power that the standard theory of democracy requires."[27]

What is most disturbing about all this is how relatively simple it was for the president to accomplish his longtime goal—the overthrow of Saddam Hussein—by distortion of information and manipulation of public opinion. The messages about WMD and al-Qaeda links sent out by the administration were so confidently stated and so persistently repeated that most Americans continued to believe that Iraq had WMD even several years into the war. Going to war is one of the most serious and consequential decisions a state can make, and for this reason the founding fathers divided war powers between the president and Congress so that war could not easily be entered into. Getting America into the Iraq War was pretty much a cakewalk for the Bush administration, though, with almost no resistance or opposition from the public, the media, or Congress and without even a formal declaration of war, as the Constitution requires. After the war began, any opposition was effectively stifled when the president declared that "you're either with us or with the terrorists." That such a weighty decision could be taken so easily does not augur well for democracy and brings to mind the advice of Nazi leader Hermann Göring to rulers who seek to enhance their power: "Whether it is a democracy or a fascist dictatorship . . . all you have to do is tell them they are being attacked and denounce the pacifists for lack of patriotism and exposing the country to danger. It works the same way in any country."[28]

The Erosion of Rights

The prosecution of the "war on terror" has led to an unprecedented expansion of presidential power, serious infringements of fundamental constitutional rights, and the employment of tactics, like torture, long considered unconscionable in most parts of the world. Cataloging these incidents could occupy a whole separate book (and has occupied many), but it is sufficient here to illustrate the general problem with three particularly egregious policies of the Bush administration: infringements on privacy, violations of habeas corpus, and the use of torture.

In December 2005, President Bush acknowledged that he had repeatedly authorized the use of wiretaps, without obtaining a warrant, to monitor the international phone calls and e-mails of American citizens. Apparently, thousands of such calls were monitored in direct violation of the Foreign Intelligence Surveillance Act (FISA), a bill passed in 1978 that allows domestic wiretaps in the interests of national security but only with a court order. As attorney and former Congresswoman Elizabeth Holtzman has pointed out, the "FISA can scarcely be claimed to create any obstacle to justified national security wiretaps. Since 1978, when the law was enacted, more than 10,000 national security warrants have been approved by the FISA court; only four have been turned down."[29] Even so, the president claimed the right to break this law based on his constitutional right as commander in chief to safeguard national security. This, of course, is an extraordinarily sweeping claim and an extremely dangerous one. The war on terror is a virtually unlimited and endless one (we will always be confronted by terrorists), so the president can assert his powers of commander in chief as long as that war continues. And if we are constantly in a state of war, he can claim the right to violate any law in the interest of national security—a term that he, as commander in chief, defines. As Holtzman points out, the extent of this claim—warrantless wiretaps of thousands of U.S. citizens—goes far beyond the few incidents of illegal incursions on privacy that led to the impeachment proceedings against President Nixon in the wake of the Watergate scandal.

Another wartime challenge to democracy has come from the Bush administration's efforts to redefine or limit the principle of habeas corpus. Habeas corpus, a principal check on arbitrary state power, allows a person who has been arrested to challenge the legality of that detention. It is a bedrock principle of human rights and the key principle of the Magna Carta of 1215 and is embodied in article I, section 9, of the U.S. Constitution. But the Bush administration has claimed the right to ignore habeas corpus for people it defines as "unlawful enemy combatants," and this principle was incorporated into the Military Commissions Act of 2006 with the assent of Congress. The government has used this assertion of state power to arrest and detain noncitizens without any formal charges or recourse to a court and to spirit off suspects (including permanent residents of the United States holding green cards) to prisons in other countries beyond U.S. legal jurisdiction, including the U.S. military base at Guantanamo Bay in Cuba. Most of these prisoners have been detained indefinitely without trial, have been deprived of contact with family members or legal counsel, and have sometimes been subject to degrading treatment or even torture. The weakening of a right so fundamental as habeas corpus is a weakening of democracy itself, but it also hurts the United States in the eyes of the rest of the world, in the one area it has been most admired through much of its history—the protection of individual rights and freedom. As *Newsweek* editor Fareed Zakaria has put it, "Our most potent weapons" in the campaign against terror "are the sense people around the world have had that the United States is an exemplar of rights and liberties and that it lives by those principles even under storm and stress. When we suspend the writ of *habeas corpus*, we cast aside these distinctive weapons and trade them for the traditional tools of dictatorships—arbitrary arrests, indefinite imprisonments and aggressive interrogations. Will this trade really help us prevail?"[30]

President Bush's assertion of executive power has gone far beyond these two examples of violations of constitutional rights. The president has repeatedly claimed that he does not need to "execute" a law that he deems unconstitutional. A study by the *Boston Globe* found that the president had disobeyed more than 750 laws passed by Congress, including military rules and regulations, affirmative action provisions, and immigration regulations.[31] Ignoring congressional legislation is a concrete manifestation of Bush's comment just after September 11 that "I'm the Commander, see . . . I do not need to explain why I say things. That's the interesting thing about being the President . . . [I] don't feel like I owe anybody an explanation."[32] This is a startling assertion of executive power and calls into question the checks and balances among the presidency, the courts, and Congress that are at the heart of the American political system.

To be sure, the judiciary has begun to take notice of these trends, and courts have recently issued rulings that curtail the excesses of executive power. In 2006, a federal judge found that warrantless wiretapping violated both the Constitution and the FISA. In her ruling on the case, U.S. federal district court judge Anna Diggs Taylor sharply rebuked the administration: "It was never the intent of the framers to give the president such unfettered control, particularly when his actions blatantly disregard the parameters clearly enumerated in the Bill of Rights. . . . The three separate branches of government were developed as a check and balance for one another."[33] About the same time, the Supreme Court struck down the administration's plans to try detainees in Guantanamo for war crimes (in *Hamdan v. Rumsfeld*).

While the courts have tried to redress checks and balances, Congress has been almost comatose in the face of this expansion of executive power. Congress rushed to authorize the USA Patriot Act just six weeks after September 11, with almost no debate and by overwhelming majorities in both houses. Only one senator, Russ Feingold (D-Wis.), voted against the bill. Some of our representatives admitted that they had not even read the bill before voting on it, yet it contained provisions regarding law enforcement and domestic surveillance that raised serious questions of constitutionality. Similarly, the Iraq War authorization bill sailed through Congress in 2002 with only desultory debate.

Since that time, Congress has been virtually silent on issue after issue, including those mentioned previously (habeas corpus and domestic surveillance) and questions about U.S. employment of torture, the conduct of the Iraq War, and abuse of executive authority by the president and members of his cabinet, among others. In the words of Senator Robert Byrd (D-W.Va.), Congress has been "unwilling to assert its power, cowed, timid and deferential toward the Bush administration, a virtual paralytic."[34] Nothing much changed after the Democrats won control of Congress in 2006.

Part of the problem here, of course, is the fear (terror?) occasioned by the attacks of September 11. But as pointed out in the aptly titled book *The Broken Branch* by Thomas Mann and Norman Ornstein, the growing impotence and ineffectualness of Congress predates September 11, the Bush administration, and even the Republican control of Congress. Before the Democrats won back control of Congress, the number of days that Congress met and the number of days scheduled for votes were at their lowest level in sixty years. The decline in deliberations is accompanied by a host of other problems, including a decline in civility and bipartisanship, the disappearance of oversight, the tolerance of executive secrecy, the explosion of "earmarks" (as discussed previously), and the growth in the role of money and "machine politics." The two seasoned political analysts who wrote this book, one Democrat and one Republican, believe that these problems diminish Congress in the constitutional scheme and encourage "more unilateral and less responsible behavior in the executive."[35] Unilateralism, of course, is as much an issue in the international arena as in the domestic one, as we explore in a later chapter.

Bush's assertion of extraordinary presidential powers has continued unabated and threatens to become embedded in the American political system. His nominee for attorney general, Michael Mukasey, told the Senate Judiciary Committee that the president's authority as commander in chief might allow him to supersede laws written by Congress.[36] Charlie Savage, the *Boston Globe* reporter who won a Pulitzer Prize for the series of stories he wrote about executive power and Bush's use of "signing statements," believes that "the expansive presidential powers claimed and exercised by the Bush-Cheney White House are now an immutable part of American history—not controversies, but facts," and those powers will be difficult to roll back, even after a new president takes over. He quotes Supreme Court Justice Robert Jackson, who once warned that any new claim of executive power, once validated into precedent, "lies about like a loaded weapon ready for the hand of any authority that can bring forward a plausible claim of an urgent need. Every repetition embeds that principle more deeply in our law and thinking and expands it to new purposes."[37]

Becoming Like Our Enemies?

On virtually every dimension, democratic principles are on the wane and in jeopardy in the United States. If one thinks of liberty, equality, and popular sovereignty as the essential principles of democracy (as I tell my students in an introductory class in political science), we see major changes, for the worse, in all three. Citizens are increasingly less interested in and knowledgeable about politics and political issues, less trusting and confident in their political leaders and institutions, and less likely to participate in the democratic political process, even with the low-cost avenue of voting. Popular sovereignty is being surrendered to professionals, bureaucrats, and lobbyists. The basic principles of liberty, including habeas corpus and freedom of the press, enshrined in the Constitution and its Bill of Rights, are being eroded in the name of national security during an undeclared war with no obvious end point. The goal of equality, which the United States advanced more than any other country in world history, has seen reversals in the past twenty years as the poor, the uneducated, and minorities are increasingly disenfranchised either de jure or de facto.

The consequences of these changes are serious both for American society and for its position in the world. Domestically, the country risks losing exactly the democratic principles that it claims to be fighting for. The goal of the jihadists who attacked the United States was to weaken the country, not to destroy it. There is no way that a small group of extremists could take on the full force of the United States of America. Terrorism is the weapon of the weak, and its main tool is to plant the seeds that will weaken its enemy from within. Terrorists hope that their target state will use repression internally, which will incite resistance or reaction from its own population and thereby prompt division or conflict. So when the U.S. government attempts to restrict civil liberties, silence dissent, co-opt the media, enhance executive power, and instill fear, it plays into the hands of those who would weaken the country from within. In the words of the humorist Garrison Keillor (not in his usual jocular frame of mind), "Our enemies have succeeded beyond their wildest dreams. They have made us become like them."[38]

The erosion of American democracy has also affected the country's stance and reputation in the rest of the world. During the American Century, the freedom, equality, and democratic political system of the United States were the primary sources of admiration for this country from peoples and governments around the world. The United States and its laws and civil rights were models for the advocates of democracy almost everywhere. But the United States no longer stands out—is no longer exceptional—on virtually any measure of democratic politics. There are many other countries that have more political equality, more political participation, more genuine competition, more freedom of the press, and more trust in their own political institutions. The United States is no longer seen as the only model for democracy or even the best one. After the 1989 anticommunist revolutions in Eastern Europe, for example, when people were asked which country should be a model for the construction of their own fledgling democracies, the most frequently named countries were in Europe (e.g., Sweden and Germany) rather than the United States. A series of coordinated polls conducted in ten countries (including the closest allies of the United States) in 2004 found only 52 percent agreeing that American democracy remained a model for other nations.[39] Even in this area where the United States was most exceptional, we were not really so exceptional after all.

Notes

1. American Political Science Association, *American Democracy in an Age of Rising Inequality* (Washington, D.C.: American Political Science Association, 2004), 7.

2. Sidney Verba, Kay Lehman Schlozman, and Henry E. Brady, *Voice and Equality* (Cambridge, Mass.: Harvard University Press, 1995).

3. *American Democracy in an Age of Rising Inequality*, 14.

4. *American Democracy in an Age of Rising Inequality*, 1.

5. Data on campaign finance are available at the Center for Responsive Politics website at http://www.opensecrets.org.

6. Quoted in the *New York Times*, November 25, 1984.

7. Data on women in national legislatures are available at http://www.ipu.org/wmn-e/classif.htm.

8. Bill Moyers, "A Time for Heresy," March 22, 2006, http://www.tompaine.com/articles/2006/03/22/a_time_for_heresy.php.

9. Michael Parenti, *Democracy for the Few*, 8th ed. (Boston: Thomson-Wadsworth, 2008), 212.

10. "In New Congress, Pork May Linger," *New York Times*, November 26, 2006, 1, 22.

11. Transparency International's annual report is accessible at http://www.transparency.org/news_room/in_focus/2007/ar2006.

12. For voter turnout data, see the website for the International Institute for Democracy and Electoral Assistance at http://www.idea.int/vt/survey/voter_turnout_pop2-2.cfm.

13. See the Eurobarometer surveys at http://ec.europa.eu/public_opinion.

14. Quoting the 2000 *Better Together* report of the Saguaro Seminar, "Civic Engagement in America," in *Broken Engagement: America's Civic Health Index*, report of the National Conference on Citizenship (Washington, D.C.: National Conference on Citizenship, 2006), 4.

15. Michael X. Delli Carpini and Scott Keeter, *What Americans Know about Politics and Why It Matters* (New Haven, Conn.: Yale University Press, 1989), 99.

16. "Public Knowledge of Current Affairs Little Changed by News and Information Revolutions," report of the Pew Center for the People and the Press, April 15, 2007, http://people-press.org/reports/display.php3?ReportID=319.

17. William Galston, "Political Knowledge, Political Engagement, and Civic Education," *Annual Review of Political Science*, June 2001, 217.

18. Galston, "Political Knowledge, Political Engagement, and Civic Education."

19. February 24, 2006, Harris poll available at http://www.harrisinteractive.com/harris_poll/index.asp?PID=644.

20. Parenti, *Democracy for the Few*, 173, citing data from Ben Bagdikian, *The New Media Monopoly* (Boston: Beacon Press, 2004).

21. Bagdikian, *The New Media Monopoly*, 121.

22. For these global press freedom rankings, see http://www.freedomhouse.org.

23. See the Reporters without Borders website at http://www.rsf.org.

24. "State of the First Amendment 2006" (final annotated survey), http://www.freedomforum.org.

25. See Bob Woodward, *State of Denial* (New York: Simon and Schuster, 2006), 209–10, 216.

26. The transcript of El Baradei's report to the Security Council is available at http://www.cnn.com/2003/US/03/07/sprj.irq.un.transcript.elbaradei.

27. *Media Coverage of Weapons of Mass Destruction*, study released March 2004 by the Phillip Merrill College of Journalism, University of Maryland, as cited in Eric Boehlert, *Lapdogs: How the Press Rolled Over for Bush* (New York: Free Press, 2006), 219.

28. Cited in Robert C. Byrd, *Losing America: Confronting a Reckless and Arrogant Presidency* (New York: Norton, 2004), 178.

29. Elizabeth Holtzman, "The Impeachment of George W. Bush," *The Nation*, January 30, 2006, 13.

30. Fareed Zakaria, "The Enemy Within" (book review), *New York Times Book Review*, December 17, 2006, 10.

31. "President Claims Power to Disregard 750 Statutes," *Indianapolis Star*, April 20, 2006, A1.

32. Cited in Bob Woodward, *Bush at War* (New York: Simon and Schuster, 2002), 145–46.

33. *New York Times*, August 18, 2006, A1.

34. Byrd, *Losing America*, 67.

35. Thomas E. Mann and Norman J. Ornstein, *The Broken Branch: How Congress Is Failing America and How to Get It Back on Track* (New York: Oxford University Press, 2006), 217.

36. Philip Shenon, "Senators Clash with Nominee about Torture," *New York Times*, October 19, 2007, A1.

37. Charlie Savage, *Takeover: The Return of the Imperial Presidency and the Subversion of American Democracy* (New York: Little, Brown, 2007), 330.

38. Garrison Keillor, "Mark Their Names," *International Herald Tribune*, October 2, 2006, http://www.iht.com/articles/2006/10/02/opinion/edkeillor.php.

39. "World Polls: U.S. Reputation Falls," October 15, 2004, http://www.cbsnews.com/stories/2004/10/15/world/printable649513.shtml. These and other foreign attitudes about the United States are explored in more depth in chapter 8.

~

CHAPTER SIX

Abandoning International Order
Unilateralism and International Law

The structure of world peace cannot be the work of one man, or one party, or one nation. It must be a peace which rests on the cooperative effort of the whole world.

—Franklin Delano Roosevelt, 1945

I don't care what the international lawyers say; we are going to kick some ass.

—President George W. Bush, 2001

In 1941, Henry Luce asserted that the United States was "the most powerful and vital nation in the world" and that we had a special mission to help the rest of the world become more like us. Presidents Roosevelt and Truman shared this vision of the United States and helped build a postwar order based on a strong U.S. presence but also a network of intergovernmental organizations, multilateral institutions, and international law. All during the Cold War, most countries either accepted American leadership or bowed to its power. There was a tacit if not explicit recognition that the United States had the status, influence, and power to lead "the free world."

By the turn of the millennium, however, and even more after September 11, all these elements of American influence began to wane. As we have seen in earlier chapters, America could no longer rely on its reputation as the most successful democracy, the strongest economy, or the most healthy society. Furthermore, other countries were beginning to challenge America's efforts to shape the rest of the world and its domination of international political and economic institutions. To make matters worse, the United States was backing away from the multilateral institutions and international norms that it had championed and pioneered in the early postwar years. America's "soft power" was eroding at the very time that its "hard power" was becoming less effective.

U.S. Exceptionalism

From its beginning, the United States perceived itself as different or exceptional from other countries and indeed has been unique. The Puritan colonists felt a providential role, with Massachusetts Bay Colony Governor John Winthrop proclaiming that they would be "as a city upon a hill" with "the eyes of all people upon us." Alexis de Tocqueville, the French aristocrat who visited the United States in the 1830s, called attention to America's distinctiveness in his book *Democracy in America*, pointing to the country's individualism, entrepreneurship, religiosity, decentralization, and tendencies to join multiple clubs, groups, and associations. As the eminent American social scientist Seymour Martin Lipset has argued, these distinctive American characteristics can be a "double-edged sword." On the one hand, they have helped the United States develop into an affluent, dynamic, democratic, egalitarian, and powerful state. On the other hand, they have fostered "income inequality, high crime rates, low levels of electoral participation, [and] a powerful tendency to moralize which at times verges on intolerance toward political and ethnic minorities."[1]

Since the time of de Tocqueville, the idea of American exceptionalism has been embraced by every American president. But while de Tocqueville (and many social scientists following him) simply described the United States as being qualitatively *different*, most politicians (and many Americans) interpret these differences as aspects of American *superiority*. This sense of superiority, especially in conjunction with the strong strain of religiosity in American political life, has often given American politics and foreign policy a messianic element. With the country's rise to global power in the "American Century," American exceptionalism became globalist with "the imperative not just to preserve America's safety and ensure its economic development but to reorganize the world to spread American values," according to Siobhan McEvoy-Levy.[2] The United States had a special mission to "make the world safe for democracy" (Woodrow Wilson), to be the "arsenal of democracy" (Franklin Roosevelt), "to support free people who are resisting attempted subjugation" (Harry Truman), and "to support any friend, oppose any foe, in order to assure the survival and the success of liberty" (John Kennedy). Ronald Reagan even revived the language of John Winthrop by proclaiming the United States to be "a shining city on a hill."

In this global exceptionalism, American citizens and policymakers alike see American values as universal ones and the United States as the only country that can really promote and protect those values. As Secretary of State Condoleezza Rice wrote before she went to Washington, "American values are universal . . . the triumph of these values is most assuredly easier when the international balance of power favors those who believe in them."[3] Another (former) secretary of state, Madeleine Albright, has characterized the United States as "the indispensable nation." And a prominent foreign policy analyst, Michael Mandelbaum, argues that the rest of the world *needs* the United States to play the role of "the world's government" and that the United States is the best and only real source of global governance. "If America is a Goliath," he contends, "it is a benign one" in that it is promoting goals—peace, democracy, and free markets—for which there is "a broad and unprecedented consensus" around the world. In Mandelbaum's view, the U.S. role in the world "has something in common with the sun's relationship to the rest of the solar system."[4] This phraseology is hauntingly familiar to the longtime belief in imperial China that China was at the center of the earth and that all other countries and civilizations radiated out from that center.

This sense of American exceptionalism and the benevolence of American intentions and policies is virtually an article of faith among both political elites and ordinary citizens in the United States. As such, it has provided a rationalization for America's global leadership, its worldwide military presence, and its global interventionism. There is, as Stephen Kinzer puts it, a "deep-seated belief of most Americans that their country is a force for good in the world" and that when the United States intervenes abroad, "their actions will benefit not only the United States but also the citizens of the country in which they are intervening—and, by extension, the causes of peace and justice in the world."[5] The U.S. belief in its exceptionalism, mission, and altruism has led it to intervene militarily in more countries than any other great power in modern times. In his book *Overthrow*, Kinzer documents fourteen cases in the past century when the United States has arranged to depose foreign leaders. "No nation in modern history has done this so often, in so many places so far from its own shores."[6] Iraq is by no means an isolated case.

Through the whole Cold War era, the United States was able to play the role of the world's government and its police force for a number of reasons. It was, first of all, the primary military power in the world and the only one with the capability to extend that power to every corner of the globe. Even if U.S. power was feared and resented by some countries and peoples, it was also seen, properly, as the only real counterbalance to Soviet military power. Besides, in many parts of the world, there was a tacit if grudging acceptance of U.S. primacy and of Washington's professions of altruism and benevolence. In the two most sustained postwar U.S. overseas interventions— Vietnam and Iraq—the United States was largely able to go it alone, in spite of resistance from the United Nations and other great powers, because of these factors.

With the end of the Cold War and the end of the millennium, however, much had changed. With the disappearance of the Soviet Union and the perceived threat of communism, the United States was no longer necessary as the "defender of the free world." And while the United States remained the lone military superpower, there were growing doubts both in the United States and worldwide about the effectiveness of the military instrument in addressing the world's most pressing threats. Global warming, ethnic conflict, and nuclear proliferation, for example, hardly seemed susceptible to military solutions. September 11 showed that the greatest military power in the world was vulnerable even to a small band of alien extremists. American military power was unable to subdue and stabilize Iraq, a small, poor country, even after five years of intensive operations. And despite a huge U.S. commitment to "the war on terror," the incidents of terrorism grew substantially in the years after the invasion of Iraq. Abundant military power no longer translated into political power or national security.

The rest of the world was changing mightily, but the United States was not. Globalization was drawing the world closer together but also raising new issues and fostering new animosities and conflicts. The rising power of China and India, the expansion and integration of Europe, and the growth and revival of Islam all posed new challenges to the world order and to the place of the United States in it. With the end of the Cold War, there seemed a new opportunity for international cooperation and negotiation, especially through multilateral institutions like the United Nations. The United States, in contrast, seemed to favor unilateralist approaches to foreign policy and continued reliance on the military instrument—at least under the presidency of George W. Bush.

The combination of a changed world environment, domestic decline in the United States, and a U.S. foreign policy that was out of step with much of the rest of the world led to increasing ambivalence and even hostility toward the United States from other countries. As we will see in chapter 8, positive attitudes about the United States declined sharply around the world in the early years of the millennium and especially after the U.S. invasion of Iraq in 2003. Even in many allied states, a majority of the population saw the United States as the greatest threat to world peace. And in many Arab and Muslim countries, more people had a favorable opinion of Osama bin Laden than of George W. Bush.[7] So while many Americans saw the United States as a force for peace, stability, and world order, few others outside our borders felt that way.

Turning Away from International Law

In March 2001, President Bush, in one of his first major acts as president, declared that the Kyoto Protocol on climate change (the Kyoto treaty) was "fatally flawed" and "dead" and that the United States would revoke its signature of the treaty and refuse to ratify it. This international treaty, aimed at stemming the carbon emissions that were causing an alarming increase in global warming, had been years in the making and had been signed by most countries in the world. Bush's blunt rejection of the treaty caused a storm of protest worldwide, especially in Europe, with newspaper headlines and street demonstrators alike declaiming America's dismissal of scientific findings, global opinion, and international rules.

Much of this animosity was directed against the American president, who was, indeed, exhibiting considerable disdain for international law and international organizations well before September 11 and 2003. The Kyoto treaty was a particularly prominent and controversial treaty. But President Bush's actions reflected a pattern of turning away from international law that preceded his administration. As with so many other issues addressed in this book, President Bush exacerbated the problem but did not cause it. The growing hostility to the United States from around the world predated him, September 11, and the Iraq War, and much of this was due to the refusal of the United States to sign on to international covenants that had achieved broad consensus around the world. American exceptionalism was becoming a liability rather than an asset.

The list of treaties rejected or unsigned by the United States is a long one, but some of them are particularly revealing of America's maverick status and particularly problematic in terms of world opinion (see table 6.1). The United States is one of only a few countries that have not ratified the 1979 UN Convention on the Elimination of All Forms of Discrimination against Women. One of the others is Afghanistan. The United States has not ratified the 1989 UN Convention on the Rights of the Child, which protects the economic and social rights of children. The only other country not to ratify

Table 6.1. International Treaties Rejected by the United States

Treaty	Description	Concluded	Number of Parties
Convention on the Elimination of All Forms of Discrimination against Women	A commitment between governments to end discrimination against women	1979	185
UN Convention on the Law of the Sea	Establishes framework for commercial, navigational, and environmental use of the oceans	1982	152
Convention on Biological Diversity	Commits governments to sustaining and protecting plants and animals	1992	190
Antiballistic Missile Treaty	Treaty to stop the use of antiballistic missiles	2001	None (agreement made between the United States and the Soviet Union; after the United States withdrew, Russia followed)
UN Agreement to Curb the International Flow of Illicit Small Arms	Treaty to end the international distribution of illicit small arms	2001	191 (all UN nations except the United States)
International Criminal Court (ICC) Treaty	Sets up the ICC in The Hague to try individuals for war crimes, crimes against humanity, and genocide	1998	104
Land Mine Treaty	Bans land mines	1997	122
Kyoto Protocol of 1997	Helps control global warming	1997	169
Comprehensive Nuclear Test	Bans all nuclear explosions	1996	164

Protocol to the UN International Covenant on Civil and Political Rights	Aimed at ending the death penalty and specifically prohibits executing those under the age of eighteen	1989	165
UN International Covenant on Economic, Social and Cultural Rights	Protects economic, social, and cultural rights	1966	155
UN Convention on the Prevention and Punishment of the Crime of Genocide	Defines and outlaws genocide and requires prosecution for genocide	1948	137
UN Convention on the Rights of the Child	Protects the economic, civil, and social rights of children	1989	The only country in the world to reject the treaty (besides the United States) is Somalia, with no functioning government

this treaty is Somalia, which has no functioning government. A principal objection by the United States to this treaty was that it might pose a problem for the application of capital punishment for minors. The United States was then one of the few states in the world that permitted this (until such executions were finally banned by the Supreme Court in 2005). The execution of minors in the United States was a stain on the country's global reputation, which was not much helped when, in 2007, the United Nations took up a resolution calling for the abolition of life imprisonment without possibility of parole for children and young teenagers. The vote was 185 to 1, with the United States the only dissenter.[8]

The United States refused to sign the treaty banning land mines, signed by 122 nations in 1997 after tens of thousands of civilians, including many children, had lost their legs or lives stepping on land mines left over from previous conflicts. Other countries refusing to sign included Russia, China, India, Pakistan, Iran, Iraq, Vietnam, and Egypt—hardly the best of company.

In all these cases, as for most of the treaties listed in table 6.1, the U.S. government raised seemingly legitimate concerns about how U.S. accession to them might conflict with the U.S. Constitution or laws or impinge on U.S. sovereignty and freedom of action. But that is the nature of all law, both domestic and international—that it restricts actions considered reprehensible by the broader community and in the interests of the community. For the United States to abstain from these international agreements—most of them reflecting very broad global consensus—suggested to many people that the United States considered itself above the law or beyond it and outside the moral constraints of the rest of humanity.

It is all the more paradoxical that it was the United States that was so skeptical and defiant of international law because it was this county that pioneered the framework of international law and international institutions after World War II. Before that time, there were few international organizations and a very weak and undeveloped corpus of international law. The starting point for a new rule-based international order was the Atlantic Charter, signed by Franklin Roosevelt and Winston Churchill in August 1941 (just a few months after the appearance of Luce's "American Century" essay). The principles of the Atlantic Charter included commitments by states to refrain from the use of force, to respect the "equal and unalienable rights" of all peoples, and to promote economic liberalization and free trade. These principles were later enshrined in the UN Charter and became the "guidelines for a new world order" that was to last for the next sixty years.[9] The commitment of the United States to these principles and to an international order that promoted them was a major source of the country's global authority, legitimacy, and popularity during the American Century. The movement away from them is a major factor in America's declining power and influence in the world.

As mentioned previously, the United States has been backing away from international standards and multilateral commitments for years. But this movement was given a jolting boost by the administration of George W. Bush from the very beginning. Even before his presidency, Bush was heavily influenced by the neoconservative group of intellectuals and policymakers that formed the Project for the New American Century (PNAC) in 1997 (see the introduction to this book). The PNAC had called for a more muscular and assertive American foreign and defense policy "to shape a new century favorable to American principles and interests." Statements and publications by members of the PNAC opposed the "utopian internationalism" of presidents Clinton, Carter, and Wilson, arguing that the United States needed to pay attention first and foremost to its own national interests and security. Two principle adherents of the PNAC, William Kristol and Robert Kagan, penned a 1999 op-ed piece for the New York Times titled "Reject the Global Buddy System," in which they asserted "that American security cannot be safeguarded by international conventions."[10] Another member of the PNAC, John Bolton, who would later be appointed by President Bush as U.S. ambassador to the United Nations, challenged a central tenet of international law in writing that international treaties (the primary component of international law) were simply political and "not legally binding."[11]

When Bush became president in 2001, he brought with him many members of the PNAC as his principal foreign policy advisers, including Donald Rumsfeld, Dick Cheney, Paul Wolfowitz, and John Bolton. Their impact on the president and his policies was dramatic and immediate, particularly in respect to international law and international institutions (like the United Nations). In the words of Philippe Sands, a British international lawyer and professor, the new administration was "outspoken in its determination to challenge global rules" and soon initiated "a full-scale assault, a war on law."[12] The two most prominent targets of the Bush administration were the Kyoto treaty on climate change and the treaty constituting an International Criminal Court (ICC). Both of these were high-profile treaties and strongly supported by most countries in the world, including virtually all the allies of the United States.

The ICC, which is already up and running in The Hague, Netherlands, was constituted to prosecute individuals for genocide, war crimes, and crimes against humanity. It is different from the International Court of Justice (the World Court), which is part of the United Nations and is meant to adjudicate issues between countries rather than individuals. The ICC followed limited but successful experiences with several ad hoc courts set up to try those accused of genocide or war crimes in Yugoslavia and Rwanda. Ironically, given the U.S. hostility to the new court, one of the inspirations for the ICC was the original war crimes tribunal constituted by the United States in Nuremberg to try Nazi war criminals after World War II.

President Clinton signed the Rome Statute of 1998 to create the ICC, but such a signature is only the first step of the process, which also includes ratification. In the United States, ratification requires approval by the U.S. Senate. But the treaty never got to the Senate. In May 2002, President Bush took the unusual step of "unsigning" the Rome Statute, announced that the United States would never be a party to the treaty, and began a campaign to discredit and weaken the ICC. The main concern of the Bush administration was that the ICC might be used for "politicized prosecutions of American service members and officials," in the words of Secretary of Defense Donald Rumsfeld.[13] This concern was heightened, of course, after the beginning of the U.S. war on terror and some of the unorthodox methods associated with that enterprise, including abuse of suspected terrorists by American soldiers and civilians and the use of torture against prisoners in Iraq and Afghanistan and against suspected terrorists apprehended elsewhere.

The Bush administration did not just withdraw from the ICC; it also launched a sustained campaign to discredit and weaken it. Shortly after the president announced the unsigning of the Rome Statute, Congress passed the American Servicemembers Protection Act, which prohibits any American cooperation with the ICC, prohibits U.S. participation in any UN peacekeeping operations unless American troops are guaranteed immunity from prosecution by the ICC, and prohibits the United States from providing military assistance to governments that are parties to the ICC. Although some exceptions are made on this last provision for the North Atlantic Treaty Organization and other important allies of the United States, in effect the legislation has been used to pressure other countries not to join the ICC or to agree not to enforce its provisions against Americans. This has led some wags to dub the U.S. legislation "the Hague Invasion Act."[14]

The intensity and even the ferocity of American resistance to the ICC has badly hurt the image of the United States in the eyes of friends and foes alike. The European Union released an official statement expressing "disappointment and regret" over the U.S. decision, which it thought would have "undesirable consequences on multilateral treaty-making and generally on the rule of law in international relations."[15] The European Union also objected strongly to the immunity agreements for Americans, and other countries and international organizations have protested the punitive actions of the United States on countries who are ICC members but refused to sign immunity agreements with the United States. But besides the general issue of U.S. arrogance and high-handedness is the very seaminess of the U.S. position—appearing to protect its own people who might commit war crimes and therefore perhaps even to be implicitly sanctioning such crimes. The United States, which with the Nuremberg trials had created the idea of individual war crimes and given legal validity to individual responsibility for such crimes, was now attempting to absolve American citizens from such responsibility. All this became more real than hypothetical with the revelations of torture and abuse of prisoners by American soldiers at Abu Ghraib in Iraq and Guantanamo Bay in Cuba.

The Kyoto Protocol on climate change is another high-profile treaty rejected by the United States in the face of widespread and overwhelming global support for the agreement. As discussed in chapter 4, a major reason for the U.S. inaction on global warming is the combination of widespread scientific illiteracy in the population and efforts by conservative politicians and industry groups to cast doubts on the science of climate change. As pointed out there, though, almost all climate scientists and professional scientific groups, both in the United States and elsewhere, have reached consensus that global warming is real and that it is a man-made problem, caused mostly by carbon emissions generated by the use of fossil fuels.

As with other aspects of international law until the 1990s, the United States was a leader in the promotion of global rules to protect the environment and working with other countries to first investigate and then stem global warming. For example, the United States led international efforts to address the issue of ozone depletion and to achieve signature of a landmark treaty, the Montreal Protocol of 1987, to ban substances (like the coolant freon) that hurt the ozone layer. Delegates from the United States played an active role in the early rounds of negotiations for a framework agreement on climate change, adopted in 1992, and in the three years of negotiations that led to the adoption in Japan of the Kyoto Protocol in 1997. This treaty aims at getting thirty-nine industrialized countries, those with the highest per capita emissions of carbon, to reduce those emissions by 2012 to roughly the levels that they were in 1990 in each country.

President Clinton signed the treaty in November 1998, hailing it as a "historic agreement" to address global warming and both "environmentally strong and economically sound."[16] But he never submitted it to Congress for ratification in the face of strong bipartisan opposition, particularly from conservatives. Much of the opposition focused on the perceived negative impact of the carbon limits on American economic growth. But from some quarters, there were hints of the next administration's hostility to international law generally. Dick Cheney, a member of the PNAC and the future vice president, signed a letter to Clinton asserting that the Kyoto Protocol would "hamstring" American military operations (though he did not explain how) and undermine U.S. sovereignty.[17]

When President Bush took office in 2001, one of his first major actions was to snuff out any prospects of the United States ratifying the protocol, in essence revoking Clinton's signature of the treaty (as he had done with the ICC). Bush's objections were threefold: that there was no "scientific consensus" on global warming, that the treaty would hurt the American economy, and that it was "unfair" in imposing restrictions on rich countries but not poor ones (especially China and India, which were also big carbon emitters). The first of these arguments, on science, was largely political and bogus (as discussed in chapter 4). The third one, on the undeveloped countries, was probably mostly a smoke screen for the second one, on the economy. It was true that the huge populations of China and India were contributing to global warming, but the idea behind the Kyoto negotiations was that the rich countries had been the primary source of the problem and were in the best position to initiate the program of carbon emission reductions. And the United States is hardly in a position to blame the rest of the world for being unfair. This country continues to generate far more greenhouse gas emissions than any other country in the world (including China) and has the second-highest per capita emissions of carbon, after only Australia—which is the only other developed country not to ratify the Kyoto Protocol. Furthermore, the United States fares very badly compared to other countries in its efforts to protect against environmental deterioration and climate change. An international study of how well countries are doing to protect against climate change has the United States ranked fifty-third out of fifty-six countries, with only China, Malaysia, and Saudi Arabia faring worse.[18] In another study of nation-by-nation environmental performance, including greenhouse gas emissions but also other indicators like clean water and low ozone levels, the United States ranked twenty-eighth in the world, behind almost all other developed countries in the world.[19]

The U.S. absenteeism on global warming and climate change has caused a host of problems both for the U.S. role in the world and for the world itself. President Bush's rejection of the Kyoto treaty occasioned a rash of condemnation and protests in the United States and worldwide. Christine Todd Wittman, former head of the Environmental Protection Agency, observed that Bush's withdrawal from the Kyoto treaty was equivalent to "flipping the bird to the rest of the world."[20] Japan's prime minister, Junichiro Koizumi, said that U.S. rejection of the treaty was "deplorable."[21] In Europe, the criticism was focused mostly on the perceived U.S. arrogance and narrow national self-interest. But there was much criticism from developing countries as well, which saw Bush's "unfair" comments as being hypocritical and as part of a broader pattern of U.S. disinterest (or even opposition to) economic development in poor countries. When the UN panel on climate change issued its newest (and most definitive) report in late 2007, UN Secretary-General Ban Ki-moon described climate change as "the defining challenge of our age" and called on the United States and China to play "a more constructive role."[22]

As with the ICC, it seemed to many that the United States was turning its back on the rest of the world or, even worse, actually snubbing its nose at the globe. And the potential consequences, in the case of global climate change, were monumental. As a distinguished Australian scientist has warned about global warming, "if humans pursue a business-as-usual course for the first half of this century, I believe the collapse of civilization due to climate change becomes inevitable."[23] If this happens, God forbid, the United States will have been a major cause.

The Bush Doctrine and Preemptive War

Even before the terrorist attacks of September 11 and indeed even before the inauguration of President Bush, the U.S. government had begun to flout important elements of international law and to lose some of its reputation as a global leader. As we have seen, the Bush administration accelerated this trend but did not initiate it. After September 11, however, there was a whole new dimension to U.S. exceptionalism, unilateralism, and rejection of international law and international institutions. This did not happen immediately after the attacks, however. The first response of the White House was to capitalize on the overwhelmingly supportive and sympathetic worldwide response to the attacks: "We are all Americans," proclaimed France's newspaper *Le Monde* on its front page of September 12. The same day, the United States went to the UN Security Council and quickly received a unanimous resolution implicitly authorizing the United States to use force, under international law, "to prevent and suppress terrorist attacks." Within the month, the United States had launched air strikes against Afghanistan and by mid-November had destroyed the al-Qaeda training camps there and brought down the government of the Taliban, which had harbored and supported Osama bin Laden and al-Qaeda. The United Nations and most of the rest of the world, with the exception of some Arab and Muslim states, sympathized with and supported the U.S. attack on Afghanistan.

Soon thereafter, though, the rhetoric, policies, and actions of Washington went far beyond the goal of bringing to justice the perpetrators of the September 11 attacks. In his State of the Union Address to Congress in January 2002, President Bush identified North Korea, Iran, and Iraq as part of an "axis of evil, arming to threaten the peace of the world."[24] Six months later, in a commencement address at West Point, the president first enunciated what came to be known as the "Bush doctrine" of "preemptive defense":

> The war on terror will not be won on the defensive. We must take the battle to the enemy, disrupt his plans, and confront the worst threats *before they emerge* [italics added]. In the world we have entered, the only path to safety is the path of action. And this nation will act.[25]

This idea of preemptive war—attacking a perceived enemy before it had taken hostile action—was developed and institutionalized later that year in the official National Security Strategy, which stated that "as a matter of common sense and self-defense, America will act against such emerging threats before they are fully formed."[26]

These were startling and disturbing assertions of American power and unilateralism and together seemed to suggest an American intent to use military force against all three members of the "axis of evil" even though not one of them had the slightest connection to the September 11 attackers, all of whom were from either Saudi Arabia or Egypt. The Bush Doctrine was also a radical departure both from the long-standing American defensive posture of "deterrence" and from fundamental principles of international law, which outlaws the use of force except under very limited conditions. The UN Charter, for example, declares that "all members shall refrain in their international relations from the threat or use of force against the territorial integrity or political independence of any state, or in any other manner inconsistent with the Purposes of the United Nations." The two major exceptions to this are self-defense against an armed attack and military force authorized by the United Nations. The Bush Doctrine, at least in application against the axis-of-evil states, was inconsistent with both of these exceptions, and therefore with the overall prohibition on the threat or use of force. Once again, the United States was setting itself outside, and above, the global community and global rules of behavior.

There was much consternation about the Bush Doctrine both in the United States and abroad. The historian Arthur Schlesinger Jr. wrote that the policy of "anticipatory self-defense" adopted by the president "is alarmingly similar to the policy that imperial Japan employed at Pearl Harbor on a date which, as an earlier American president said it would, lives in infamy. Franklin D. Roosevelt was right, but today it is we Americans who live in infamy."[27] Then UN Secretary-General Kofi Annan perhaps reflected global opinion on the strategy of preemption in a speech to the UN General Assembly in September 2003—after the doctrine had been implemented with the invasion of Iraq. Without mentioning the United States by name, Annan questioned U.S. arguments that nations have the "right and obligation to use force preemptively." "My concern is that, if it were to be adopted, it could set precedents that resulted in a proliferation of the unilateral and lawless use of force, with or without credible justification," he warned. The logic of preemption, he contended, "represents a fundamental challenge to the principles, on which, however imperfectly, world peace and stability have rested for the last 58 years."[28]

The Invasion of Iraq

The U.S. invasion of Iraq in March 2003 was a logical and perhaps inevitable outcome of all these trends and policies: the U.S. rejection of international norms and institutions; the determination of Bush, influenced by neoconservatives of the PNAC, to push a more aggressive and militaristic foreign policy; the adoption of the tool of preemption; and the particular, even peculiar, obsession with Iraq from the very beginning of the Bush presidency. It also became the most dramatic example of the U.S. willingness to disregard international law, to snub its allies, and to ignore global opinion, leading to a further and precipitous decline in world public opinion about the United States. Here we consider only these aspects of the U.S. invasion of Iraq; the next chapter addresses the broader consequences and impact of the Iraq war and the war on terror.

In retrospect, perhaps a U.S. invasion of Iraq was inevitable even without September 11. According to Ron Suskind in his book *The One Percent Doctrine*, the very first meeting of the National Security Council of the Bush administration, in January 2001, dealt with the overthrow of Saddam Hussein, as did the second. "It was a matter of *how*, not *whether*," according to Suskind.[29] The attacks of September 11 brought the issue of Iraq to the fore and provided a convenient justification for the president's goal to finish the work his father had begun a decade before with Operation Desert Storm. The horror, anger, and fear in the American public caused by the attacks on the World Trade Center and the Pentagon allowed the administration to dispense with the niceties of both the U.S. Constitution and international law. On September 12, when Secretary of Defense Donald Rumsfeld briefed the president on the limits that international law would place on a military response to the terrorist attacks, Bush retorted, "I don't care what the international lawyers say; we are going to kick some ass."[30] Richard Clarke, President Bush's chief counterterrorism specialist, recounts that a few days after September 11, the president told a group of his advisers to "see if Saddam did this. See if he is linked in any way." Clarke, astonished, replied, "But, Mr. President, Al Qaeda did this." When Clarke reminded him that U.S. intelligence had previously investigated this and found no links between al-Qaeda and Iraq, the president insisted that they look again.[31]

The president was determined to act forcefully in reaction to September 11, to "kick some ass," and the first and most obvious target was Afghanistan, where there indeed were strong and clear links to Osama bin Laden and al-Qaeda. Even here, though, the president dismissed an opportunity to apprehend bin Laden, offered by the Taliban government, in favor of the more overwhelming military action to overthrow the government itself. Just days before the launch of U.S. air strikes on Afghanistan, the Taliban's ambassador to Pakistan announced at a news conference that the Taliban would detain bin Laden and try him under Islamic law if the United States made a formal request and presented evidence of bin Laden's links to the September 11 attacks.[32] The United States rejected this offer, insisting that bin Laden be turned over unconditionally, and the war on Afghanistan commenced. If the apprehension of bin Laden was really that important, the United States missed an opportunity.

But the president's ultimate and more important goal was the removal of Saddam Hussein in Iraq, and as soon as the Afghanistan campaign was concluded, in six short weeks, preparations were under way for the next stage in the war on terror, the invasion of Iraq. In this case, however, there was not a shred of evidence that Hussein was linked to the September 11 attacks or to al-Qaeda. In fact, most analysts both inside the government and outside believed that any such relationship between Hussein and bin Laden was one of antagonism and hostility rather than friendship or common purpose. Bin Laden's main goal was the replacement of pro-Western (e.g., Saudi Arabia) or secular (e.g., Iraq) Arab governments with Islamist ones like that of the Taliban in Afghanistan. In 1990, bin Laden had even offered to help Saudi Arabia expel Hussein's forces from Kuwait. Saudi Arabia's refusal and acceptance instead of U.S. assistance turned bin Laden (himself a Saudi) against the kingdom, and after that the governments of both Iraq and Saudi Arabia were understandably distrustful of bin Laden and of al-Qaeda.

But apparently none of President Bush's close advisers brought these facts to the president's attention, and none tried to dissuade him from the planned attack on Iraq. Instead, they shifted the focus of accusation against Iraq from the country's alleged connections to September 11, to Iraq's alleged possession of weapons of mass destruction (WMD). As discussed in chapter 4, almost all the reliable intelligence at the time suggested that there were no such weapons in Iraq and that the WMD that had been there in the early 1990s had all been dismantled or destroyed under UN supervision by 1995. When the United States insisted that UN weapons inspection teams be reinserted into Iraq in the fall of 2002, the UN Security Council unanimously adopted Resolution 1441, which provided for a renewed, enhanced inspection regime in Iraq and for periodic reports on the results of those inspections to the Security Council. It concluded with the warning that Iraq "will face serious consequences as a result of its continued violations of its obligations," but it did not authorize the use of force to implement its requirements.[33]

To most people's surprise (and the dismay of some), Hussein quickly agreed to the inspections, insisting that Iraq was "a country devoid of weapons of mass destruction."[34] After five months of such inspections, both the chief UN weapons inspector and the head of the International Atomic Energy Agency testified before the UN Security Council that they had found no evidence of any nuclear, chemical, or biological weapons in Iraq.

The Bush administration brushed aside these findings and continued the drumbeat of war, insisting that Hussein had such weapons and was in a position to use them. The other members of the UN Security Council were not so sure, with some of them arguing that in the absence of any evidence of WMD so far, it would be prudent to simply continue and intensify the international inspections of Iraq. Washington attempted to persuade the Security Council to adopt a second resolution authorizing the use of force against Iraq. There was little support for that resolution, despite heavy-handed U.S. pressure on Security Council member states, including promises of enhanced foreign aid to countries that voted with the United States.

By this time, early 2003, the White House had already decided to invade Iraq and had begun preparations for that operation, and it was still hoping for some kind of international cover and legitimacy for the invasion. So Bush administration officials now began to argue that Resolution 1441, adopted in November 2002, implicitly authorized the use of force if Hussein failed to comply with its provisions. Almost no other members of the Security Council agreed with this interpretation, believing instead that the Security Council would have to authorize the use of force, in a follow-up resolution, when and if it considered such action necessary. The overwhelming majority of international lawyers in both Britain and the United States rejected the U.S. interpretation of Resolution 1441, issuing statements that "there is no justification under international law for the use of military force against Iraq."[35] But President Bush had already made it clear that he would act with or without the sanction of international law. On March 7, the head of the UN weapons inspection team, Hans Blix, gave his third report to the Security Council, repeating that so far no WMD had been found in Iraq, nor was there evidence of any "proscribed activities" in this regard, but asking for more time to complete the inspections. But ten days later, President Bush announced the initiation of Operation Iraqi Freedom. The government of the United Kingdom was the only major country to support the invasion.

If the governments of most countries were opposed to the U.S. war on Iraq, their populations were even more so. Even before the war started, there were massive demonstrations worldwide against the imminent attack. On the weekend of February 15–16, between 6 million and 10 million people marched against the war in sixty countries worldwide in the largest demonstrations since the Vietnam War. Some of the largest demonstrations, numbering over a million people in each, took place in countries whose governments supported the Bush administration's war plans, including London, Barcelona, and Rome.[36]

There were many more demonstrations, some of the largest in world history, in the months surrounding the beginning of the war. One estimate suggests that some 36 million people participated in 3,000 protests worldwide between January and April 2003.[37] In almost every country where polls were conducted, large majorities of the population opposed the war. In almost every country polled by the Pew Global Attitudes Project after the invasion, a majority thought that the world was "more dangerous" without Saddam Hussein.[38] Nobel Prize winner Archbishop Desmond Tutu denounced the war as "immoral," and then UN Secretary-General Kofi Annan asserted that the invasion was "illegal." The war, even before it descended into chaos and fiasco, was another devastating blow to America's global image and reputation.

The Question of Torture

There was yet another issue, though, that was even more damaging to the United States and the nail in the coffin of the American Century—the issue of torture. In the spring of 2004, the Pulitzer Prize–winning journalist Seymour Hirsch published a story in *The New Yorker Magazine* titled "Torture at Abu Ghraib," which documented the torture and abuse of Iraqi prisoners by American soldiers and intelligence officers at the U.S. military prison outside

Baghdad. Hirsch based his story on a detailed report by Major General Antonio Taguba that was not meant for public release. Taguba's report listed some of the appalling abuse that had taken place at Abu Ghraib:

> Breaking chemical lights and pouring the phosphoric liquid on detainees; pouring cold water on naked detainees; beating detainees with a broom handle and a chair; threatening male detainees with rape; allowing a military police guard to stitch the wound of a detainee who was injured after being slammed against the wall in his cell; sodomizing a detainee with a chemical light and perhaps a broom stick, and using military working dogs to frighten and intimidate detainees with threats of attack, and in one instance actually biting a detainee.[39]

The report mentioned photographs and film taken of some of these activities by the soldiers during the abuse but did not include them because of their "extremely sensitive nature." But a few days before, the CBS television news program 60 Minutes II had broadcast several of these photographs. As Hirsch says, "The photographs tell it all":

> In one, Private England, a cigarette dangling from her mouth, is giving a jaunty thumbs-up sign and pointing at the genitals of a young Iraqi, who is naked except for a sandbag over his head, as he masturbates. Three other hooded and naked Iraqi prisoners are shown, hands reflexively crossed over their genitals. A fifth prisoner has his hands at his sides. In another, England stands arm in arm with Specialist Graner; both are grinning and giving the thumbs-up behind a cluster of perhaps seven naked Iraqis, knees bent, piled clumsily on top of each other in a pyramid. There is another photograph of a cluster of naked prisoners, again piled in a pyramid. Near them stands Graner, smiling, his arms crossed; a woman soldier stands in front of him, bending over, and she, too, is smiling. Then, there is another cluster of hooded bodies, with a female soldier standing in front, taking photographs. Yet another photograph shows a kneeling, naked, unhooded male prisoner, head momentarily turned away from the camera, posed to make it appear that he is performing oral sex on another male prisoner, who is naked and hooded.[40]

As Hirsch notes, such sexual humiliation would be unacceptable in any culture but is especially so in the Arab world, where homosexuality is prohibited by Islamic law and where it is considered humiliating for men to appear naked in front of other men.

The story and the photographs quickly spread around the world. Americans were shocked and mortified, Arabs were angry, and people all around the world were appalled. President Bush, Secretary of Defense Rumsfeld, and

U.S. military commanders all expressed regret about the abuse, and the culpable soldiers were dismissed, court-martialed, or lightly punished. But the question of initiative and responsibility for the crimes of Abu Ghraib bubbled higher up. Hirsch wrote that even the Taguba report faulted "army leadership at the highest levels" and that "interrogating prisoners and getting intelligence, including by intimidation and torture, was the priority."

The revelations about Abu Ghraib came hard on the heels of accusations of prisoner abuse and torture at another American military base, Guantanamo Bay in Cuba. In May 2004, the *Washington Post* reported on classified military documents that showed Pentagon approval for the use of sleep deprivation, exposure to hot and cold, bright lights, and loud music during interrogations at Guantanamo.[41] Guantanamo had already been a source of controversy because of the government's use of extrajudicial detention of prisoners, most of whom were suspected Taliban or al-Qaeda fighters or supporters captured in Afghanistan. The Bush administration described these prisoners as "unlawful enemy combatants" rather than prisoners of war and therefore outside the protection of the Geneva Conventions, a set of international treaties that include guidelines on the treatment of prisoners during war. In addition, the administration argued that because they were in Cuba rather than the United States, they were also not subject to the protections of U.S. law. Prisoners at Guantanamo were not granted the right of habeas corpus, were not subject to the process or protection of either U.S. law or international law, and were often not even allowed contact or communication with family members or lawyers.

At both Abu Ghraib and Guantanamo, the United States was once again skirting around if not in direct violation of international law and even of U.S. law and military regulations. Torture and other inhumane treatments have been outlawed in many international treaties and conventions since World War II. Article 5 of the 1948 Universal Declaration of Human Rights states flatly that "no one shall be subjected to torture or to cruel, inhuman or degrading treatment or punishment." There are no exceptions. Similar language banning torture or inhumane treatment appears in the International Covenant on Civil and Human Rights, the American Convention on Human Rights, the Geneva Conventions III and IV, the 1977 Geneva Protocol I, and the 1984 Convention against Torture. Even the U.S. Army's *Field Manual* (1987), which has procedures for intelligence interrogations, prohibits the use of torture or force and, in addition, states that the use of such techniques "yields unreliable results."[42]

It was all the more disturbing, then, and an additional embarrassment for the United States worldwide when U.S. administration officials attempted to justify or excuse torture and extralegal treatment of prisoners of the war on terror. The overarching argument used by President Bush and his subordinates was that the war on terror was different than past wars, requiring different techniques and revised rules. White House general counsel Alberto Gonzales (who was later appointed attorney general) laid out this argument in a memorandum in January 2002, stating that "this new paradigm renders obsolete Geneva's strict limitations on questioning of enemy prisoners and renders quaint some of its provisions."[43] A second memorandum by Jay Bybee, then an assistant attorney general (but subsequently appointed by Bush as a federal judge), attempted to narrow the definition of torture. "Where the pain is physical, it must be of an intensity akin to that which accompanies serious physical injury such as death or organ failure." Anything less, he contended, would not be torture and was therefore permissible.[44] Under this definition, then, the abuses of both Abu Ghraib and Guantanamo are perfectly acceptable.

In October 2003, conservative legal scholar Jack Goldsmith was appointed head of the Justice Department's Office of Legal Counsel, which advises the president and the attorney general about the legality of executive actions. Looking into the issue of torture, he and his Justice Department colleagues, in consultation with lawyers from the Defense Department, State Department, Central Intelligence Agency, and National Security Council, reached a consensus that the Geneva Conventions afford protection to all Iraqis, including those who are terrorists. When he presented these findings to the White House, David Addington (Vice President Dick Cheney's legal adviser then and now his chief of staff) exploded in anger: "The president has already decided that terrorists do not receive Geneva Convention protections. You cannot question his decision."[45]

World reactions to all of this were understandably negative. The initial reports of torture—and especially the Abu Ghraib pictures—were offensive enough, but in some ways the efforts of the administration to excuse or justify these actions were even worse, implying a deeper moral malaise within the United States. The foreign minister of the Vatican, Giovanni Lajolo, said that the torture scandal was "a heavier blow to the United States than September 11, particularly [because] the blow was not inflicted by terrorists but by the Americans on themselves."[46] The editor of an influential Arabic-language newspaper in London asserted that "the liberators are worse than the dictators. This is the straw that broke the camel's back for America."[47] As to Guantanamo, several UN committees, the European Union Parliament, and the United Kingdom's Attorney General Lord Goldsmith all called for the United States to close down the camp. But as of mid-2007, the camp was still in operation, with more than 300 detainees.

The Impact on America

We have seen in earlier chapters that the domestic situation of the United States has weakened in recent decades and increasingly compares unfavorably with other countries. To some extent, this has been recognized by people outside the United States and has contributed to some disillusionment about America as a model for the rest of the world. But it is the way the United States has treated the rest of the world that has really turned the world against the United States and eroded the American role as global leader. At the same time that the world has become more globalized and interconnected and increasingly faces problems that require global cooperation and multilateral solutions, the United States has gone the other direction, rejecting international cooperation, international law, multilateral institutions, and even global standards of morality.

It could be argued that these problems are largely temporary and will disappear with a new administration in Washington that is more committed to international law and international cooperation. Indeed, this would be a welcome change and improvement, but for several reasons it seems unlikely to reverse the damage already done. First, the exceptionally belligerent behavior and insensitive rhetoric of the Bush administration has, for many people in the rest of the world, acted to pull back the curtain on the American Wizard of Oz. It has caused people to take a second look at the United States and to recognize the less positive aspects of America's domestic situation quite apart from its international behavior. As we will see in chapter 8 on world opinion of the United States, people in other countries are increasingly critical not only of the U.S. government but also of the country's people, society, and culture. The United States is no longer seen as the "beacon on the hill." Given the huge underlying social, economic, and political problems in the United States, it will be difficult even for a more conciliatory and internationalist president to convince others that the United States is "the indispensable nation." Furthermore, the fiasco of the Iraq War and the war on terror has revealed the hollowness of America's hard power as well as its soft power. Through the American Century, the country's global influence was built on other countries either loving or fearing it. Increasingly, neither can be relied on.

Second, many of the international problems caused by the Bush administration were underlying ones to begin with and were simply made much worse since 2001. Those problems will not disappear, and some of them have become virtually irreversible. It is difficult to see how they could be "solved" by an administration, Democrat or Republican, with a different worldview.

The problem of global warming, for example, has accelerated and deepened since the U.S. abandonment of the Kyoto treaty. The two biggest contributors of greenhouse gases, the United States and China, are unconstrained by the limits of the treaty (though for different reasons). Even if the United States, under a different leadership, did eventually adhere to the treaty, it will probably be too late to avoid catastrophic consequences of climate change. Many climate scientists believe that the world has already passed the tipping point.

A similar argument could be made about the threat of terror and of Islamic fundamentalism. The United States, like the rest of the world, had confronted these issues for many years before 2001. The Islamic revival, after all, took wing with the Iranian Revolution of 1979. The misbegotten U.S. invasion of Iraq, which was intended to squelch both terrorism and fundamentalism while planting the seeds of democracy in the Middle East, has had the exact opposite effect on all counts. Iraq has provided a breeding ground for terrorism, fundamentalism, sectarianism, and antidemocratic movements. Terrorist attacks have increased sharply across the world since 2003. And some of the few secular (and potentially democratic) regimes in the Middle East, like Egypt, Palestine, and Lebanon, have suffered reversals in their efforts at democratization. The U.S. presence in Iraq has fueled Islamism in that country and throughout the Middle East and the rest of the Muslim world. Islam, fundamentalist and otherwise, is a growing and momentous force in the world and will pose many new challenges to the United States. A new president or a new Congress is unlikely to have much impact on this. These growing threats to American primacy are the subject of the following chapter.

Notes

1. Seymour Martin Lipset, *American Exceptionalism: A Double-Edged Sword* (New York: Norton, 1996), 13.

2. Siobhan McEvoy-Levy, *American Exceptionalism and US Foreign Policy* (New York: Palgrave, 2001), 25.

3. Condoleezza Rice, "Campaign 2000: Promoting the National Interest," *Foreign Affairs*, January/February 2000, http://www.foreignaffairs.org.

4. Michael Mandelbaum, *The Case for Goliath: How America Acts as the World's Government in the 21st Century* (New York: Public Affairs, 2005), xvi.

5. Stephen Kinzer, *Overthrow: America's Century of Regime Change from Hawaii to Iraq* (New York: Times Books, 2006), 107.

6. Kinzer, *Overthrow*, 1–2.

7. These polls will be cited and discussed more fully in chapter 8.

8. *New York Times*, October 17, 2007, A1.

9. Philippe Sands, *Lawless World: America and the Making and Breaking of Global Rules from FDR's Atlantic Charter to George W. Bush's Illegal War* (New York: Viking, 2005), 9.

10. *New York Times*, October 25, 1999, also available at the PNAC's website at http://www.newamericancentury.org/def_natl_sec_044.htm.

11. Cited in Sands, *Lawless World*, 20.

12. Sands, *Lawless World*, xii.

13. "Secretary Rumsfeld Statement on the ICC Treaty," U.S. Department of Defense news release, May 6, 2002.

14. Sands, *Lawless World*, 62–63.

15. "Statement of the European Union on the Position of the United States of America towards the International Criminal Court," submitted by Spain to the Preparatory Commission for the International Criminal Court, May 20, 2002.

16. "President Clinton Written Statement," White House briefing, December 11, 1997.

17. Sands, *Lawless World*, 89.

18. Calculations by the environmental group Germanwatch, taking into account greenhouse gas emission levels and trends and climate policy, reported at the website of the Climate Action Network at http://www.climnet.org.

19. The "2006 Environmental Performance Index" produced jointly by Yale and Columbia universities, reported in the *New York Times*, January 23, 2006, A3.

20. From the PBS *Frontline* show "Hot Politics" airing on April 29, 2007.

21. *Japan Times*, June 14, 2001, http://search.japantimes.co.jp/cgi-bin/nn20010614a7.html.

22. *New York Times*, November 18, 2007.

23. From a review by Carl Zimmer of Tim Flannery's book *The Weather Makers* (New York: Atlantic Monthly Press, 2006) in *New York Times Book Review*, March 12, 2006, 8.

24. This speech is available at http://www.whitehouse.gov/news/releases/2002/01/20020129-11.html.

25. This is speech available at http://www.whitehouse.gov/news/releases/2002/06/20020601-3.html.

26. Available at the White House website at http://www.whitehouse.gov/hsc/nss.html.

27. Arthur Schlesinger Jr., "Good Foreign Policy a Casualty of War," *Los Angeles Times*, March 23, 2003.

28. Evelyn Leopold, "Annan Challenges U.S. Doctrine of Preventive Action," Reuters, September 23, 2003, available at CommonDreams.org newscenter.

29. Ron Suskind, *The One Percent Doctrine* (New York: Simon & Schuster, 2006), 26.

30. Quoted in Richard Clarke, *Against All Enemies* (New York: Free Press, 2004), 24.

31. Clarke, *Against All Enemies*, 32–33.

32. "U.S. Rejects Taliban Offer to Try bin Laden," CNN.com, October 7, 2001.

33. Sands, *Lawless World*, 185.

34. Cited in Kinzer, *Overthrow*, 295.

35. Sands, *Lawless World*, 187; see also the letter of the New York City Bar Association, sent to President Bush on October 15, 2002, which found no "facts justifying the use of force in self-defense under Article 51 of the United Nations Charter" and urged the president to obtain authorization from the UN Security Council before any military action against Iraq. In James R. Silkenat and Mark R. Shulman, eds., *The Imperial Presidency and the Consequences of 9/11* (Westport, Conn.: Praeger, 2007), 54–56.

36. "Millions Join Global Anti-war Protests," BBC Online, February 17, 2003, http://news.bbc.co.uk/1/hi/world/europe/2765215.stm#map.

37. Estimate by the French political scientist Dominique Reynie, in his *La Fracture occidentale: Naissance d'une opinion européenne*. (Paris: Editions de La Table Ronde, 2004), 37.

38. See details and references to these Pew surveys in chapter 8.

39. Seymour M. Hirsch, "Torture at Abu Ghraib," *The New Yorker*, May 10, 2004, http://www.newyorker.com/archive/2004/05/10/040510fa_fact.

40. Hirsch, "Torture at Abu Ghraib."

41. "Pentagon Approved Tougher Interrogation," *Washington Post*, May 9, 2004, http://www.washingtonpost.com/ac2/wp-dyn/A11017-2004May8?language=printer.

42. Sands, *Lawless World*, 210.

43. Gonzales's memo to the president appears in Mark Danner, *Torture and Truth: America, Abu Ghraib, and the War on Terror* (New York: New York Review of Books, 2004), 84.

44. Bybee's memo appears in Danner, *Torture and Truth*, 115–66.

45. Jeffrey Rosen, "Conscience of a Conservative," *New York Times Magazine*, September 9, 2007, 43; Jack Goldsmith has published a book recounting all of this in *The Terror Presidency* (New York: Norton, 2007).

46. "Catholics, Protestants, Urge New Iraq Policy," *The Christian Century*, June 1, 2004.

47. Paul Majendie, "Iraqi Prison Photos Mar U.S. Image," Reuters, April 30, 2004.

CHAPTER SEVEN

The Last Gasp of U.S. Supremacy

The Iraq War and Terrorism

The Iraq war has become a "cause célèbre" for jihadists, breeding a deep resentment of U.S. involvement in the Muslim world and cultivating supporters for the global jihadist movement.

—U.S. National Intelligence Estimate, 2006

Four years into the Iraq War, it has finally become clear to most people what almost all experts knew would be the case before the war began. The war is a *Fiasco*—the title of a devastating critique of the war by the Pulitzer Prize–winning Pentagon correspondent for the *Washington Post*, Thomas E. Ricks. Ricks sees the decision to invade Iraq as "one of the most profligate actions in the history of American foreign policy."[1] Lieutenant General Ricardo Sanchez, the former top commander of American forces in Iraq, describes the war effort as "a nightmare with no end in sight."[2] It is hard to disagree with these assessments. The decision to invade was based on false information and taken without international support. It has claimed the lives of more than 3,800 American soldiers and hundreds of thousands of Iraqis and has cost the United States, so far, more than $500 billion. And far from bringing democracy to Iraq or to the region, it has triggered economic and social collapse, sectarian animosity, political fragmentation, civil war, and regional instability. It has also inflamed anti-Americanism and stimulated terrorism both in the Middle East and worldwide.

To have hinted at such possible outcomes in 2003 or 2004 would have seemed almost treasonous, but to describe them now is so commonplace as to be almost trite. The scale of the disaster is so enormous that one could hardly do justice to the topic in a short space. Rather, this chapter focuses on the consequences of the Iraq War for the American role in the world. On this problematic issue, perhaps more than any other in the catalog of problems facing the United States, it is difficult to separate the failures of the Bush presidency from the more deep-seated and long-term issues confronting the country. As for the Iraq War, Ricks argues, "none of this was inevitable" except for the extremely bad decisions of the Bush White House. General Sanchez calls the Bush administration's handling of the war "incompetent." This war, more than any other in U.S. history, can be laid at the doorstep of one man and a few of his closest advisers. So it may hardly seem right to blame this fiasco on the United States rather than on George W. Bush. But many of the social and political problems afflicting the country—the decline of education, the withering of democracy, and the timidity of the mass media—made it much easier for the White House to lead the country into war. And no matter the cause, the country as a whole is stuck with the consequences of this war, which have exacerbated these social and political problems as well as the country's economic ones. The war cannot be undone, and it will be extremely difficult even to bring it to a close. The Iraq War and the violence, animosity, and instability that it has bred constitute a closing chapter of the "American Century."

False Premises and Bad Information

As we saw in the previous chapter, the entire premise of the Iraq invasion was flawed. There were no weapons of mass destruction (WMD) in Iraq, Iraq was not threatening any of America's allies, and there were no connections between al-Qaeda or the September 11 terrorists and the government of Saddam Hussein. This did not stop the White House from making claims on all three of these counts and for reaching for all sorts of evidence to substantiate those claims. In some cases, the evidence was so far fetched as to be almost laughable. In other cases, the president deliberately used inflammatory "facts" that he already knew to be in dispute. The overall effect, though, was to intimidate a frightened public and Congress into supporting a war that made no sense.

The most controversial of these claims was President Bush's assertion in his State of the Union Address in January 2003 that "the British government has learned that Saddam Hussein recently sought significant quantities of uranium from Africa." He was referring to rumors, from as early as 2002, that Iraq was acquiring uranium from the African country of Niger for possible use in the construction of nuclear weapons. This became a central piece of the argument from the White House that Hussein was close to developing nuclear weapons. But the evidence was flimsy to begin with and completely discredited before the United States launched Operation Iraqi Freedom in March 2003. A full year before the State of the Union Address, French intelligence had conveyed to Washington that there was no hard evidence of any such Iraq–Niger connection.[3]

Furthermore, in February 2002, the Central Intelligence Agency (CIA) had sent Ambassador Joseph Wilson to Niger to investigate the claims, and when Wilson reported he found no such evidence, the CIA passed this finding on to the White House. Finally, on March 7, 2003, Mohammed El Baradei, the head of the International Atomic Energy Agency (IAEA), reported to the UN Security Council that after examining the documents of the Niger uranium connection, IAEA experts determined that they were "not authentic."[4] Apparently, it had taken IAEA analysts only a few hours to discover the documents were crude forgeries, including incorrect names of Nigerian officials, though U.S. intelligence officials had extensively reviewed the documents.[5] The Niger uranium claim was a slender reed indeed on which to base a major war.

President Bush made an even more preposterous claim in an October 2002 speech in Cincinnati, where he warned that "Iraq has a growing fleet of manned and unmanned aerial vehicles that could be used to disperse chemical and biological weapons across broad areas" and expressed concern that they could be used "for missions targeting the United States." The vehicles he was referring to, though, were jet training aircraft purchased from Czechoslovakia decades earlier, the Soviet-bloc equivalent of America's Cessna, with a range of about 840 miles and a top speed of 145 miles per hour. As journalist and author Chalmers Johnson puts it, "The president did not explain how these slow-moving aircraft could reach Maine, the nearest point on the U.S. mainland to Iraq, some 5,500 miles away, or why they would not be shot down the moment they crossed Iraq's borders."[6] In combination with the assertions about Hussein's links to al-Qaeda and his alleged development of WMD, the idea that the U.S. mainland might be vulnerable to WMD attacks was particularly terrifying and was effective in eliciting support for the war. But it was not true.

In the run-up to the invasion of Iraq, the Bush White House also attempted to link Hussein with the September 11 attacks, if not with detailed evidence at least through innuendo. In the fall of 2002, Secretary of Defense Donald Rumsfeld asserted that "there are al-Qaeda in Iraq," that the government had "bulletproof" evidence of links between Iraq and al-Qaeda, and suggested that Hussein's Iraq had offered safe haven to Osama bin Laden and Taliban leader Mullah Mohammed Omar. In a speech in October 2002, President Bush said that "some al-Qaeda leaders who fled Afghanistan went to Iraq."[7] In his State of the Union Address in January 2003, when the president made the case for an attack on Iraq, he asserted that "Saddam Hussein aids and protects terrorists, including members of al Qaeda." While not directly blaming Hussein for the September 11 attacks, he implied such connections, frequently mentioning that date and Hussein's name in the same sentence or paragraph and asking us "to imagine those 19 hijackers with other weapons and other plans—this time armed by Saddam Hussein."[8]

There was no evidence of any such links, and the president and his cabinet had been warned numerous times by CIA head George Tenet and National Security Council counterterrorism director Richard Clarke that there was no evidence of any connection between September 11 and Hussein. A congressional joint inquiry that investigated the September 11 attacks similarly found no evidence linking Iraq to the hijackers or the attacks. As with the issues of WMD and Hussein's hostile intents on the United States, in the absence of real evidence, the administration reached for straws on the Iraq links to September 11. Vice President Dick Cheney, in particular, frequently referred to allegations that Mohamed Atta, the leader of the September 11 attacks, had met with an Iraqi intelligence officer in Prague as many as four times in the spring of 2001. Cheney continued to make these assertions even after Czech intelligence services, then Czech President Vaclav Havel, the Federal Bureau of Investigation (FBI), and the CIA all told the White House that there was no evidence of any such meeting in Prague. Indeed, U.S. records at the time showed that Atta was living in Virginia Beach, Virginia, during the alleged meetings in Prague, and the FBI could find no record of him having left the United States during the time in question.[9] Later reports suggested that it was a different Mohammed Atta, a Pakistani, who was in Prague in early 2001.

That the case for war could be built on such flimsy evidence raises disturbing questions about the integrity of our leaders. Beyond that, though, it also paints a dismal picture of government manipulation of data, intelligence, and public opinion; the failure of the U.S. mass media to challenge such dubious and transparent allegations; the temerity of Congress; and the gullibility of the American public. As discussed in chapter 4, in 2003 an overwhelming majority of Americans accepted the assertions of the White House about Iraq's WMD. On the eve of the war, 58 percent believed either that Iraq was "directly involved" in carrying out the September 11 attacks or that Iraq had provided "substantial support" to al-Qaeda. Even more astounding is the fact that a full year into the war, during which time no evidence of either al-Qaeda or WMD had been found in the country, these poll numbers had hardly changed at all: Americans still believed that Hussein was behind the terrorists and possessed WMD. The persistence of misinformation is quite stunning because even in 2006, half of all Americans still believed Iraq had WMD at the time of the U.S. invasion.

Perhaps American citizens can be excused for being so uncritical and gullible, given the barrage of disinformation and propaganda thrown at them from authoritative sources, including their president, and given the failure of the mass media to provide any correctives, at least in the year surrounding the beginning of the war. But the senior officials in the government and members of Congress have no such excuse and have plenty of resources to find out the truth and understand the situation. However, from the top to the bottom, there was an appalling level of ignorance about Iraq, the Middle East, and Islam among the very people who were making policy and who planned and implemented the war.

Once again, in this case the problem is particularly evident at the very top with President Bush himself, but it spreads far wider than the White House. President Bush is famously a nonreader and does not, reportedly, even read a newspaper. He has said that he may glance at newspaper headlines but rarely reads the articles, asserting that "the best way to get the news is from objective sources," and "the most objective sources I have are the people on my staff who tell me what's happening in the world."[10] But his staff seems mostly interested in protecting him from unpleasant news rather than providing him with a broad panoply of sources, views, or opinions. Journalist Ron Suskind, author of *The One Percent Doctrine*, reports that a senior Bush aide derisively dismissed him as "a member of the reality-based community." "That's not the way the world really works anymore," said the official. "We're an empire now, and when we act, we create our own reality. And while you're studying that reality . . . we'll act again, creating other new realities, which you can study too, and that's how things will sort out. We're history's actors . . . and you, all of you, will be left to just study what we do."[11]

As the United States prepared to invade Iraq, there were few people in positions of power who knew enough about the Middle East to challenge the White House's version of reality. Even well into the war, most members of Congress quizzed by a reporter could not define the difference between Sunni and Shiite Muslims and did not know whether al-Qaeda or Hezbollah were predominantly Sunni or Shiite.[12] This kind of high-level ignorance is dangerous both for the country contemplating intervention in the region and for the targets of such intervention. An example of this that would be funny were it not tragic was the visit of an American congressional delegation led by Senator John McCain to Baghdad's central market in April 2007. Using the visit as evidence of the success of the U.S. military's new security plan for the city, McCain and his colleagues described the market as a safe, bustling place full of hopeful and welcoming Iraqis. Representative Mike Pence, an Indiana Republican and member of the delegation, said it was "like a normal outdoor market in Indiana in the summertime."[13] The visit received widespread coverage in the news media, essentially parroting the delegation's rosy reports. What was not initially reported was that the four-man delegation was protected by more than one hundred American soldiers, three Black Hawk helicopters, and two Apache gunships. The market was closed off, traffic was redirected, sharpshooters were posted on roofs, and the congressional tourists sported bulletproof vests. Iraqi shop owners interviewed the next day were incredulous about the Americans' conclusions: "The area is very dangerous," said one. "They cannot secure it." Several merchants said the Americans' visit might have made the market a more inviting target for insurgents. And indeed, the *Times* of London reported that twenty-one of the market's workers and merchants were "ambushed, bound and shot dead" the day after the congressmen's visit.[14] In many ways, the Shorja market visit is a case study representing the broader U.S. experience in Iraq: Americans waltz into the country on a flimsy pretext, ill informed and naive about the situation and spouting platitudes and inanities, and leave resentment, death, and destruction in their wake.

The American misadventure in Iraq is due partly to the hubris and arrogance of the Bush administration, partly to the refusal of the administration to listen to experts on Iraq and the Muslim world, and partly to a dearth of expertise in places where it is needed. The 2006 bipartisan Iraq Study Group Report argued that "all our efforts in Iraq, military and civilian, are handicapped by Americans' lack of language and cultural understanding." It noted that the U.S. embassy in Baghdad, with more than 1,000 employees, had only thirty-three Arabic speakers, just six of whom were fluent.[15] In 2003, the U.S. State Department had fewer than sixty employees who were fluent in Arabic, and only five of those had skills sufficient to participate in a television or radio interview.[16] Fewer than ten analysts in the Defense Intelligence Agency have more than two years' experience in analyzing the insurgency that is tearing Iraq apart. Few American soldiers in Iraq have language abilities or even much training in Arabic or Muslim culture. This does not help the American mission on the ground. A painful example of this was depicted in the PBS television documentary *America at a Crossroads* when a young lieutenant—a West Point graduate and intelligence officer stationed at a camp near Baghdad—decides to venture outside the camp to interact with some of the locals. When asked by a reporter to speak some Arabic, she provides this example: "So you think I'm stupid? I know you're lying, coward."[17] This was the first Arabic phrase that came to mind for her, apparently, but hardly seems the kind of language that will endear Americans to Iraqis.

The other part of this equation is that those people who were experts were either kept at a distance or ignored by the Bush White House. President Bush tended to surround himself with like-minded thinkers and did not welcome contrary opinions. His advisers told him what he wanted to hear, and the president dismissed critics as "Monday morning quarterbacks." But there were plenty of informed people who warned against the invasion of Iraq. Thomas Ricks's book *Fiasco* recounts many warnings from Middle East experts and military veterans, like General Anthony C. Zinni and General H. Norman Schwarzkopf, who cautioned that the invasion and aftermath would not be as quick or simple as the administration predicted. Ricks reports that in late 2002, seventy national security experts and Middle East scholars met at the National Defense University to discuss the impending war and concluded that occupying Iraq would "be the most daunting and complex task the U.S. and the international community will have undertaken since the end of World War II."[18] Most U.S. academic specialists on international relations and Middle East politics also opposed the decision to go to war with Iraq. A survey in 2004 of more than 1,000 international relations faculty in the United States and Canada found that more than three-quarters had opposed the U.S. decision prior to the invasion, and a similar survey two years later found almost 90 percent believing that the war would "decrease international security."[19] Perhaps the most prescient warning, though, came from retired General Brent Scowcroft, who had been national security adviser to the first President Bush, in a 2002 op-ed piece titled "Don't Attack Saddam" in the *Wall Street Journal*. It is worth quoting the column at length both because it sums up so much of what we have discussed here and because so much of what he predicted turned out to be true:

There is scant evidence to tie Saddam to terrorist organizations, and even less to the Sept. 11 attacks. Indeed, Saddam's goals have little in common with the terrorists who threaten us, and there is little incentive for him to make common cause with them. He is unlikely to risk his investment in weapons of mass destruction, much less his country, by handing such weapons to terrorists who would use them for their own purposes and leave Baghdad as the return address. . . . The central point is that any campaign against Iraq, whatever the strategy, costs and risks, is certain to divert us for some indefinite period from our war on terrorism. Worse, there is a virtual consensus in the world against an attack on Iraq at this time. . . . Ignoring that clear sentiment would result in a serious degradation in international cooperation with us against terrorism. And make no mistake, we simply cannot win that war without enthusiastic cooperation, especially on intelligence.[20]

Failure in Iraq

The failure of the American effort in Iraq is staggering in both its breadth and its depth. The United States has lost more than 3,800 soldiers in the conflict—more people than died in the destruction of the World Trade Center in September 2001. Hundreds of thousands of Iraqis have died, and millions have become refugees. As Sunni and Shiite factions attack each other, sectarian violence has soared, and the country has degenerated into civil war. Iraq has become a magnet and breeding ground for terrorists who have also escalated their attacks worldwide. Oil production, which was supposed to pay for the rebuilding of the country, is far below prewar levels. The war has further hurt U.S. relations and the U.S. reputation with other countries, including its allies. In the view of former national security adviser Zbigniew Brzezinski, the war has been "a geopolitical disaster" and "has caused calamitous damage to America's global standing."[21]

As virtually every analysis of Iraq has pointed out, a principal problem was the failure by the administration to adequately plan for the postwar reconstruction of Iraq. The initial military conquest was relatively quick, easy, and straightforward. Within six weeks of the beginning of combat operations, President Bush was able to stand on the deck of the aircraft carrier USS *Abraham Lincoln*, in front of a banner proclaiming "Mission Accomplished," and assert that "in the battle of Iraq, the United States and our allies have prevailed." Given the overwhelming military superiority of the United States (population 300 million) compared to Iraq (27 million), the military victory was not in doubt, but there was almost no consideration in the White House about what would come after the overthrow of the Hussein government, and the United States was ill prepared in terms of plans, expertise, or personnel to handle the postwar situation. In the immediate aftermath of the invasion, the country descended into virtual anarchy. There was widespread looting and vandalism, including the National Museum of Iraq in Baghdad and other archaeological sites containing treasures dating to the dawn of civilization. Defense Secretary Rumsfeld brushed off the stories about looting, saying "stuff happens" and "freedom's untidy."[22] But the stories and images of the looting and the apparent unwillingness or inability of U.S. forces to stop it did much to hurt the U.S. cause and its reputation. As Fred Ikle, the Pentagon's policy chief under President Reagan, wrote, "America lost most of its prestige and respect in that episode. To pacify a conquered country, the victor's prestige and dignity is absolutely critical."[23]

American postwar planning for Iraq focused primarily on removing the Baathist regime of Hussein and putting in place a broadly representative democracy. In fact, after it became apparent that there were neither WMD nor connections to al-Qaeda in Hussein's Iraq, the administration's justification for the invasion shifted subtly to this one goal: to bring freedom and democracy to Iraq and to use Iraq as a proving ground and incubator for democracy throughout the Middle East. In a speech in November 2003 commemorating the twentieth anniversary of the National Endowment for Democracy, the president laid out his "forward strategy for freedom in the Middle East": "Iraqi democracy will succeed—and that success will send forth the news, from Damascus to Teheran—that freedom can be the future of every nation. The establishment of a free Iraq at the heart of the Middle East will be a watershed event in the global democratic revolution."[24]

Even in this primary and essential goal of the Iraqi operation, promoting democracy, the accomplishments after five years were dismal. The country did come up with a constitution, held elections, and formed a government of national unity (in 2006) that was broadly representative of the Iraqi people. But the form was much more impressive than the substance. The bipartisan *Iraq Study Group Report* of 2006 provided a sobering assessment of the political situation in the country.[25] "The composition of the Iraqi government is basically sectarian," it found, with key players in the government acting in their sectarian interests. The Shiites, who dominate the government, have gained political power for the first time in 1,300 years, and many are determined to preserve that power. Shiite militias are seen as "legitimate vehicles of political action" and are used not only to secure order in neighborhoods but also to fight against Sunnis, often in revenge or retaliation for Sunni attacks on Shiites.

The Iraqi constitution was approved without the resolution of some fundamental issues, with the idea that these issues would be settled at a later time through amendments. The issues included the nature of the federal structure, the control of oil and oil revenues, and the source of federal government revenues and taxation authority. These are bedrock issues for any government, but they are still unresolved despite the passing of several deadlines on them set by both the Iraqi government and the U.S. government. The core issue is federalism. The Kurds in the north and many Shiites, mostly in the south, favor a highly decentralized system of government, perhaps with autonomous zones for Kurds, Shiites, and Sunnis. But most Sunnis oppose such a structure, in part because most of Iraq's energy sources (especially oil) lie within the Kurdish and Shiite areas. There is also concern that an autonomous Shiite region would fall even more under the sway of Shiite Iran (with which Iraq fought a long and bitter war in the 1980s) or that Iraq could be dismembered altogether.

These issues of unity, autonomy, revenue, and oil are the most fundamental political ones for Iraq and seem no closer to resolution in 2008 than they were in 2004. But the *Iraq Study Group Report* lists a host of other issues of governance, including the tendency of the Shiite-dominated government to withhold government services from Sunni neighborhoods, the lack of security, rampant corruption, a weak judiciary, and the lack of bureaucratic and technocratic capacity due to the "de-Baathification" policy and middle-class emigration that has deprived the country of competent, experienced, and educated administrators. The Iraqi Ministry of Displacement and Migration estimated in 2007 that almost a third of all professors, doctors, pharmacists, and engineers had fled the country since 2003. Hundreds of students and professors had been killed or kidnapped, and Iraq's universities were near paralysis.[26] The medical profession was similarly under siege. Some 2,250 doctors had been murdered or kidnapped, and another 12,000 had fled the country.[27] By the beginning of 2007, more than 2 million Iraqis had fled the country, and a staggering 1.7 million had been "internally displaced." This massive exodus, the biggest refugee crisis in the Middle East since the dislocations caused by the formation of Israel in 1948, intensifies the chaos inside Iraq and places in jeopardy the stability of its neighbors.

In February 2007, the release of a new "National Intelligence Estimate" (an analysis by American intelligence agencies) expressed serious doubts about the ability of Iraqi's political leaders to hold the country together and about whether the Iraqi military could assert control over the powerful sectarian militias. The assessment judged "that the term 'civil war' does not adequately capture the complexity of the conflict in Iraq, which includes extensive Shia-on-Shia violence, Al Qaeda and Sunni insurgent attacks on coalition forces, and widespread criminally motivated violence." The report also warned that further sectarian splintering of the country could invite involvement or intervention by other Middle Eastern countries and suggested the possibility of "a period of sustained, bloody fighting leading to partition of Iraq along ethnic lines."[28] A no less sobering assessment was issued at the end of 2007 by the Office of the Inspector General for Iraq Reconstruction, which found that "attempts by American-led reconstruction teams to forge political reconciliation, foster economic growth and build an effective police force and court system in Iraq have failed to show significant progress" in nearly every region of the country.[29]

Impact on Iraqis and Daily Life

While the number of U.S. combat deaths climbed steadily after the "conclusion" of hostilities in 2003, the American casualties and suffering are miniscule compared to that of Iraqis. Insurgent and militia attacks on civilians doubled between 2004 and 2006, reaching 800 per week by the fall of 2006. Average casualties for Iraqi civilian and security forces reached more than 100 per day in that time period, more than three times the rate in early 2004.[30] By early 2007, there were fifteen to thirty bodies found on Baghdad streets every day.[31] "Multiple-fatality bombings" grew from seventeen per month in February 2004 to fifty-four per month in February 2007 (see figure 7.1). The average daily casualties in the country remained high even after the "surge" that sent an additional 30,000 U.S. troops to Iraq beginning in February 2007 (see figure 7.2).

It is estimated that the number of insurgents in Iraq has increased by five times since 2003 to some 25,000 and that the strength of Shiite militias has

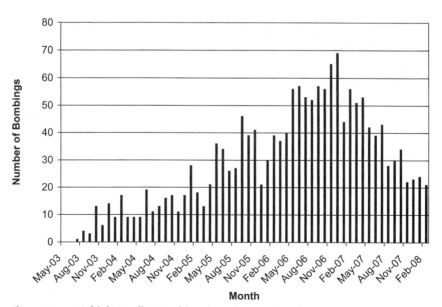

Figure 7.1. Multiple Fatality Bombings in Iraq, 2003–2007
Source: Iraq Index (Washington, D.C.: Brookings Institution, 2008)

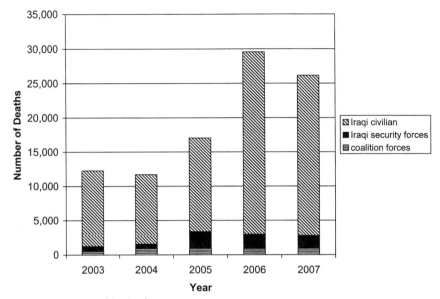

Figure 7.2.   Casualties in the Iraq War, 2003–2007
Source: http://www.icasualties.org and http://www.iraqbodycount.org/analysis/numbers/2007.

grown tenfold during that time to 50,000.[32] Although there are no reliable figures on the total number of Iraqi deaths since the U.S. invasion (and the U.S. government deliberately suppresses this information), estimates vary from 60,000 (by the website http://www.iraqbodycount.org) to 655,000 (by the Johns Hopkins School of Public Health).

The country's deadly violence is only the beginning of the problems for most Iraqis. More than a third of Iraqi citizens are without jobs. The war has damaged most hospitals and health care facilities, and many doctors have been killed or fled the country, so the level of health care has declined precipitously. The child mortality rate has doubled since 1990, and a quarter of all children under five years of age are malnourished. Life expectancy for Iraqis is eight years below the average for surrounding countries. A quarter of all Iraqis are totally dependent on food rations. Less than a third of the population has access to clean drinking water. Electricity output is below prewar levels and meets less than half the demand. Most residents of Baghdad receive only a few hours of electric power each day. Three-quarters of the children in Baghdad do not attend school, and between 30 and 70 percent of all the country's schools are closed because of insecurity, targeting of teachers, bombings, and kidnappings.[33] All these statistics, it might be necessary to point out, are far worse than before the U.S. invasion of March 2003.

Given the violence, chaos, and disruption in the country, it is not surprising that most Iraqis have turned against the Americans and the U.S. involvement in the war. The Iraq Study Group reported that only 36 percent of Iraqi citizens feel their country is headed in the right direction, and 79 percent have a "mostly negative" view of the U.S. role in their country. Even more alarming, 61 percent approve of attacks on U.S.-led forces.[34] A large-scale national poll conducted in Iraq in the spring of 2007 found sharply divided opinions about the war and the United States among different regions and sects, but none of them provide much encouragement for the United States. In Baghdad, half of those sampled agreed that "attacks on coalition forces are justified." In Anbar province, a Sunni stronghold, 100 percent agreed with such attacks. Sixty-one percent of all Arabs in the country (Sunni and Shiite) felt that a withdrawal of coalition troops would "make things better." There were substantial differences on this question between Shiites (62 percent), Sunnis (43 percent), and Kurds (15 percent), who have been protected by the Americans since the end of the Gulf War in 1991. In Anbar, Baghdad, and Basra, 100 percent agreed with the statement that "it is not safe in my own neighborhood."[35]

What is even more alarming is the extent of alienation and hostility among young people in Iraq. Like most of its neighbors, Iraq is a young country, with almost half the population under eighteen years of age, and a sizable numbers of these youngsters have been scarred or traumatized by the war. Recent studies of children in Iraq have found, for example, that almost half the children in Baghdad reported "exposure to a major traumatic event," that 30 percent of children in Mosul were suffering from posttraumatic stress disorder, and that 92 percent of Iraqi children showed signs of learning impediments.[36] It is not surprising that these children increasingly turn to violence, having lost parents or homes and seen their communities torn apart by sectarian violence and occupied by foreign troops. A State Department poll in the summer of 2006 found that nine out of ten young Iraqis, both Sunni and Shiite, saw the United States as an occupying force. American forces repeatedly encounter underage fighters on the battlefield. In 2004, the United States revealed that it was holding 107 suspected insurgents under the age of sixteen in detention camps in Iraq, but since then the government has refused to release figures about the number of such kids in detention.[37] A whole new generation of jihadists is being bred, enemies of the United States who will likely be fighting America all over the Middle East in the decades ahead.

Increasing Incidents and Threats of Terrorism

One of the great ironies and tragedies of the Iraq War is that rather than stemming terrorism, it has vastly increased both the incidence of terrorism and the likelihood of future terrorist attacks. President Bush has been fond of saying that we must stay in Iraq to defeat the terrorists and to keep terrorism from spreading, particularly to the United States. "It's better to fight them there than here," the president has said. But virtually all analysts, both inside the government and outside, believe that the war has contributed to the growth of terrorism rather than stemming it.

In the first place, of course, Iraq itself has become the centerpiece of the global war on terror. The number of attacks against U.S. forces, Iraqi security forces, and civilians have all increased steadily since the U.S. invasion of 2003, averaging 149 per day in April 2007 and about 5,000 per month. Even these numbers and the estimates of sectarian violence are probably significantly undercounting the real levels of such attacks. *The Iraq Study Group Report* states that "there is significant underreporting of the violence in Iraq" and gives an example of one day in July 2006 when there were ninety-three acts of violence reported, but "a careful review of the reports for that single day brought to light 1,100 acts of violence."[38] As noted previously, the number of insurgents in the country has grown from an estimated 5,000 in 2003 to 25,000 in late 2006. Iraq has become a magnet for jihadists from all over the world, with the number of "foreign fighters" among the insurgents growing from an estimated 250 in 2003 to 1,350 in 2006.[39]

President Bush seems to feel that fighting terrorism in Iraq has inhibited terrorist attacks elsewhere in the world, but the evidence points in the other direction. We have all been witness through television coverage of the horrific terrorist attacks on civilians in Madrid, London, Riyadh, Casablanca, Sharm el-Sheikh, and Bali, all of which were connected to al-Qaeda or its sympathizers. These, though, were simply the most deadly of a rash of terrorist incidents worldwide, and the number of such attacks has been increasing in recent years (see figure 7.3).

A study by the RAND Corporation estimates that of all the suicide bombings worldwide since 1968, three-quarters of them have taken place since September 11.[40] According to the U.S. government's National Counterterrorism Center, global terrorist attacks tripled from 2003 to 2004 and then quadrupled from 2004 to 2005. They rose again by about 25 percent in 2006, reaching 14,000 attacks worldwide, claiming the lives of some 20,000 noncombatants.

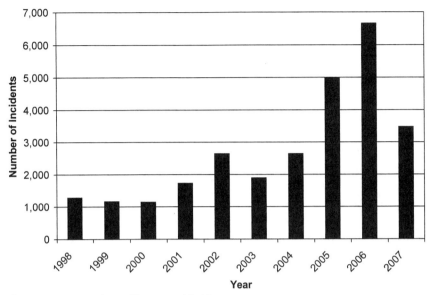

Figure 7.3.   Terrorist Incidents Worldwide, 2003–2007
Source: Terrorism Knowledge Base at http://tkb.org/Home.jsp.

These grim statistics confirm expert analysis of the impact of the Iraq War on global terrorism. The National Intelligence Estimate for 2006, produced by U.S. intelligence agencies, found that "the global jihadist movement . . . is spreading and adapting" and that "the Iraq jihad is shaping a new generation of terrorist leaders and operatives." It pointedly argued that the Iraq War had become "a 'cause célèbre' for jihadists, breeding a deep resentment of U.S. involvement in the Muslim world and cultivating supporters for the global jihadist movement."[41] The bipartisan Iraq Study Group reached similar conclusions in 2006, quoting an Iraqi official who told them that "Al Qaeda is now a franchise in Iraq, like McDonald's." The group worried that a chaotic Iraq would provide "a still stronger base of operations for terrorists who seek to act regionally or even globally."[42]

Not only has the Iraq War provided a stimulus and training ground for terrorists, but it has also diverted U.S. attention from other important potential venues for terrorism. The war has been a diversion for U.S. attention, U.S. troops, and U.S. resources, from places or methods that are far more likely to cause serious damage to the United States or its allies. There are many possibilities here, but the most alarming is of a terrorist smuggling a nuclear weapon into a U.S. seaport, perhaps in one of the 9 million containers that pass through U.S. ports each year. It is estimated that only about 6 percent of these are inspected by Customs and Border Protection officials. If a relatively "small" Hiroshima-sized weapon (ten to twenty kilotons) were detonated in the harbor of a large city, it would kill 50,000 to 1 million people, cause hundreds of billions of dollars in property damage, and disrupt trade sufficiently to threaten economic collapse in many countries.[43] Before the Iraq War, the Bush administration was worried about Saddam Hussein supplying nuclear weapons to terrorists. Hussein had neither the capacity, the motivation, nor the intent to do so, but there are numerous other places where terrorists could get nuclear weapons or nuclear materials to build such a weapon. In Russia, for example, thousands of low-yield "tactical" nuclear weapons (some of which are as powerful as the Hiroshima bomb) are not well secured, and even their numbers and locations are uncertain. A terrorist group could buy or steal such a weapon. There is concern about the security of nuclear weapons in both India and Pakistan as well. There are many sympathizers with both al-Qaeda and the Taliban within the Pakistani army, and should an Islamist government come to power in Pakistan (an increasingly likely possibility), terrorist groups would find even more opportunities to obtain such weapons from Pakistan.

Instability in the Middle East

The goal of the Bush administration in Iraq was to defeat radical Islam, reestablish American prestige, create a "demonstration model" of democracy for other Arab states, and unleash a "democratic tsunami" across the Islamic world. In the words of the journalist Mark Danner, this was a "war of the imagination" that had little connection to reality, and the results have been the polar opposite of the ambitions.[44] Instead, radical Islam has been strengthened, with its major target and enemy, the United States, invading and occupying Arab territory, its "infidel" soldiers killing Muslims. American prestige, already weakened by a decade of flouting world opinion and international law, reached a new low, both in the region and worldwide, with an illegal war built on manufactured evidence. Democracy in Iraq seems farther away than ever, assuming that the country even continues to exist as a unitary state. And to the extent that democracy is flourishing elsewhere, for example, with democratic elections in Iran and the Palestinian territories, it is bringing to power individuals (like President Ahmadinejad of Iran) or parties (like Hamas in Palestine) that are more hostile than their predecessors to American interests and policy in the region.

Indeed, the outcome of the U.S. invasion of Iraq is more in tune with the goals of Osama bin Laden than those of George W. Bush. In the view of most analysts, bin Laden's main hope with the September 11 attacks was to draw the United States into a long war on Arab territory that would drain and weaken the United States militarily and economically and eventually weaken U.S. allies in the region, particularly Saudi Arabia. Bin Laden's main targets were the secular (non-Islamist) Arab states like Iraq and those friendly to the United States like Saudi Arabia. But probably from his point of view, any American military presence in the region would both enhance the possibilities for jihad and increase political instability, fertilizing the seedbed of Islamic fundamentalism. Surely he expected a U.S. attack on Afghanistan; the invasion of Iraq must have seemed to him a godsend. In fact, these goals are reflected and even portended in a short book, *The Future of Iraq and the Arabian Peninsula after the Fall of Baghdad*, apparently written by an al-Qaeda insider on the eve of the U.S. invasion in 2003. This book, as described by Ron Suskind in *The One Percent Doctrine*, said "that an American invasion of Iraq would be the best possible outcome for al Qaeda, stoking extremism throughout the Persian Gulf and South Asia, and achieving precisely the radicalizing quagmire that bin Laden had hoped would occur in Afghanistan."[45]

The possibilities for disruption and chaos go far beyond Iraq, however. Even in Afghanistan, where the military victory was quick and easy, as was the installation of a mostly democratic government, the situation has deteriorated badly. The Taliban, which the United States deposed with its 2001 invasion of the country, is resurgent and now controls much of the south and east of the country and even great swaths of territory in neighboring Pakistan. The north of Afghanistan is controlled mostly by tribal warlords, with the pro-American government of Hamid Karzai effectively controlling only the area around the capital city of Kabul. Thirty percent of Afghanis suffer serious "food insecurity." At the same time, Afghanistan now produces 92 percent of the world's illicit opium. And, of course, both the former Taliban president, Mullah Omar, and the man he protected, Osama bin Laden, are still at large, even after six years of intense bounty hunting. Afghanistan, with its rebellious and independent population, has always been a thorn in the side of great powers, including both the British and the Soviets in the past, and it promises to remain so for the Americans.

An even more destabilizing development will be the breakup of Iraq, which by now seems virtually inevitable. As we saw earlier in this chapter, the possibilities for a unified and democratic Iraq have withered away in the face of increasing sectarian divisions and violence that are likely to be passed on to the next generation of young people. The "national" government now is effectively a Shiite one, with the Sunnis essentially boycotting both the elections and the constitutional process. In the north, the Kurds (who are not Arabs) have created a de facto autonomous Kurdistan. The country is already, in essence, three separate and irreconcilable zones. Some analysts suggest that we should simply formalize the inevitable and allow for the emergence of a "three-state solution."[46]

While a partition of Iraq may be inevitable and perhaps even the best solution, it brings with it a host of new problems. As Mark Danner trenchantly points out, "Iraq sits on the critical sectarian fault line of the Middle East," and "a conflict there gains powerful momentum from the involvement of neighboring states, with Iran strongly supporting the Shia and with Saudi Arabia, Kuwait, Jordan and Syria strongly sympathetic to the Sunnis."[47] Many Iraqi Shiites view Iran as a friend, a coreligionist, and a model for a powerful Shiite Islamic state. Iran has protected and supported Iraq's Shiite leaders for decades, and Iran's Khomeini regime sponsored the founding of Iraq's largest Shiite party, the Supreme Council for the Islamic Revolution of Iraq.[48] So a separate and powerful oil-rich Shiite Islamic state would be a boost both to Iran and to Islamism throughout the Shiite Arab world. The rise of Shiism was evident in 2006 when the Hezbollah of Lebanon (with support from Iran) engaged in a prolonged and violent conflict with Israel and effectively fought the powerful Israeli army to a draw.

An independent Kurdistan arising out of a dismembered Iraq could also be a problem for neighboring states. The Kurds, numbering about 35 million, are spread mostly across four states—Turkey, Iran, Syria, and Iraq—with about half the total in Turkey. An independent Kurdistan on Turkey's border would provide a magnet for separatist sentiments among Kurds in Turkey, where there is already a decades-long movement for Kurdish independence. Through most of the 1980s and 1990s, there was open war between the Kurdish separatist group, the Kurdistan Workers' Party, and Turkey's military. A revival of that movement could potentially dismember Turkey (a member of the North Atlantic Treaty Organization and a candidate for membership in the European Union) as well as Iraq.

Iraq and the End of the American Century

The Iraq War and global terrorism have hurt the United States in many ways and have diminished its power, influence, and authority in the world. As we have seen in earlier chapters, the decline of the United States was already in progress well before the Iraq War, but this war has accelerated the process and brought a conclusive end to the American Century. Washington's cavalier disregard of international law, the United Nations, and U.S. allies in the run-up to the war contributed to the country's already diminished standing in the eyes of the rest of the world. The mistreatment of prisoners of war in Iraq, Afghanistan, and Guantanamo, including the use of torture (apparently sanctioned by the U.S. government), horrified people around the world. The infringement of fundamental rights in pursuit of national security, including the bedrock principle of habeas corpus, eroded America's status as a beacon of democracy and freedom. The utter failure of the United States to achieve its goals in Afghanistan and Iraq has shattered the illusion of American power, even its military prowess. And these botched military and diplomatic efforts have contributed to the growth of anti-Americanism, terrorism, regional instability, and Islamic fundamentalism, all of which will continue to gnaw at American power and influence in the years ahead.

There is one more hugely important aspect of the impact of the Iraq War on American decline—the economic one. As we saw in chapter 1, the central element of the end of the American Century, around which almost all others revolve, is the alarming growth of U.S. deficits and debt. Both the U.S. government and American consumers have been spending far beyond their means for a generation. On top of these preexisting and systemic problems are added the massive and growing costs of the Iraq War and the "war on terror." Before the war started, the White House budget director, Mitch Daniels (now governor of Indiana), declared that the war would be "an affordable endeavor." He rejected an estimate by the chief White House economic adviser that the war would cost between $100 billion and $200 billion as "very very high."[49] But with the fiscal year 2008 budget, Congress will already have authorized $626 billion for the war in Iraq.[50] A Congressional Research Service study estimated that even with a phased pullout of troops, the costs of the wars in Iraq and Afghanistan could rise by an additional $371 billion. These total costs for both wars far exceed the inflation-adjusted cost of the Vietnam War.[51] They also account for about a quarter of the ballooning federal budget deficit. American military spending makes up over half of all "discretionary spending" in the U.S. budget. At a time when the United States is already deeply in debt and is struggling to provide basic health care, education, and retirement benefits to its citizens, it can hardly afford a costly and prolonged war.

This brings us back to the theme of the rise and fall of great powers, so presciently analyzed by Paul Kennedy years ago. What Kennedy had to say about "imperial overstretch" and the decline of great powers in the past is increasingly true of the United States today. "Great Powers in relative decline," wrote Kennedy, "instinctively respond by spending more on 'security' and thereby divert potential resources from 'investment' and compound their long-term dilemma."[52] The response of the United States to the September 11 attacks has been this kind of "instinctive" reaction—one based on fear and insecurity. It also reflects a nation trying to stem its own decline by acting with muscular power and imperial arrogance—showing the world its stuff, so to speak. But in the process, it has weakened itself internally, perhaps fatally so. Kennedy describes the way it has happened to other great powers in the past when "too large a proportion of the state's resources is diverted from wealth creation and allocated instead to military purposes," leading to "a weakening of national power over the longer term." This problem "becomes acute if the nation concerned has entered a period of relative economic decline."[53]

The United States was already in a period of "relative economic decline," as we saw in earlier chapters. This extremely costly war—costly in terms of men and women, material, money, and national prestige—is closing the book on America's century of great power. In the words of former National Security Adviser Zbigniew Brzezinski, "Fifteen years after its coronation as global leader, America is becoming a fearful and lonely democracy in a politically antagonistic world."[54]

Notes

1. Thomas E. Ricks, *Fiasco: The American Military Adventure in Iraq* (New York: Penguin, 2006), 3.

2. David S. Cloud, "Ex-Commander Calls Iraq Effort 'a Nightmare,'" *New York Times*, October 13, 2007, A1.

3. "Niger Uranium Rumors Wouldn't Die," *Los Angeles Times*, February 17, 2006.

4. "Transcript of El Baradei's U.N. Presentation," March 7, 2003, http://www.cnn.com.

5. Chalmers Johnson, *The Sorrows of Empire* (New York: Metropolitan Books, 2004), 304.

6. Johnson, *The Sorrows of Empire*, 231.

7. Citations in Johnson, *The Sorrows of Empire*, 231.

8. The State of the Union Address is available online at http://www.whitehouse.gov/news/releases/2003/01/20030128-19.html.

9. Dana Priest and Glenn Kessler, "Iraq, 9/11 Still Linked by Cheney," *Washington Post*, September 29, 2003.

10. Quoted in a review of Craig Crawford's book, *Attack the Messenger: How Politicians Turn You against the Media* (Boulder, Colo.: Rowman & Littlefield, 2005), in *New York Times*, November 11, 2005, B29.

11. Ron Suskind, "Faith, Certainty and the Presidency of George W. Bush," *New York Times Magazine*, October 17, 2004.

12. Jeff Stein, "Democrats' New Intelligence Chairman Needs a Crash Course on al Qaeda," December 8, 2006, http://www.cq.com.

13. *New York Times*, April 3, 2007, A1, A10.

14. "Lorry Bomb Kills Children in School," *Times* (London), April 3, 2007.

15. James A. Baker III and Lee H. Hamilton, cochairs, *The Iraq Study Group Report* (New York: Vintage, 2006), 92.

16. "Lack of Arabic Translators Hurting U.S.," November 19, 2003, http://www.abcnews.go.com.

17. "Warriors," from *America at a Crossroads*, aired on PBS, April 16, 2007.

18. Ricks, *Fiasco*, 72.

19. Daniel Maliniak et al., *The View from the Ivory Tower: TRIP Survey of International Relations Faculty in the United States and Canada* (Williamsburg, Va.: College of William and Mary, 2007).

20. Brent Scowcroft, "Don't Attack Saddam," *Wall Street Journal*, August 15, 2002.

21. Zbigniew Brzezinski, *Second Chance: Three Presidents and the Crisis of American Superpower* (New York: Basic Books, 2007), 146–48.

22. Cited in Ricks, *Fiasco*, 136.

23. Cited in Ricks, *Fiasco*, 136.

24. The speech is available online at http://www.whitehouse.gov/news/releases/2003/11/20031106-2.html.

25. Baker and Hamilton, *The Iraq Study Group Report*, 12–21.

26. Zvika Krieger, "Iraq's Universities Near Collapse," *Chronicle of Higher Education*, May 18, 2007, A35–A39.

27. Nina Camp, Michael O'Hanlon, and Amy Unikewicz, "The State of Iraq: An Update," *New York Times*, December 20, 2006.

28. Mark Mazzetti, "Analysis Is Bleak on Iraq's Future," *New York Times*, February 3, 2007.

29. Summary of the report in James Glanz, "Head of Reconstruction Teams in Iraq Reports Little Progress throughout Country," *New York Times*, October 19, 2007, A10.

30. *New York Times*, September 2, 2006, A6.

31. "Gangs of Iraq," from *America at a Crossroads*, aired on PBS, April 17, 2007.

32. Camp et al., "The State of Iraq."

33. "Life in Iraq," http://news.bbc.co.uk/2/shared/spl/hi/in_depth/post_saddam_iraq/html/2.stm.

34. Baker and Hamilton, *The Iraq Study Group Report*, 35.

35. "Fraying Nation, Divided Opinions," *Washington Post*, May 13, 2007, B2.

36. Christian Caryl, "Iraq's Young Blood," *Newsweek*, January 22, 2007, 25–32.

37. Caryl, "Iraq's Young Blood," 32.

38. Baker and Hamilton, *The Iraq Study Group Report*, 95.

39. Camp et al., "The State of Iraq."

40. Daniel Benjamin and Steven Simon, *The Next Attack* (New York: Times Books, 2005), 72–73.

41. Declassified excerpts from the report are available online at http://news .bbc.co.uk/2/hi/americas/5383614.stm.

42. Baker and Hamilton, *The Iraq Study Group Report*, 34.

43. See the Congressional Research Service report to Congress by Jonathan Medalia, *Terrorist Nuclear Attacks on Seaports: Threat and Response*, January 2005, http://www.fas.org/irp/crs/RS21293.pdf.

44. Mark Danner, "Iraq: The War of the Imagination," *New York Review of Books*, December 21, 2006.

45. Ron Suskind, *The One Percent Doctrine: Deep Inside America's Pursuit of Its Enemies since 9/11* (New York: Simon & Schuster, 2006), 235.

46. For example, former U.S. ambassador to Croatia Peter Galbraith, in his book *The End of Iraq* (New York: Simon & Schuster, 2006).

47. Mark Danner, "Taking Stock of the Forever War," *New York Times Magazine*, September 11, 2005, 44–87.

48. Galbraith, *The End of Iraq*, 173.

49. "Report: Iraq War Costs Could Top $2 Trillion," *Christian Science Monitor*, January 10, 2006, http://www.csmonitor.com.

50. Congressional Research Service, *CRS Report for Congress: The Cost of Iraq, Afghanistan, and Other Global War on Terror Operations since 9/11* (Washington, D.C.: Congressional Research Service, November 2007).

51. Jonathan Weisman, "Projected Iraq War Costs Soar," *Washington Post*, April 27, 2006, A16.

52. Paul Kennedy, *The Rise and Fall of the Great Powers* (New York: Random House, 1987), xxiii.

53. Kennedy, *The Rise and Fall of the Great Powers*, xvi. It is chilling to know that top al-Qaeda ideologist Ayman Al-Zawahiri is a reader and "great admirer" of Kennedy's book. See Adam Elkus, "Surging Right into bin Laden's Hands," *Foreign Policy in Focus*, February 2, 2007, http://www.fpif.org.

54. Zbigniew Brzezinski, *Second Chance*, 181.

CHAPTER EIGHT

⁓

The World Sours
on the United States

The Americans, in their intercourse with strangers, appear impatient of the smallest censure and insatiable of praise. . . . They unceasingly harass you to extort praise, and if you resist their entreaties they fall to praising themselves. It would seem as if, doubting their own merit, they wished to have it constantly exhibited before their eyes.

—Alexis de Tocqueville, 1835[1]

Fifteen years after its coronation as global leader, America is becoming a fearful and lonely democracy in a politically antagonistic world.

—Former National Security Advisor Zbigniew Brzezinski, 2007[2]

The Iraq War and the unilateralist behavior of the United States, especially during the Bush administration, have turned much of the world against the country. Even most Americans now recognize the pervasiveness of anti-American sentiment in the world, as we are bombarded with television images of anti-American demonstrations and global public opinion poll results. In part, these are a reflection of current U.S. policies and leadership, but the shift in attitudes is much deeper, broader, and more enduring than that. It reflects the more general collapse of U.S. power and influence in the world. We have seen that the United States has lost (or is losing) most of the elements that undergirded its postwar domination of the world, including its economic prosperity, its dynamic and egalitarian society, its broadly participatory democracy, and its commitment to global international rules. As the country has lost ground in those areas that occasioned the most admiration from other countries, it has lost stature, status, and influence worldwide. The Iraq War and the foreign policies of the Bush administration have simply exacerbated all this and made more open and clear what it is about the United States that bothers the rest of the world. So the setbacks in America's "hard power" are being compounded by the decline in its "soft power."

The declining image of the United States is not something mentioned only by people or pundits in other countries. In 2005, a congressionally mandated advisory report issued by the U.S. Department of State concluded that "America's image and reputation abroad could hardly be worse" and that the country "is viewed in much of the world less as a beacon of hope than as a dangerous force to be countered."[3] This is a far cry from the image of the United States proffered, in different ways, by both Henry Luce and Franklin Roosevelt at the beginning of the "American Century." And while the American way of life and its ideals were widely admired around the world during most of the postwar era, it should be pointed out that there were places in the world and episodes in time where there was considerable anti-Americanism. In Latin America, for example, where the United States has thrown its weight around since the enunciation of the Monroe Doctrine in 1823, there has always been fear, resentment, and anger at the "colossus of the North." The numerous American military interventions in Central and South America have reinforced this sentiment. As Stephen Kinzer put it in his history of U.S. interventionism, "Almost every American overthrow of a foreign government has left in its wake a bitter residue of pain and anger."[4] This became shockingly evident to Americans early on in the Cold War, when Vice President Richard Nixon's automobile convoy was stoned by angry crowds in Caracas, Venezuela, in 1958.

Throughout the American Century, Europe was the bulwark of support and admiration for the United States. In western Europe, this was due in part to the decisive American contribution in liberating the continent from Nazi Germany and to U.S. support and aid in rebuilding the Continent after the war. In Eastern Europe, there was much popular gratitude for the anticommunist rhetoric of U.S. presidents during the Cold War. But even in Europe, there were bouts of fervent anti-Americanism, with large-scale protests, for example, against the deployment of U.S. nuclear weapons on the Continent, against U.S. military bases (and nuclear facilities) in England and elsewhere, and against the creeping influence of American culture and commerce (especially in France). In the 1960s, President Charles de Gaulle of France pulled France out of the military component of the North Atlantic Treaty

Organization (NATO) and began the development of France's own deterrent nuclear force (the *force de frappe*), rejecting the notion that the United States would risk its own safety and security in defense of a European country.

Thus, foreign perceptions of the United States were never as glowing or constant as most Americans assumed they were. Nevertheless, they were pretty positive, in most parts of the world, and especially in Europe. A 1983 Gallup European poll, for example, showed substantial opposition to U.S. government policies but widespread approval of the American people and way of life. A *Newsweek* cover story summed up the poll results as showing that "Americans are seen as a good and productive people with an erratic or even dangerous government" and that while there was skepticism of American power and policies, "the world guilelessly embraces America's products and popular culture."[5] A generation later, global surveys sponsored by the U.S. Department of State in 1999–2000 showed substantial majorities having a favorable view of the United States in twenty-two of twenty-five countries surveyed. The ratings were the highest, as might be expected, in Europe but were also very strong in Latin America and in some countries in Africa and Asia as well.[6]

But in 2003, with the U.S. invasion of Iraq, the favorability ratings of the United States declined sharply in almost every country in the world and in most countries have continued to decline since then (see table 8.1).[7] Only in Africa did opinions about the United States remain positive.

Much of this hostility, of course, comes from the almost universal opposition to the U.S. invasion of Iraq. As we saw in the previous chapter, there were massive public demonstrations against the war all over the world and especially large ones in many European cities. The continued opposition to the war in other countries is evident in many global public opinion surveys. One such survey, conducted for the BBC in late 2006, found that nearly three-quarters of those polled in twenty-five countries disapprove of U.S. policies toward Iraq and that more than two-thirds thought the U.S. military presence in the Middle East does more harm than good.[8] Another BBC poll conducted a year earlier found that in thirty-three of thirty-five countries, the most common view was that the war had increased the likelihood of terrorist attacks around the world.[9] And in Pew Center surveys in various countries that asked if the war in Iraq to remove Saddam Hussein made the world a safer place or a more dangerous place, only in the United States did a majority agree that it made the world a safer place (see figure 8.1). Support for the U.S.-led "war on terror" has dropped off sharply in the past few years in virtually every country.

Table 8.1.   Favorable Views of the United States, 2002 and 2007

| Country | Percentage Favorable or Somewhat Favorable | |
	2002	2007
Canada	72	55
Argentina	34	16
Brazil	51	44
Mexico	64	56
Venezuela	82	56
Britain	75	51
France	62	39
Germany	60	30
Italy	70	53
Czech Republic	71	45
Poland	79	61
Russia	61	41
Ukraine	80	54
Turkey	30	9
Jordan	25	20
Pakistan	10	15
Indonesia	61	29
India	66	59
Japan	72	61
Kenya	80	87
Nigeria	76	70
South Africa	70	61

Source: Pew Global Attitudes Project, *Global Unease with Major World Powers* (Washington, D.C.: Pew Global Attitudes Project, 2007), 13; http://www.pewglobal.org.

While the Iraq War may have sharpened anti-American sentiments around the world, the hostility toward the United States and its policies goes far beyond that war. In a 2006 BBC poll of twenty-five countries, about two-thirds disapproved of U.S. handling of detainees at Guantanamo Bay and disliked the U.S. stance on that year's military conflict between Israel and the Hezbollah militia in Lebanon. Sixty percent opposed U.S. policies on Iran's nuclear program, 56 percent were opposed to Washington's stance on global climate change, and 54 percent disapproved U.S. policies toward North Korea.[10] Nearly half of those polled felt that the United States is now playing a mostly negative role in the world. In the eighteen countries surveyed in earlier years by BBC, the percentage of those saying the United States had a generally positive influence in the world had declined steadily from 40 percent in 2004 to 36 percent in 2005 and to just 29 percent in 2006.[11] Steven Kull, the director of the Program of International Policy Attitudes (which

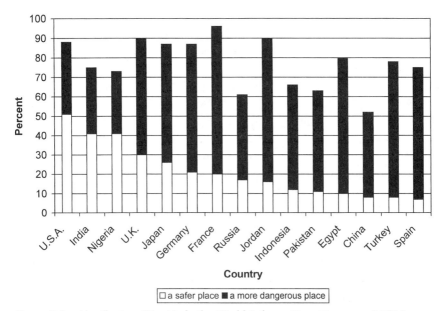

Figure 8.1.   Has the Iraq War Made the World Safer or More Dangerous? 2006
Source: Andrew Kohut, "America's Image in the World: Findings from the Pew Global Attitudes Project," Testimony before the Committee on Foreign Affairs of the U.S. House of Representatives, March 14, 2007.

fields the Pew surveys), expressed surprise at how much opinion of the United States had deteriorated. "I thought it had bottomed out a year ago, but it's gotten worse, and we really are at historic lows." "The thing that comes up repeatedly is not just anger about Iraq," according to Kull. "The common theme is hypocrisy. The reaction tends to be: 'You were a champion of a certain set of rules. Now you are breaking your own rules, so you are being hypocritical.'"[12]

What is even more extraordinary than this sharp dropoff in approval for the United States and its policies is a widespread belief in other countries that the United States is itself a major threat to world peace. Since the Iraq War began, this sentiment is particularly strong in Arab and Muslim countries. In a 2005 Pew study, in each of the five predominantly Muslim countries surveyed (Indonesia, Pakistan, Turkey, Jordan, and Lebanon), large majorities expressed worry that the United States might become a military threat to their country. Even more startling was a large-scale Gallup poll in Europe in 2003 in which 53 percent of Europeans considered the United States "a threat to world peace." In every one of the fifteen countries polled, at least 40 percent expressed that view, and in some countries, including

Spain, Finland, Austria, Holland, and Greece, more than 60 percent did.[13] This was a far cry from the way the United States viewed itself in the world and even from the way most other countries had viewed the United States in previous decades. And these views came from citizens of our closest allies.

It may be that most of this negativity about the United States could be attributed to the presidency of George W. Bush and that with a different president most of these bad feelings would wither away. Indeed, Bush was deeply unpopular in much of the rest of the world, even before his popularity ratings plunged within the United States. In the Pew surveys, there is only one country (India) where a majority of the population had confidence in Bush's leadership, with both Britain's Tony Blair and France's Jacques Chirac faring much better in global opinions.[14] In some countries, particularly in Muslim ones, Bush's unfavorable ratings exceeded those of Osama bin Laden.

When the Pew surveys ask those who have an unfavorable opinion of the United States if the problem was more with President Bush or with America in general, most people in Western countries place the blame on the president (see figure 8.2). However, in most non-European countries, more people were likely to say "America in general" or "both" than to pin the blame on Bush. Furthermore, in almost every country, there was an increase over

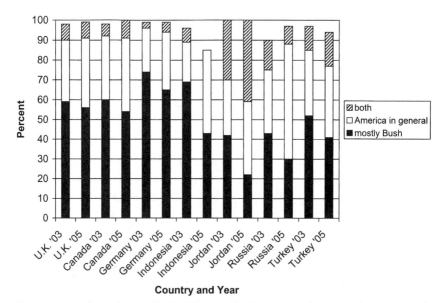

Figure 8.2. What's the Problem with the United States: Bush or America in General? 2003 and 2005

Source: Pew Global Attitudes Project, *U.S. Image Up Slightly, but Still Negative* (Washington, D.C.: Pew Global Attitudes Project, June 2005).

time in those assigning blame to America rather than its president. As the Pew Center's Andrew Kohut observes, this dislike of the American people themselves is something new in international surveys, and "the negative image of many things American seems unlikely to change anytime soon in much of the world."[15] Thus, reinforcing tendencies we have observed elsewhere in this book, it seems that while President Bush has exacerbated the problems facing the United States, the problems are increasingly lodged with the United States itself and are unlikely to leave the scene when he does.

Losing Global Public Opinion

Americans could take some comfort in the fact that, in the face of all these negative views about the United States, its policies, and its leadership, global views about the American people are much more positive. Indeed, this has been the case for many years in many parts of the world. Even during the years of the Cold War, in countries that were hostile to the United States or its policies (e.g., in the Soviet Union or Nicaragua), the populations of those countries typically looked favorably on American citizens. The Pew surveys do show that in most other countries, views of "the American people" are much more favorable than those of "the United States" as a country. But even here, the image of the United States has been losing ground rapidly since the turn of the millennium. In almost every country where Pew asked this question, there was a decline in those having a favorable view of the American people from 2002 to 2007. And in those countries where there was no such decline, the numbers were pretty low to begin with.[16]

People in other countries tend to see Americans as hardworking and inventive but also as greedy and violent, according to the Pew surveys, and there is increasing resistance to the spread of American culture, customs, and ideas in their countries. While people in most parts of the world (with the notable exception of predominantly Muslim countries) acknowledge that they like American movies, music, and television, substantial majorities in almost every country view negatively the spread of American ideas and customs (see figure 8.3).

This is a striking turnaround from the heyday of the American Century when all things American, from Marlboro cigarettes to multiparty elections, were admired and coveted in most places in the world. Even more striking is that the very ideals and institutions that the United States was most trying to promote—democracy and free market capitalism—are also going out of favor. These principles were at the heart of the idea of the American Century in the mid-twentieth century and were the mainstay of presidential inaugural addresses and speeches up to the present. All American presidents and most

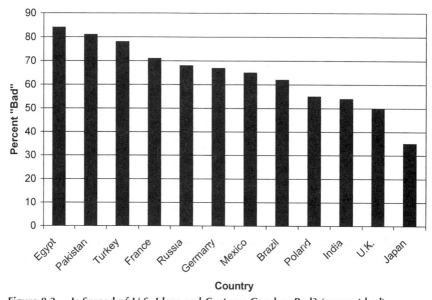

Figure 8.3.   Is Spread of U.S. Ideas and Customs Good or Bad? (percent bad)

Source: Pew Research Center, "Global Opinion: The Spread of Anti-Americanism," chapter 7 in *Trends 2005*, produced by the Pew Research Center, released January 2005; online at http://www.pewglobal.org.

Americans assumed that people in other countries wanted to be like the United States and to have American-style political and economic institutions. But if this was ever the case—and it certainly was in some countries at least—it is increasingly less true. The Pew surveys show that while people in most countries embrace the democratic ideal and democratic values, there is little enthusiasm for "American-style democracy," particularly in the Middle East.[17] There is even less support for American ways of doing business. The highest degree of support for both American democracy and American business practices came from formerly communist countries like Uzbekistan, Ukraine, and the Czech Republic. But many other surveys of opinions in the postcommunist states show that people in those countries are much more inclined toward the "social market" economies of western Europe than to the more unfettered capitalism of the United States.[18] In the postcommunist states of Europe, the favored model is the social welfare state, such as in Scandinavia.

This leads us back to the issue of "American exceptionalism." As we saw in chapter 6, Americans tend to see themselves—and people in other countries see them—as being "exceptional" in certain key respects. Fundamental among those are individualism, competitiveness, and religiosity. These values helped produce and perpetuate an economy relatively free of government intervention and a messianic strain in American foreign policy that calls for the spreading of

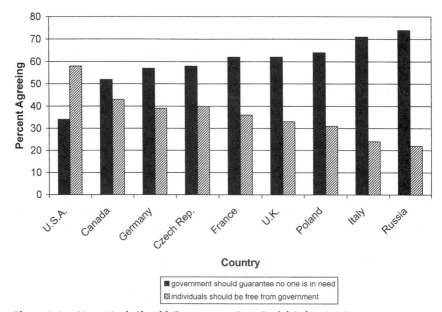

Figure 8.4. How Much Should Government Be a Social Safety Net?
Source: Pew Research Center, "Global Opinion: The Spread of Anti-Americanism," chapter 7 in *Trends 2005*, produced by the Pew Research Center, released January 2005; online at http://www.pewglobal.org.

these ideals. For much of the American Century, these characteristics and ideals were admired by people around the world who lived mostly under governments that restricted individual rights, economic competition, and religious freedom. But as the world has changed and matured and more and more peoples have begun building their own political and economic structures based on their own values, the "exceptional" values and practices of the United States increasingly become either irrelevant or unwelcome.

In comparative public opinion surveys that include a U.S. sample, the United States often appears as an "outlier" with opinions quite different from any of the other nationalities in the sample. Americans, for example, are much more likely than those in other developed countries to be very religious and to believe in sin and in moral absolutes, to believe that poverty is due to laziness, and to favor freedom over equality.[19] This reflects American exceptionalism but can also be seen as Americans being out of step with the rest of the world (which, indeed, is the way many non-Americans see it). A significant example of this is the question of the role of government in society, particularly in terms of providing for people's basic needs. As one can see from figure 8.4, only 34 percent of Americans believe that "the government should guarantee that no one is in need." In every other country in the sample, at least a majority accepted that principle. On the flip side, measuring individualism, Americans are far more likely than others to agree that individuals should be "free from government" to pursue their own goals. On both of these issues, the United States is an outlier. In most other parts of the world, there is much more emphasis put on "community," whether that takes the form of the village, the religious group, or the state, than on the individual. Thus, rugged individualism, so prized in the United States, is often seen as a societal flaw or even as an indication of heartlessness in many other cultures.

Arab and Muslim Hostility to the United States

As is apparent from all of these global surveys, the United States has a particular public relations problem in the Middle East and among Muslim populations all over the world. There are at least 1.2 billion Muslims worldwide, constituting about a fifth of the world's population and one of the fastest-growing segments of global population. While fundamentalists constitute a small portion of all Muslims and those Muslims who advocate and practice terrorism are an even more miniscule part, their numbers appear to be growing as well. Many experts on both the Islamic world and terrorism believe that the only long-term solution to terrorism is an improvement in relations between the United States and the Islamic world. But the feelings among Muslims toward the United States are so broadly and overwhelmingly negative that it seems unlikely there will be any understanding or reconciliation anytime soon. And even apart from the issue of terrorism, the United States will have increasingly little influence over Arab and Muslim countries, where there is so much distrust and hostility toward that country.

In the Muslim world, opinions about the United States have been negative for decades, but there was little real awareness in the United States about the depths of this hostility until after September 11. After that catastrophe, numerous American magazines and newspapers ran stories asking "Why Do They Hate Us?" with no very good answers. A Pew survey of opinion leaders around the world just three months after the attack found that more than three-quarters of those in the Middle East and other Islamic states believed that U.S. policies were a major cause of the attacks. More than two-thirds in those countries believed it was good for Americans to know what it feels like to be vulnerable.[20] Since that time and particularly since the U.S. invasion of Iraq, attitudes toward the United States from Arab and Muslim countries have become even more negative. A recent book, *What the Arabs Think of America*, points out that "the two main political-intellectual camps in the Arab world today, political Islam and Arab nationalism," are both "virulently anti-American."[21]

It is instructive to look at public opinion about the United States not only in the mostly Muslim countries of the Middle East but also in the countries in the world with the largest Muslim populations (Indonesia, Pakistan, Bangladesh, India, and Turkey), none of which are Arab (see table 8.2). Only in the South Asian countries of India and Bangladesh is there much sympathy for the United States. Surveys by Pew and other organizations in Arab and Muslim states show large majorities thinking the Iraq War will make Iraqis worse off, will make the region less peaceful, will breed more terrorism, and will worsen the prospects for settling the Arab–Israeli dispute. There is also deep distrust of American motives in the Iraq War and the war on terror, with large majorities in all Arab and Muslim states thinking that U.S. policy was driven by a desire not to spread democracy but to control Mideast oil, to protect Israel, to weaken the Muslim world, or to "dominate the world."[22] In Iraq itself, as we saw in chapter 7, most people (with the exception of the Kurds) favor the departure of U.S. forces, and in some areas a majority of the population even believes that attacks on coalition forces are justified.

The intensity of dislike and fear of the United States among Muslims is reflected in the high degree of support for Osama bin Laden in many countries. A Pew survey in 2004 found about half the respondents expressing "favorable" views of bin Laden in three of the four Muslim countries in the poll: Pakistan, Jordan, and Morocco (the fourth was Turkey).[23] Such numbers are shocking to Americans and may be one reason why the Pew project has not widely publicized this particular poll question. But for those who know Islam

Table 8.2.   Arab and Muslim Views of the United States, 2007

Country	Percentage Favorable
Indonesia	29
Pakistan	15
Bangladesh	53
India	59
Turkey	9
Jordan	20
Egypt	21
Morocco	15

Source: Pew Global Attitudes Project, *Global Unease with Major World Powers* (Washington, D.C.: Pew Global Attitudes Project, 2007), http://www.pewglobal.org.

and the Middle East, it is not so surprising. Muslims have experienced and resent a long history of Western domination and intervention in their lands, with the United States simply being the most recent manifestation of this. For many, it is not only their countries that are under threat or attack but Islam itself. Many Muslims see bin Laden as a heroic figure for claiming to defend Islam against the apostate, the infidel, and the West. As Michael Scheur, the former chief of the bin Laden unit of the Central Intelligence Agency, sees it, "As bin Laden and his ilk defend the things they love—a love held by most Muslims—they are themselves loved not just for defending the faith, but as symbols of hope in a Muslim world conditioned to massive military defeats, Islamic charlatans as rulers, and U.S.-protected and coddled tyrants." Thus, while America's leaders depict bin Laden as a murderous and deranged gangster, many Muslims see the American pursuit of him "as an attempt to kill a heroic and holy man who lives and works only to protect his brethren and preserve their faith."[24] This attitude may account for the utter failure of the $5 million U.S. government bounty on bin Laden, which has yielded no results in six years.

Hostility to the United States is long standing and deep in the Arab world and has been intensified by the U.S. invasion and occupation of Iraq and even by the U.S. war on terror. When people in six Arab countries were polled in 2005, fully 87 percent thought that the Iraqi people were "worse off" than before the war, and large majorities thought the war had brought less peace, less democracy, and more terrorism to the region.[25] The U.S. treatment of prisoners from the war on terrorism, at Abu Ghraib and Guantanamo Bay, also inflamed Arab and Muslim sentiments around the world. For many Muslims, these represented "a confirmation of the low regard in which they believe the United States holds them."[26]

The difficulty in winning over people in the Arab and Muslim world is compounded by the lack of expertise on the region in the U.S. government and the consequent ineffectiveness of American public relations campaigns there. A PBS *Frontline World* program, for example, followed two U.S. military public relations specialists trying to promote the U.S. image in the Middle East. Neither one knew Arabic. They met with the news director of the Al Arabiya television, a station backed by Saudi Arabia to counter the militancy of the rival Al Jazeera network. Interviewed after the departure of the two Americans, the Al Arabiya newsman bemoaned that they were "trying to sell [an] unsellable product." On the same program, David Marash, formerly of ABC's *Nightline* and then anchor for Al Jazeera in English, asserted that "America has never been perceived as more isolated and less influential" than it is today.[27]

The United States Loses Global Clout and Respect

One could argue, perhaps, that public opinion surveys do not reflect geopolitical realities and that what people in other countries think about the United States has little bearing on America's power or influence in the world. This would be particularly true in nondemocratic countries, where public opinion is less likely to affect government officials or policies. In this case, however, public opinion is just one piece of a much bigger picture in which one sees U.S. domestic decline, the increasing isolation of the United States in a multilateral and globalizing world, catastrophic failures in U.S. foreign policy, and increasingly assertive governments worldwide willing to challenge U.S. supremacy. Negative public opinion about the United States both reflects these other changes and reinforces them.

The decline of the United States, in reality and in the global imagination, is already having an impact on the rhetoric and behavior of political and economic elites on every continent. Perceiving the United States as weakened and less influential and emboldened by public opinion polls that reflect this, foreign leaders have fewer compunctions about criticizing the United States (or its leadership). Furthermore, a less appealing, less powerful, and less influential America leads other countries to look elsewhere for political, economic, or military partners. In the following chapter, we explore some of these potential rivals to the United States. Here, we simply illustrate these trends with examples from each continent.

As seen in public opinion surveys, outside the Muslim world the U.S. image has suffered the most in Europe, the linchpin of the Atlantic Alliance. According to the writer Andrei Markovits, "Anti-Americanism has been promoted to the status of Western Europe's lingua franca." He writes in 2007 that he cannot recall a time in four decades when there has been "such a vehement aversion to everything American" on the Continent.[28] This sentiment has emboldened European leaders to confront the U.S. government and even to use an anti-American platform in (victorious) electoral campaigns, as did Gerhard Schroeder in Germany's parliamentary elections in 2002 and Jose Luis Rodriguez Zapatero in Spain's national elections the next year. At a usually amicable and staid NATO summit meeting in 2004, French President Jacques Chirac shredded diplomatic niceties by telling President Bush, to his face, that European Union affairs were none of his business (in response to Bush's call for the European Union to accept Turkey in its membership). "He has gone into a domain which is not his own," said Chirac. "He has nothing to say on the subject."[29] Even after efforts to patch up relations with Europe in Bush's second term, the United States found things rough going in the Old World. When the president visited Vienna in June 2006 for a summit with European Union officials, the *Washington Post* observed that "diplomats and experts on Europe say public opinion is a significant drag on Bush's ability to expect much from political leaders here."[30] Even more harsh comments came from former President Vladimir Putin of Russia, who bluntly criticized the United States for trying to create a unipolar world with itself at the center. In a speech in Munich, Germany, in 2007, he characterized the United States as "one single center of power; one single center of force. One single center of decision making. This is the world of one master, one sovereign."[31] In another speech a few months later, commemorating the defeat of Nazi Germany, he obliquely compared the foreign policy of the United States to the Third Reich. There are new threats in the world, he said, as during the time of Hitler, with "the same claims of exceptionality and diktat in the world." These statements, from heads of state of our most important partners and allies, are highly unusual—even shocking—in the world of diplomacy and statecraft. But they reflect the declining authority and influence of the United States and the willingness of politicians to play on anti-American sentiments and to risk alienating Washington for their own political goals.

In other parts of the world as well, America's status and influence is in decline. Countries and leaders that used to defer to Washington are no longer doing so and are often looking to other countries than the United States as partners in trade and security. In Southeast Asia, for example, a region of primary U.S. influence through much of the Cold War, China is rapidly replacing the United States as the main power broker. This is due both to declining American attention to and influence in the region and to stepped-up efforts by Beijing to win over these countries. In the aftermath of September 11, many leaders in the region were put off by Washington's single-minded focus on fighting terrorism and military issues at the expense of trade and economic development. Beijing stepped into the breach, offering trade and aid with a dollop of cultural affinity. China is offering soft power as an alternative to Washington's hard power, and the results are paying off. China's foreign aid to the Philippines is now roughly four times greater than U.S. aid, and its aid to Laos is about three times greater. In Thailand, long a close U.S. ally, 70 percent of the population views China as the country's most important external relation, and the prime minister has said the same. China has signed Southeast Asia's Treaty of Amity and Cooperation (which Washington has not signed). Southeast Asia's total trade with China has now surpassed that with the United States or Japan. And in the face of tightened visa restrictions in the United States (mostly due to the war on terror), young people in Southeast Asia are now more likely to study in China than in the United States.[32]

A similar process is at work in Africa. After a decade of relative neglect of the continent after the end of the Cold War, Washington has begun to pay more attention to the region, recognizing that poverty, misery, and instability can be a breeding ground for terrorists. The United States is providing more financial aid than ever to Africa, but even so the United States has lost a good deal of its credibility and influence. A *New York Times* article on the United States and Africa, with the title "U.S. Power Isn't So Super," reports that in much of Africa, there is "a perception that the United States is no longer the only power that counts, that it is too bogged down in the Middle East to be a real threat here, and so it can be ignored or defied with impunity."[33] In this part of the world as well, China has been asserting itself, vastly expanding its trade contacts and exercising soft-power diplomacy. (This is discussed more fully in the following chapter.) But it is not just China that is gaining influence across the continent. African leaders are seeking out other countries as "potential competitors or 'balancers' of U.S. diplomatic leverage," according to Chester Crocker, former assistant secretary of state for Africa. "It is not just China: it is Brazil, the Europeans, Malaysia, Korea, Russia, India."[34]

In Latin America, Washington's influence is also on the wane, though for different reasons in different parts of the continent. In Mexico, anti-U.S. sentiments have increased with the growing anti-immigration policies and restrictions coming from Washington due only in part to increased security concerns with the war on terror. The resurgence of leftist and populist governments in Nicaragua, Bolivia, Ecuador, and Venezuela has fueled nationalism and anti-Americanism in those countries. The leaders of those countries (Daniel Ortega, Evo Morales, Rafael Correa, and Hugo Chavez, respectively) have criticized U.S. policy in the region (including "the Washington consensus" of neoliberal economic reforms), and some have moved to nationalize their country's oil and other hydrocarbon resources, some of which are owned or controlled by U.S. companies. The most brazen and forthright challenges to the United States have come from President Hugo Chavez of Venezuela, a country that has the largest petroleum reserves in the Western Hemisphere and is the third-largest supplier of oil to the United States. On an overseas tour in August 2006 that included stops in Vietnam, Iran, and Belarus, Chavez asserted that "capitalism will lead to the destruction of humanity" and that the United States "is the devil that represents capitalism."[35] The next month, in a startling breach of diplomatic protocol in a formal address to the UN General Assembly, Chavez referred to President Bush, who had spoken from the same rostrum the day before, as "the devil himself." The president of the United States, continued Chaves, "came here, talking as if he owned the world. Truly. As the owner of the world." Rafael Correa, who was shortly to be inaugurated as the new president of Ecuador, later quipped that the comparison of Bush to the devil was unfair to the latter: "The devil may be bad, but at least he is intelligent."[36] This kind of language, from one head of state about another, is virtually unprecedented in the modern world. It reflects the hugely diminished status of the United States in the eyes of the rest of the world. As has been the case in Europe and elsewhere, it is also an indication of the usefulness of anti-American rhetoric to politicians in countries where there is already highly negative popular opinion about the United States.

Chavez, suggests David Rieff of the New York Times, is a kind of "new Castro" in that he has become "an iconic figure for many people across the world who see the United States as the principal threat to world peace, not its benevolent guarantor."[37] His frequent meetings with Iran's President Ahmadinejad, who has also been openly and bluntly critical of both President Bush and the United States, seems to be part of an effort to form an anti-American coalition of powerful states in different parts of the world. Ahmadinejad has reciprocated Chavez's visits with those of his own that included meetings with Daniel Ortega of Nicaragua, Evo Morales of Bolivia, and Rafael Correa of Ecuador. Both Chavez and Ahmadinejad have also strengthened ties and signed oil cooperation agreements with Vladimir Putin's Russia, raising the possibility of an alliance of large, powerful states with populist, nationalist, anti-American leaders—and tons of oil. Venezuela is also purchasing expensive and sophisticated military equipment from Russia, and Tehran has signed both military and nuclear cooperation agreements with Moscow. These agreements and this potential alliance (which might also include China) are built, in part, on resistance to U.S. power and hegemony and provide a possible counterweight to the United States. This is a new challenge that the United States will have to confront after the end of the American Century—a topic to be addressed in the next chapters.

The Decline of "Brand U.S."

The declining popularity of the United States around the world is hurting the United States not only in terms of global political influence but in many other ways as well, including the appeal and marketability of U.S. brands and products overseas. A number of different studies have shown a recent decline in the popularity of U.S. brand products in various parts of the world, espe-

cially among young people. In part, this is due to political boycotts or foreigners "transferring anger at the US government to anger at the US and
anger at US business," according to Keith Reinhard, the chairman of DDB
Worldwide, an agency that includes McDonald's and Budweiser as clients.[38]
But the shift also seems to be due to the dimming luster and cachet of American products among young people in Latin America, Europe, Asia, and elsewhere. Asian consumers, for example, are paying more attention to Asian
trends and products. As one Asian-based advertising executive put it, "Cool
would definitely come from Tokyo rather than Los Angeles."[39] A Nation
Brands Index poll comparing the popularity of nation brands among a worldwide panel of consumers found the United States ranked eleventh of twenty-
five countries (with Australia and Canada at the top of the list). According
to Simon Anholt, the author of the survey, the United States is still recognized as a good place to do business and the home of desirable brands and
popular culture, "but its governance, its cultural heritage and its people are
no longer widely respected or admired in the world." On the "heritage" side
of the scale, a measure of a country's "wisdom, intelligence, and integrity,"
the United States ranked dead last among twenty-five countries.[40]

In the Nation Brand Index poll, the study's American respondents consis-
tently placed the United States at the top of all six categories in the poll, reflecting both how out of step Americans are with the rest of the world and
how clueless Americans apparently are about the way others see us. There is
another aspect of this that would also surprise most Americans, who continue to embrace a popular mythology that most people in the world would
like to live in the United States if they could. Polls in other countries suggest otherwise, however. A 2003 BBC poll asked people in ten countries, "If
you had the chance, would you like to live in America?" As figure 8.5 shows,
no more than a quarter answered yes to this question in any country, though
when Americans were asked if they thought that others wanted to come live
there, 96 percent answered yes.

In one of the Pew surveys, when people in sixteen countries were asked
where young people from their country could go "to lead a good life," in only
one of the sixteen countries (India) was the United States the first choice of
destinations.[41] The United States is even becoming less attractive (and more
difficult) as a tourist destination. During a global tourism boom, the United
States is the only major country in the world to which travel has declined.[42]

Given the ambivalent and even negative worldviews about the United
States—its policies, politics, people, culture, economy, and influence—it is
not surprising that large majorities in almost every country believe it would
be better if another country or group of countries emerged to rival the United

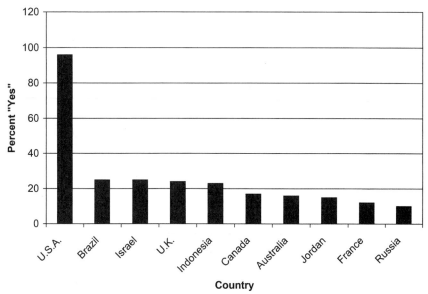

Figure 8.5.   Would You Like to Live in America?

Note: Americans were asked if they thought others wanted to live in America.

Source: BBC-ICM, "What the World Thinks of America" (June 2003), cited in Stephen Brooks, *As Others See Us* (Ontario: Broadview, 2006), 35.

States as a global military power (see figure 8.6). Only in the United States does a majority feel that the United States should remain the sole super-power. This American view is consistent with the neoconservative positions expressed by the Project for the New American Century and is the prevailing view in the Bush administration but has little support anywhere else in the world.

Worldwide, the most favored candidate for replacing the United States as the preeminent power center is "Europe." A poll conducted in twenty-three countries in late 2004 found that in twenty of them, a majority or a plurality of people think it would be "mainly positive" if Europe were to become more influential than the United States in world affairs.[43] In that survey, in every country but one, Europe is seen as having a mainly positive influence in the world, in contrast to the United States, which is viewed that way in only six countries. Even China's influence in the world is viewed more favorably than that of the United States in most countries—a testament to the increasing clout of China's economy and its soft power diplomacy in many parts of the world. These public opinion survey results portend the trends addressed in the next chapter: the gradual eclipse of American global power by Europe, China, and other powers.

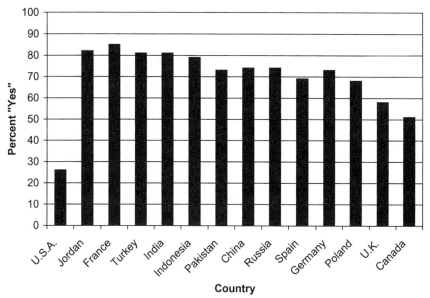

Figure 8.6. Would It Be Better If Another Rivaled U.S. Military Power?
Source: Pew Global Attitudes Project, "Bucking the Global Trend, U.S. Popularity Soared in India in '05," 2005; online at http://www.pewglobal.org.

The Anti-American Century

In the previous chapter, on Iraq and the war on terror, we saw that American military power—its hard power—has been ineffective and even counterproductive in achieving U.S. goals and enhancing the country's influence abroad. In this chapter, we have seen that the United States has also lost ground in terms of its soft power—its ability to influence other countries through the sway of its culture, political system, economy, and ideals. During the twentieth century, the United States was the dominant global superpower because of its unsurpassed strength in both hard power and soft power. Both of these are now slipping away, and that tendency has been sharply accelerated by the Iraq War. While the United States has focused on and been drained by a costly and fruitless military campaign in Iraq, the rest of the world has begun to look elsewhere for models of democracy, economic development, and global leadership.

The American Century has morphed into the "Anti-American Century," a phrase used by the independent scholar Julia Sweig.[44] It is not simply a reaction to the current American president or his policies, though these have certainly highlighted and intensified anti-Americanism. Increasingly, as international polls have indicated, anti-Americanism "runs deeper and is qualitatively different than in the past."[45] It has become more pervasive across the globe, it is increasingly directed at American ideals and the American people (rather than simply the country's policies), and it reflects increased concern about the U.S. role in the world. And, as Andrew Kohut, the director of the Pew Center surveys, points out, "This new found anti-Americanism was proving itself to be quite robust and long-lived."[46] Indeed, it signals a fundamental shift in the global status of the United States.

Quite naturally, the diminished status of the United States has opened the door for other countries and other regions to become more assertive and influential on the world stage. This is increasingly evident in every continent, with regional powers emerging to challenge the influence of the United States in their own backyards and even farther afield. The globetrotting diplomatic efforts of Venezuela's Hugo Chavez, Iran's Mahmoud Ahmadinejad, China's Hu Jintao, and Russia's Vladimir Putin are all aimed at trying to boost the global presence and influence of their countries—usually at the expense of the United States. The Europeans, increasingly powerful, confident, and unified, are also becoming more assertive and independent of Washington, and their stock has risen greatly in the eyes of peoples and leaders in other continents. It is to these rival powers, each with a potential to shape the world afer the American Century, that we now turn.

Notes

1. Alexis de Tocqueville, *Democracy in America*, ed. Richard Heffner (New York: Signet, 2001), 251.

2. Zbigniew Brzezinski, *Second Chance: Three Presidents and the Crisis of American Superpower* (New York: Basic Books, 2007), 181.

3. *Cultural Diplomacy: The Linchpin of Public Diplomacy*, Report of the Advisory Committee on Cultural Diplomacy (Washington, D.C.: U.S. Department of State, September 2005).

4. Stephen Kinzer, *Overthrow: America's Century of Regime Change from Hawaii to Iraq* (New York: Times Books, 2006), 302.

5. Jerry Adler, "What the World Thinks of America," *Newsweek*, July 11, 1983, 45.

6. State Department data cited in the Pew Global Attitudes Project, *Global Unease with Major World Powers* (Washington, D.C.: Pew Global Attitudes Project, 2007), http://www.pewglobal.org.

7. Pew Global Attitudes Project, *Global Unease with Major World Powers*.

8. Kevin Sullivan, "Views on U.S. Drop Sharply in Worldwide Opinion Poll," *Washington Post*, January 23, 2007, A14; "World View of US Role Goes from Bad to

Worse," BBC World Service Poll, http://www.globescan.com/news_archives/ bbcusop.

9. "World Public Says Iraq War Has Increased Global Terrorist Threat," reporting survey conducted for BBC World Services, http://www.worldopinion.org/incl/ printable_version.php?pnt=172.

10. Sullivan, "Views on U.S. Drop Sharply in Worldwide Opinion Poll."

11. Sullivan, "Views on U.S. Drop Sharply in Worldwide Opinion Poll."

12. Sullivan, "Views on U.S. Drop Sharply in Worldwide Opinion Poll."

13. A poll of 7,500 Europeans in October 2003 conducted by EOS Gallup Europe on behalf of the European Commission, reported in the New York Times, November 16, 2003.

14. Pew Global Attitudes Project, "U.S. Image Up Slightly but Still Negative," June 2005, http://www.pewglobal.org.

15. Andrew Kohut and Bruce Stokes, America against the World: How We Are Different and Why We Are Disliked (New York: Times Books, 2006), 25.

16. Pew Global Attitudes Project, "U.S. Image Slightly Up but Still Negative" and Global Unease with Major World Powers.

17. Kohut and Stokes, America against the World, 124.

18. See, for example, David S. Mason and James R. Kluegel, Marketing Democracy: Changing Opinion about Equality and Politics in East Central Europe (Lanham, Md.: Rowman & Littlefield, 2000), esp. 240–41.

19. Data from the World Values Surveys cited in Stephen Brooks, As Others See Us (Ontario: Broadview, 2006), 83–95.

20. Pew Research Center, "Global Opinion."

21. Andrew Hammond, What the Arabs Think of America (Westport, Conn.: Greenwood, 2007), 205.

22. Andrew Kohut, "America's Image in the World," testimony to Congress, 2007, and reports of a 2005 Zogby International poll in Daniel Yankelovich, "The Tipping Points," Foreign Affairs, May/June 2006, http://www.foreignaffairs.org.

23. Pew Research Center, "A Year after the Iraq War," 2004, http://people-press .org/reports/display.php3?PageID=796.

24. Anonymous (Michael Scheur), Imperial Hubris: Why the West Is Losing the War on Terrorism (Washington, D.C.: Brassey's, 2004), 19.

25. "Arab Attitudes toward Political and Social Issues, Foreign Policy and the Media," a 2005 poll conducted by Professor Shibley Telhami, University of Maryland, and Zogby International, http://www.bsos.umd.edu/sadat/pub/arab-attitudes-2005 .htm.

26. Somini Sengupta and Salman Masood, "Guantanamo Comes to Define U.S. to Muslims," New York Times, May 21, 2005.

27. Frontline World, aired on PBS, March 27, 2007.

28. Andrei Markovits, "Western Europe's America Problem," Chronicle of Higher Education, January 19, 2007, B6.

29. "Chirac Tells Bush to Keep His Nose Out," *Daily Telegraph* (London), June 29, 2004, http://www.telegraph.co.uk.

30. Michale Abramowitz, "Bush's Unpopularity in Europe Hangs over Summit," *Washington Post*, June 21, 2006, A15.

31. *New York Times*, May 10, 2007, A6.

32. Joshua Kurlantzick, "China's Charm: Implications of Chinese Soft Power," Carnegie Endowment for International Peace *Policy Brief*, no. 47 (June 2006), http://www.carnegieendowment.org.

33. Jeffrey Gettleman, "Across Africa, a Sense That U.S. Power Isn't So Super," *New York Times*, December 24, 2006, sec. 4, p. 1.

34. Gettleman, "Across Africa, a Sense That U.S. Power Isn't So Super," 10.

35. *New York Times*, August 16, 2006, A3.

36. *Financial Times* (London), October 2, 2006.

37. David Rieff, "A New Castro?" *New York Times Magazine*, January 28, 2007, 16.

38. Quoted in Dan Roberts, "Is the World Falling Out of Love with US Brands?" *Financial Times* (London), January 5, 2005.

39. Roberts, "Is the World Falling Out of Love with US Brands?"

40. Kevin Allison, "World Turning Its Back on Brand America," *Financial Times* (London), July 31, 2005; for details on the Nation Brands Index, see http://www.nationbrandindex.com.

41. Pew Global Attitudes Project, "U.S. Image Up Slightly but Still Negative."

42. Fareed Zakaria, "America the Unwelcoming," *Newsweek*, November 26, 2007, 42.

43. A poll of 23,518 people conducted by Globescan and the Program on International Policy Attitudes at the University of Maryland reported in "In 20 of 23 Countries Polled, Citizens Want Europe to Be More Influential than US," http://worldpublicopinion.org/pipa/articles/home_page.

44. In her book *Friendly Fire: Losing Friends and Making Enemies in the Anti-American Century* (New York: Public Affairs, 2006).

45. Kohut and Stokes, *America against the World*, xviii.

46. Kohut and Stokes, *America against the World*, xix.

~

CHAPTER NINE

America's New Rivals

Europe, China, and Others

To the citizens of unified Europe, military power seems an outmoded concept.

—T. R. Reid[1]

If any country is going to supplant the U.S. in the world marketplace, China is it.

—Ted Fishman[2]

The United States has deteriorated economically, socially, and politically and compares unfavorably with other affluent countries on most measures of societal health and welfare. In other countries, the United States is no longer seen as the beacon of democracy, the defender of human rights, or the model of capitalism. Even its awe-inspiring military has proved incapable of delivering desirable outcomes or even of quashing America's enemies. The country no longer has the right stuff to qualify as a superpower.

But if not the United States, then who? Some would argue, as former Secretary of State Madeleine Albright has, that there is no real alternative to the United States as "the indispensable nation." Similarly, in *The Case for Goliath*, Michael Mandelbaum contends that there is no other country that could fill the shoes of the United States in acting as "the world's government." But these views are both shortsighted and ethnocentric. They ignore both the dynamics of the rise and fall of states and the perceptions and wishes of people outside the United States—which, as we have seen, can be quite different from those of Americans themselves.

Europe and China, in particular, are two regions that have witnessed startling change in recent decades, where leaders and citizens alike are skeptical of U.S. supremacy and increasingly willing to assert a greater role for themselves in the world. Europe has integrated twenty-seven separate countries into a flourishing European Union (EU), with more people, a bigger economy, and more trade than the United States. China, the most populous country in the world, has emerged as an economic dynamo and powerhouse with the most rapid and sustained economic growth of any country in world history and the potential to replace both the United States and the EU as the globe's economic juggernaut. In much of the world, the EU and China are looked on more favorably than is the United States.

The EU and China are not the only entities likely to challenge U.S. supremacy. China is only one of the four so-called BRIC countries—the regional up-and-coming powers that also include Brazil, Russia, and India. Japan, which seemed poised to take on the United States a generation ago, is once again resurgent. And one cannot rule out the feisty oil-rich countries of Venezuela and Iran. Iran, one should point out, is twice as populous as Iraq and is the world's fourth-largest oil producer, with twice the production of Iraq. It could also be the case that none of these powers—not the United States, China, India, or the EU—will dominate the world, or will feel the need to, once the United States is no longer throwing its weight around.

The European Superpower?

There is no doubt that Europe has, once again, become an imposing force in the world economy and international politics. The titles of recent books show which way the wind is blowing: *The United States of Europe: The New Superpower and the End of American Supremacy* by the journalist T. R. Reid, *The European Superpower* by political scientist John McCormick, and *The Next Superpower?* (but note the question mark) by former U.S. ambassador to the EU Rockwell Schnabel.[3] The EU, now including twenty-seven countries with a combined population of 490 million and a gross domestic product (GDP) of $13.5 trillion, is larger on both counts than the United States. Besides the United States, no other country in the world comes close to matching its combination of size and wealth.

The two biggest countries and the first- and third-largest economies in the EU are Germany and France, which U.S. Secretary of Defense Donald Rumsfeld brushed off as "Old Europe" when they objected in 2003 to the U.S. invasion of Iraq. Despite Rumsfeld's assertion, those two countries have been at the core of some of the most dynamic changes in modern history, as they fostered the birth and growth of an integrated Europe. The idea for European unification came after World War II, when Britain's Prime Minister Winston Churchill appealed for "a kind of United States of Europe" beginning with a partnership between France and Germany, countries that had fought three wars with each other in the course of seventy-five years.

But Churchill did not envision England being part of this partnership, and it took two visionary Frenchmen, Jean Monnet and Robert Schuman, to ac-tually implement the idea. The European Coal and Steel Community (ECSC) started operation in 1952 with six member states (Germany, France, Italy, Belgium, the Netherlands, and Luxembourg) with the very limited goal of coordinating coal and steel production. But for Monnet and Schuman, the idea was that this very prosaic cooperation would spill over into other areas, create patterns of peaceful interaction among these former enemies, and eventually lead to broader and deeper cooperation and integration. Schuman saw the ECSC as "a first step in the federation of Europe."[4]

The ECSC was indeed so successful both politically and economically that it led the six nations to the formation in 1958 of the European Eco-nomic Community (EEC), which took the principles of the ECSC and ap-plied them to the whole of their economies. With the aim of eliminating bar-riers to trade (like tariffs and quotas) among the six countries, it came to be known as the Common Market. Both trade and the standard of living grew rapidly in the EEC in the 1950s and 1960s, generating "economic miracles" all over the Continent. The success of the organization drew other states to apply to join, and membership grew to nine, then twelve, then fifteen by 1995, with the organization now renamed the European Union. As member-ship expanded, so did the organization's scope, with free movement of peo-ples as well as goods, harmonized social policies, a European-wide parlia-ment, a European flag, and in 2002 the adoption by most countries of a common currency, the euro. The EU even adopted an anthem, with the stir-ring melody of Beethoven's *Ode to Joy*. Although the lyrics themselves were not formally adopted—only the music—everyone knew the famous phrase *Alle Menschen werden Brüder* contained in the stanza "With your magic, reunite us / Whom the times did once divide / Then we all shall stand as brothers / Where your gentle wings spread wide."

With the inclusion of countries like Greece, Spain, and Portugal, all much poorer than the original six and all with recent authoritarian pasts, the EEC began to set both political and economic criteria for joining. Now countries had to demonstrate markers of both a free market economy and democratic politics, including respect for human rights. These criteria became important elements in the democratization of the former communist states of Eastern Europe when they began applying for EU membership in the 1990s. In 2004, eight of these were part of the ten-nation expansion of membership, and in 2006 Bulgaria and Romania joined as well. Virtually the whole of Europe was now united in one assembly of democratic polities and market economies, living in peace.

This was a quite amazing achievement. Countries and peoples that had been on opposite sides of World War II or the Cold War or divided by race or ideology were now trading and traveling freely throughout the Continent. Young people in particular—what T. R. Reid calls "Generation E"— are "creating a unified European society of their own" and thinking of the entire continent, not just one country, to be "home."[5] For the first time in history, countries have given up significant chunks of their sovereignty in the interest of this common enterprise. As former officer of the Central Intelligence Agency Graham Fuller puts it, we have witnessed for the first time an "empire" built on "consensus and common desire rather than power and conquest. . . . Hardly the stuff of the 'Old Europe.'"[6] The EU also represents an amazingly successful "melting pot" of nationalities, perhaps even more so than the U.S. one. As Fuller observes, the U.S. experiment is built on immigrants who have *left* their homelands. The EU is built right on top of these traditional ethnic homelands—a much harder task—and represents "a model for a world of ethnic homelands" in a world that is increasingly riven by tribalism, national chauvinism, and ethnic conflict.

European Economic Powerhouse

With the most recent expansion of the European Union, the community has become "the biggest and richest capitalist marketplace in the world."[7] The EU accounts for about a third of the world's GDP and contains about half of the industrial world's consumer population. It is also, by far, the world's biggest trading power, accounting for about 40 percent of global exports, compared to less than 10 percent for the United States. And this gap is widening: between 1993 and 2006, the EU's share of global exports grew while that of the United States declined.[8]

European corporations are increasingly making inroads into the dominant global role played by American corporations during the "American Century." In 1969, 60 percent of the world's largest corporations were American, and only 27 percent were from Europe. By 2007, the playing field was leveled, with exactly 162 American corporations and 162 EU ones (32 percent) on the *Fortune* Global 500 list of the world's biggest corporations.

Europe has also become the world's biggest magnet and biggest source of investments. In the decade before the 2004 expansion of the EU, the EU-15 attracted twice the amount of foreign direct investments as the United States and invested in other countries more than three times the amount of the United States.[9] European countries are also the biggest source of investments in the U.S. economy and in U.S. debt instruments. This has become an extremely important factor in keeping the debt-ridden U.S. economy afloat for as long as it has been. As we saw in chapter 1, the United States has been "running on empty" for a long time now, accumulating huge budget deficits and unprecedented trade deficits. The United States imports far more goods than it exports, causing this trade deficit. Foreign investments in the United States help bring those dollars home. Europe (and, as we will see, China) are the biggest sources for foreign investment in the United States and are among the biggest foreign owners of the huge U.S. debt. So, in essence, Europe and China have been subsidizing the profligate spending of the U.S. government and the American consumer. In a switch in roles from the early Cold War years, Europe has been keeping the United States afloat.

Then there is the euro. In 1999, twelve EU countries representing three-quarters of the GDP of the EU-15 adopted the euro as a common currency, and in 2002, with much fanfare and surprisingly few glitches, they replaced their marks, lira, francs, and other national currencies with the new euro coins and banknotes. Immediately, the euro became a rival for the U.S. dollar as countries in Europe and elsewhere began to use the euro for foreign transactions, foreign investments, and national reserves. Even in EU countries that had not yet adopted the euro, it became a major currency for consumer purchases. When the euro was launched in 2002, the American columnist George Will proclaimed that "it will not work,"[10] but within two years the euro was solidly entrenched in Europe and had risen by 60 percent against the dollar. At the beginning, the euro was worth 86 U.S. cents; two years later, it was equivalent to $1.30; and in early 2008, it was going for $1.52—a record (see figure 9.1). In another switch from earlier decades, Americans were finding Europe expensive, and Europeans were reveling in budget vacations to the United States.

The role of the euro, though, and its potential impact on the United States went far beyond the relative price of tourism. Because the U.S. dollar has been the world's major source of international transactions and of foreign government currency holdings (or reserves), the demand for the dollar has been high. Both private investors and governments have used the dollar and U.S.

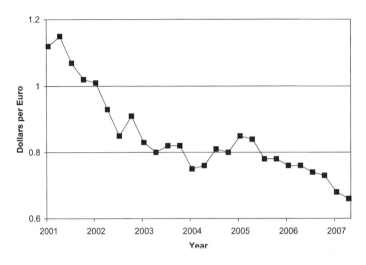

Figure 9.1. Dollar–Euro Exchange Rate, 2002–2008

Treasury securities as a safe haven for their excess currencies, knowing that the dollar has remained stable in value and usable for international transactions. These foreign investments in dollars and U.S. debt have, so far, helped counterbalance the U.S. trade deficit and helped float the huge U.S. federal debt.

However the euro is now challenging the supremacy of the U.S. dollar in international trade and finance. Governments and corporations alike are increasingly borrowing in euros, with investments in euro-denominated bonds now about equivalent to dollar-denominated bonds.[11] A survey of central banks in 2005 showed that about two-thirds of the world's sixty-five richest nations were planning to shift investments out of dollars into euros.[12] The dollar's share in the world's official foreign exchange reserves has declined since 2001, while that of the euro has steadily increased.[13]

The same shift is occurring in international finance and trade. About 40 percent of foreign exchange transactions are now carried out in euros rather than dollars, and that percentage is growing. Some important oil-producing countries and the Organization of Petroleum Exporting Countries have discussed selling their products in euros rather than dollars. Russia's President Vladimir Putin announced publicly that his country was considering selling its oil for euros. In 2000, Saddam Hussein's Iraq started trading oil for euros. After his government was overthrown and his country occupied, U.S. administrators quickly put oil transactions back onto the dollar standard.[14]

Some people more conspiracy minded than I suggest that this threat to American dollar dominance was one of the reasons the United States invaded Iraq. Whether or not this is the case, the growing strength, value, and influence of the euro could indeed pose a threat to the already fragile American economy. If countries and corporations begin to doubt the strength or stability of the dollar, they are likely to switch their investments and transactions to the euro. Given the enormous and growing "triple deficit" of the United States, it is not surprising that investors have already gotten skittish and begun moving toward the euro and euro-denominated securities. As with any investment, if you own dollars and think their value is declining (as they are in fact), you will sell them before the value declines even further. When there are more sellers than buyers for the dollar, the dollar becomes weaker, and the process accelerates. The U.S. Treasury would have to raise interest rates to attract more borrowers to finance the U.S. debt, which would have negative ripple effects throughout the economy and also simply add to the federal debt. A weak dollar also tends to depress the U.S. stock market as investors look for safer havens. "To put it simply," writes T. R. Reid, "the success of Europe's common currency could bring America's financial house of cards tumbling down."[15]

The European Social Model

The EU poses a different kind of challenge to the United States in the way its economy and society is organized and in the attractiveness of its social system. As we saw in chapters 2 through 4, the wealthiest European countries (i.e., most of the EU-15 before the EU expansion into eastern Europe) have less poverty, more equality, and cheaper and better health care and produce better-educated students than the United States. Poverty rates in the EU countries, even the new (and poorer) ones, are about one-half to one-third the rates in the United States (see figure 9.2). The fewer number of poor people in Europe is the main reason why there is more economic equality in those countries compared to the United States (see figure 2.2 in chapter 2). Europeans have longer life expectancy, lower rates of infant and maternal mortality (figure 3.1 in chapter 3), and lower rates of heart disease and cancer, and in every EU country, health care is available to all citizens for free or very inexpensively because it is paid for or subsidized by the governments. Even so, the overall per capita costs of health care in those countries are about half of the costs in the United States (see figure 3.2 in chapter 3). Like health care, university education in Europe is generally free or very heavily subsidized. In Britain, one of the few EU countries to charge university

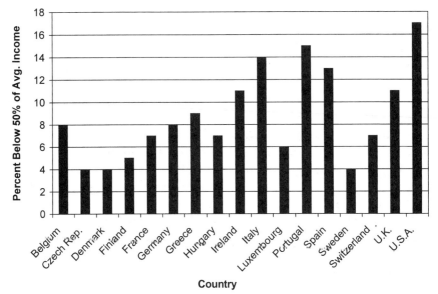

Figure 9.2. Poverty Rates in Europe and the United States

Source: Michael Forster and Marco Mira d'Ercole, *Income Distribution and Poverty in OECD Countries in the Second Half of the 1990s*, OECD Working Paper no. 22 (March 2005), online at http://www .oecd.org/dataoecd/48/9/34483698.pdf.

tuition, the undergraduate fee at Oxford University—the most prestigious university in the country—is about $6,000 per year. Harvard costs five times that much.

Most European countries also have much more generous unemployment assistance, parental leave programs, and child allowance benefits than in the United States.[16] The whole package of subsidies and benefits is part of "the welfare state"—a term that is viewed with derision by most Americans but is a source of pride for Europeans. No other countries in the world have such an advanced system of social welfare. It has come to be known as "the European social model" and is the source of envy and imitation all over the world. Indeed, the European model has essentially replaced the American one that prevailed through much of the twentieth century. As we have seen earlier, people emerging from communism or other authoritarian systems have tended to look toward Europe rather than the United States as models for what they want to achieve. And in countries all over the world, the European social, economic, and even political models are now more trusted and admired than the American.

One might object that in spite of all this, the United States still has a higher standard of living than any European country. This is both true and untrue. Measured in the usual way, as GDP per capita, the United States does indeed rank highly in the world, at $43,444 in 2006. But there are three countries that are higher—Luxembourg, Ireland, and Norway—and all are in Europe.[17] Furthermore, there are other ways of figuring standard of living besides these raw economic calculations. The United Nations, for example, has a "quality of life index," which takes into account education, health care, and life expectancy as well as income. By that measure, the United States ranks eighth in the world, with four European countries—Norway, Iceland, Ireland, and Sweden—ranked more highly. Another measure is the "World Database of Happiness," compiled by a Dutch scholar, which ranks nations in terms of "how much people enjoy their life as a whole." On this scale, the United States also does well, ranking seventh in the world; the six countries ahead of the United States are European.[18]

Postmodern Power

During the twentieth century, the global dominance of the United States was built on a combination of enormous military power and impressive "soft power" based on the attractiveness of U.S. politics, economics, culture, and ideals. In recent years, however, it has become apparent that American military power is either ineffectual (e.g., in Iraq and Afghanistan) or irrelevant (e.g., in solving threats like global warming), and U.S. soft-power influence has virtually evaporated. Europe's potential as a global superpower is based not on raw military power but rather on a reconfigured role for military forces and the growing magnetism of the European social model and the EU's own exercise of soft-power politics.

Even in conventional military terms, Europe's potential power is impressive. The EU's member countries have almost twice as many military personnel as Russia or China, and combined defense spending is far larger than in either of those substantial military powers. But compared to the United States, Europe is a "military pygmy," in the words of a former secretary-general of the North Atlantic Treaty Organization (NATO).[19] The U.S. military budget is twice that of the EU. In fact, the United States has a bigger defense budget than the next ten countries combined and accounts for about half of the world's military spending. The United States has the world's biggest nuclear arsenal, the most advanced military technology, the best-trained soldiers, and the most extensive global network of military bases. So Europe will not compete with the United States in the strictly military realm—at least not for a long while.

The EU has developed a military capability, however, that is eminently suited and in fact designed for the small-scale conflicts that are increasingly common on Europe's periphery and around the world. These would include international peacekeeping operations and the settling or monitoring of small-scale conflicts before they become big ones. In 2003, the EU authorized creation of the European Rapid Reaction Force (sometimes called the EuroArmy), which will have up to 60,000 troops on call for short-term operations in and around Europe, mostly in support of UN or other international peacekeeping, humanitarian, and rescue missions. Already EU forces have taken over peacekeeping duties from NATO troops in Macedonia and Bosnia and from UN troops in the Democratic Republic of the Congo and have played a major role in Afghanistan after the fall of the Taliban, where European troops have suffered more casualties than Americans.

For Europeans, the configuration and orientation of their military are closely tied to the European social model and to their preferences for soft-power influence in global politics. As T. R. Reid sees it, "To the citizens of unified Europe, military power seems an outmoded concept."[20] They have already achieved what Jean Monnet and Robert Schuman set out to do in the aftermath of World War II: to build a community of Europeans in which the idea of warring on each other would be unthinkable. It is accomplishment enough that Germany, France, and Britain are no longer enemies or even military rivals. Now there are twenty-seven European countries concerned more with human rights and material prosperity than with territorial conflicts or military conquest. In addition, Europe has no aggressive intentions against any countries on its borders (or anywhere else in the world for that matter), and other countries recognize this.

Instead, the Europeans are using the same carrots of soft-power attraction that worked so effectively for the United States for so many decades. In the absence of any particular military threats and without huge military capabilities of its own, the EU can rely on its strengths of economic and diplomatic prowess and the sheen of its own social and political accomplishments. In *The European Superpower*, John McCormick refers to this as "the rise of postmodern Europe," reflecting different attitudes toward government, society, and economic structures and toward international politics.[21] Europe's attractiveness to other countries and influence in global politics have been established by its own domestic successes and enhanced by its willingness and even enthusiasm for international collaboration and cooperation. The EU's unanimous support for the Kyoto Protocol on global warming, for example, helped bring Russia on board, allowing a successful implementation of the treaty (without the United States). Similarly, as the former U.S. ambassador to the EU puts it, the EU's support for the International Criminal Court "has made America seem an arrogant scofflaw for not signing on."[22] And in the UN Security Council's debates leading up to the Iraq War in 2003, when France's foreign minister, Dominique de Villepin, gave an impassioned appeal for cooperation and diplomacy rather than war, his talk was greeted by those in attendance with a standing ovation—well outside the usual stuffy protocol of such assemblies:

> This message comes to you today from an old country, France, from a continent like mine, Europe, that has known wars, occupation and barbarity. A country that does not forget and knows everything it owes to the freedom-fighters who came from America and elsewhere. And yet has never ceased to stand upright in the face of history and before mankind. Faithful to its values, it wishes resolutely to act with all the members of the international community. It believes in our ability to build together a better world.[23]

The EU is also pursuing a more active and assertive role in world affairs in terms of diplomacy, commerce, and development assistance. In 2003, the EU launched its "European Neighborhood Policy" to "create a ring of friends" along the periphery of the EU with the potential to extend European influence into some thirty-one countries with a total population of more than 500 million. Some of these are candidates for EU membership, meaning that they are already making efforts to move toward the human rights, democratic, and economic prerequisites for joining the club. Most others have signed cooperation agreements with the EU, agreeing in principle to respect such principles in exchange for enhanced access to European markets and trade.[24]

The EU's growing influence is global, not just regional. As the EU moves toward a common European foreign policy, the organization's twenty-seven national members translate into impressive political clout in international organizations like the United Nations, NATO, and the International Monetary Fund, where voting is usually counted by country. Europe is gaining more friends and influence in the developing countries of the world as well. The EU is now by far the world's biggest supplier of foreign aid ("overseas development assistance"), providing over half of the world's total of such aid and more than twice what the United States offers. The magnet of Europe's huge market economy is also affecting countries around the globe, both poor and rich. By providing EU industrial standards to developing nations and requiring rich countries to abide by EU health, safety, and environmental regulations to get access to the market, much of the world is taking baby steps, at least, toward the European social model even without joining the organization or necessarily even agreeing with these standards. Ambassador Schnabel calls attention to a poster at an EU exhibition in Brussels that proclaimed that "by creating common standards that are implemented through national institutions, Europe can take over the world without becoming a magnet for hostility."[25]

Both Europeans and much of the rest of the world seem to favor this grow-ing global influence for the EU. As we saw in chapter 8, people in most coun-tries in the world have negative feelings about U.S. influence in the world, favor a reduction in such influence, and believe it would be good if some other regions or countries came to balance American power. These senti-ments are particularly strong in Europe and in the Muslim world. In most parts of the world, Europe is the most popular candidate for a counterbal-ancing force to the United States. A survey of twenty-three countries in 2004 found that worldwide, 58 percent of those surveyed agreed that it would be a good thing if Europe were to become "more influential than the United States in world affairs."[26] In eighteen of the countries, at least half the popu-lation felt that way, and in all the European countries surveyed, over two-thirds did. Another survey conducted in six European countries in 2002 found almost two-thirds of those questioned favoring the notion that the EU should become a superpower like the United States.[27] Even Washington's best friend in Europe, former British Prime Minister Tony Blair, expressed this point of view: "A single-power world is inherently unstable. I mean, that's the rationale for Europe to unite. When we work together, the Euro-pean Union can stand on par as a superpower and a partner with the U.S. The world needs that right now."[28]

Of course, there are those who doubt the EU's ability to supplant the United States as a superpower. Some, like Robert Kagan, point to the EU's lack of raw military power and its disinclination to use it. In Kagan's colorful phrasing, "Americans are from Mars and Europeans are from Venus," but in his view, in a world still driven mostly by power, the United States holds most of the cards and can afford to "go it alone" even without Europe.[29] Oth-ers are doubtful of the EU's economic strength and future, arguing that the EU has lower economic growth rates, lower levels of labor productivity, and higher unemployment levels than the United States. In demographic terms, too, Europe may be in an even more precarious situation than the United States, with its impecunious and aging baby boomers. Europe's birthrate is much lower than that of the United States, and the population is both aging and shrinking; if nothing changes, by 2050, the median age in Europe will be fifty-two, compared to thirty-five in the United States.[30] This could pose a problem both for the European welfare state and for economic dynamism. The defeat of the EU's proposed new constitution, rejected by popular referenda in France and Holland in 2005, signaled to some a major blow to the whole idea of a united Europe.

There is some reason to be cautious about Europe's future. Its problems with debt, unemployment, and economic growth are in many respects the same as those confronted by the United States. On the other hand, as we have seen, Europe's accomplishments since World War II have been quite stunning: recovering from the destruction and hatred of World War II, rising to the top of the world in wealth and living standards, constructing societies that are both free and secure, and doing this while gradually bringing under the umbrella of the EU almost every country on the Continent. The European social model and its practice of soft power is now much more widely admired around the world than the American "neoliberal" one and its continued emphasis on "hard power." Even if Europe does not replace the United States as the world's superpower, its growing economic and political clout will certainly diminish Washington's overseas influence. And if, as seems to be occurring already, the euro begins to replace the dollar as the world's favored international currency, this could further accelerate the already imminent unraveling of the U.S. economy.

The Chinese Behemoth

If Europe poses a challenge to U.S. dominance by its wealth, social model, and soft power, China has an equally strong claim to global influence by the sheer weight of its huge population—at least 1.3 billion people—and its startlingly large and dynamic economy. Since the beginning of the liberalizing economic reforms in the 1970s, China has been the world's fastest-growing economy, expanding at an annual rate of almost 10 percent. No other country in world history has grown so fast over so sustained a period. The country is expected to overtake Germany this year as the world's third-largest economy, after only the United States and Japan.[31] China is the second-largest foreign holder of U.S. public debt (behind only Japan). It is the world's largest producer of coal, steel, and cement and produces two-thirds of the world's copiers, microwave ovens, DVD players, shoes, and toys.[32] It is also the second-largest consumer of energy and the third-largest importer of oil. The country's enormous appetite for energy and petroleum is one big reason for the rise in gasoline prices in the United States. Its export of consumer goods to the United States is the major factor in America's record large and growing trade deficit. These superlatives have led at least two recent books to envision the replacement of the American Century with the "Chinese Century." This is the title of a recent book by Ohio State University business professor Oded Shenkar[33] and of a *New York Times Magazine* article and book chapter by journalist Ted Fishman.[34]

The rapid emergence of China as a global economic power is both remarkable and surprising. For those of us who grew up at dinner tables where we had to eat the last disgusting piece of asparagus because there were "starving people in China," the new Chinese wealth and affluence is quite astounding. The essence of the change lies in two major accomplishments: the ending of widespread hunger and famine—a frequent affliction in China's long history—by the communist regime and the bringing of at least 250 million people out of poverty and into the middle class since the adoption of the economic reforms. China scholar David Lampton believes that the Chinese middle class is "growing more rapidly than any middle class ever has, anywhere."[35] But perhaps China's economic boom should not be so surprising. For most of its long history, China had the world's largest economy, and it remained so up until the middle of the nineteenth century.[36]

For the next hundred years, China was weakened, disrupted, and afflicted by Western imperialism, revolution, world war, civil war, and the various "campaigns" of Mao Zedong's communism, including the Cultural Revolution of the 1960s and 1970s. But after Mao's death in 1976, a semblance of normality was restored, and the country's new leader, Deng Xiaoping, launched a program of modernization and economic development relatively free of the ideological strictures of communism. "To get rich is glorious," he declared. "It doesn't matter if it is a black cat or a white cat. As long as it can catch mice, it is a good cat." The government increasingly opened up the economy to market forces and even to free enterprise. By 1997, the private sector made up 15 percent of the country's GDP. Eight years later, 70 percent of GDP was private, with almost 5 million privately owned companies.

China's astounding growth since the 1970s—over 9 percent a year for a quarter century—is unprecedented in modern history anywhere in the world. It has been fueled by a number of factors: the surge in private businesses, large-scale movement of people from the countryside to the cities, huge increases in exports, and impressive levels of domestic and foreign investments. Those investments, most of them for building new infrastructure and manufacturing plants, equal almost half of China's GDP. In the United States, Europe, and Japan, investments constitute less than a quarter of GDP.[37] China's continued high level of investment, along with its still booming export business, suggests that this dynamic economic growth will continue into the foreseeable future.

Some economists expect China's economy to exceed that of the United States in size within a generation or two. Amazingly, the People's Republic of China already leads the world in the number of publicly traded companies with market values of more than $200 billion—with eight among the top twenty in the world, compared to seven for the United States.[38]

China's biggest impact on the rest of the globe comes through its burgeoning trade, especially in the years since it joined the World Trade Organization in 2001. From being almost a nonfactor in international trade, China is now the world's third most active trading nation, behind only the United States and Germany but ahead of Japan. China alone has accounted for about 12 percent of the growth of global trade in recent years.[39] China has now displaced the United States as Japan's leading trade partner. In the words of Ted Fishman, author of *China Inc.*, "If any country is going to supplant the U.S. in the world marketplace, China is it."[40]

The United States has played a particularly large role in the growth of China's trade and also therefore in the growth of China's domestic economy. The United States is China's largest trade partner, and China ranks third among U.S. trading partners. But there is a huge imbalance in this trading relationship, with the United States importing from China almost six times as much as it exports to that country. The U.S. trade deficit with China has increased steadily since the mid-1980s, reaching $256 billion in 2007 (see figure 9.3). China is now the single largest source of the overall U.S. balance of trade deficit, accounting for more than a quarter of the total trade deficit.[41] As we saw in chapter 1, the trade deficit is one of the many components of the deepening crisis of the U.S. economy. The Chinese are a big factor in that, but, as we will see, China has also been helping to postpone the crisis by a virtual loan to the U.S. consumer.

The problem is that American consumers are purchasing products made in China at record levels, but American workers are not producing much that the Chinese want to buy. China is now producing much of the world's television sets, desktop computers, audio equipment, cameras, cell phones, shoes, and toys, and much of that is being purchased by consumers in the United States and a lot of it at Wal-Mart. Wal-Mart sells things cheaply, largely by importing from China, where labor costs are a fraction of what they are in the United States—typically less than $200 per month for assembly-line workers. Of Wal-Mart's 6,000 suppliers, 80 percent are in China.[42] This has multiple effects on the American consumer and the U.S. economy—some good and some bad but all extremely consequential. It contributes mightily to "outsourcing" and the consequent loss of jobs and decline

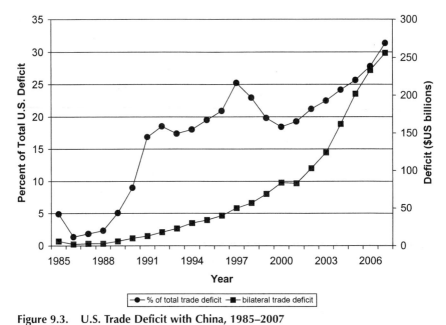

Figure 9.3.   U.S. Trade Deficit with China, 1985–2007

Source: U.S. Census Bureau, Foreign Trade Statistics, online at http://www.census.gov/foreign-trade/balance/c5700.html.

in wages here in the United States. On the other hand, it subsidizes the American consumers and their standard of living by providing an abundant array of consumer goods at low prices. And then there is the impact on the trade deficit. In 2003, Wal-Mart alone imported $15 billion in merchandise from China, equivalent to about 15 percent of the U.S. trade deficit with that country.[43]

This continuing bilateral trade deficit has potential consequences for the stability and value of the U.S. dollar and consequently for interest rates, inflation, and the stock market in the United States. When most countries trade, over time there is a rough balance in trade, and the currencies flow back and forth in roughly equal purchases. That is not the case with China and the United States, with a net of more than $200 billion each year moving from the United States to China. Most economists think that this kind of trade imbalance cannot be sustained over a long period without some significant adjustments in either trade or currency valuations. China has mitigated the potential effects, though, by sending dollars back to the United States in the form of purchases of U.S. Treasury bonds and other securities. This has helped keep the dollar from declining in value but also means that China is, in effect, subsidizing the record-setting U.S. federal budget deficits.

Almost half of U.S. public debt is now held by foreigners. Japan and China are by far the largest foreign holders of such debt. This is not a particular problem at the moment, but if China decided to diversify its foreign currency holdings and move out of the dollar and dollar-denominated securities, it is likely that the value of the dollar would decrease, perhaps precipitously. As we saw in our discussion of Europe, the euro, and the U.S. dollar, this has already begun happening, as other countries have shifted out of the dollar over concern about the burgeoning U.S. debt and the trade deficit. Even more ominous is the possibility that China could use this financial leverage in negotiations with the United States. A senior Chinese financial official recently suggested that the country's foreign reserves could be used as a "bargaining chip" in talks with the United States.[44]

A primary reason both for the rising purchase of Chinese-made products in the United States and for the stagnant exports of the United States is that the United States is not actually producing very much. American manufacturing, which fueled global economic growth through much of the twentieth century, now accounts for only about 12 percent of U.S. GDP—about half the level of the 1970s. In his book *American Theocracy*, Kevin Phillips talks about the "financialization of the U.S." in showing that financial services have increasingly replaced the production of goods in the United States.[45] The growth in the financial sector, along with huge salaries and profit margins there, have contributed to declining wages for most workers, growing inequality, and growing debt in the United States. It is more difficult to export financial services than manufactured goods, particularly to a highly regulated country like China, so the United States has less to offer China in exchange for manufactured consumer goods that are imported from that country. As one Shanghai economist puts it, "The U.S. has little to sell back to China but Boeing and beef."[46] Clyde Prestowitz paints a grim picture of the remedy for the huge U.S. trade deficit, the largest component of which is trade with China. In order to cut the trade deficit by half, the United States would have to increase exports of both manufacturing and services by 30 percent, a task that seems unlikely given that both sectors are already running at close to capacity. "This suggests that when the adjustment comes, it almost surely will be largely through reduced consumption, which very likely means a recession if not worse."[47]

The reduced U.S. manufacturing base also means that American businesses are not in a very good position to take advantage of the domestic Chinese market, which is poised to become the largest in the world. On average, Chinese incomes and consumption levels are still low by world standards. But there are already at least 250 million people in the middle class in

China—more than in the United States—and some 300,000 millionaires, and both of these numbers are expanding rapidly. China has 300 million mobile-phone users—the largest such market in the world. There is a boom in car ownership and highway construction in China, with the number of passenger cars more than tripling since 2000 and the total miles of highway more than doubling in that period. The government plans to have 53,000 freeway miles by 2035, more than the fifty-year-old U.S. interstate highway system. According to some estimates, by that year there will be as many cars in China as in the United States.[48]

The rapid growth of the Chinese economy and of middle-class spending will have obvious impacts on the global economy. As the biggest domestic market, China will increasingly become a magnet for investments and trade, perhaps rivaling and surpassing both the United States and Europe. Already China has passed the United States as the leading recipient of direct foreign investment. Unable to produce or compete, the United States will increasingly become marginalized as a major player in the global economy. There are other less benign consequences of China's emerging economic muscle. Its enormous appetite for energy and particularly for automobile gasoline has already put pressure on global supplies of petroleum and is a major factor in the rising price of gasoline in the United States. Over the past decade, China's share of world energy consumption has increased from 9 to 12 percent.[49] China is likely to become a strategic competitor with the United States in the Middle East, where so much of the world's petroleum is located. China's mounting use of petroleum and other fossil fuels will also complicate the worrisome problem of global warming. Only the United States emits more greenhouse gases than China, and China is rapidly approaching U.S. levels.

Attracting Friends, Influencing People

China's burgeoning economy and trade and its emphasis on trade over ideology and politics have boosted the country's image, reputation, and attractiveness to other countries in the region and around the globe. In many respects, China is like the EU in emphasizing its soft-power approach to international politics. China is now the leading trading partner of the other economic powerhouse in the region, Japan, and China's leaders have stressed the development of "good-neighborly relationship and partnership" with countries on its borders. Beijing recently signed a Treaty of Amity and Cooperation with the ten-nation Association of South East Asian Nations, a treaty that the United States did not sign. It has also resolved virtually all its territorial disputes with bordering states (though Tibet and Taiwan remain thorny issues). Beijing has greatly increased its development assistance for other countries, particularly those in the region. In recent years, China's aid to the Philippines was four times greater than that of the United States; aid to Laos was three times greater, and aid to Indonesia was twice the U.S. aid.[50] New middle-class Chinese tourists in the region are carrying a different image of China as richer, more confident, and more influential. "Among some countries, China fever seems to be replacing China fear," says Wang Gungwu, the director of the East Asian Institute at National University in Singapore.[51]

Beijing has worked to extend its influence further afield as well, particularly in areas where there is oil. China was a founding member of the Shanghai Cooperation Organization (SCO), consisting originally of China, Russia, and the four central Asian states (and former Soviet republics) of Kazakhstan, Uzbekistan, Tajikistan, and Kyrgyzstan, though in 2006, Iran, India, Pakistan, and Mongolia were inducted as observers and expected to become full members soon. The U.S. application for observer status was rejected. The SCO is nominally an alliance of "good neighborliness and friendly cooperation," but many observers see it as a counterbalance to NATO and perhaps to the EU. In 2003, the Chinese Premier Wen Jiabao proposed a long-term goal of turning the organization into a free trade area, reminiscent of the early phases of the EU.

The alliance already includes countries occupying three-fifths of the Eurasian landmass, and an expansion that would bring together China, Russia, India, and Iran would be an imposing global force. Furthermore, it would bring together some of the world's major oil reserves in Iran, Russia, and the Caspian Sea. Some analysts see a strategic and economic effort among these countries to reduce the U.S. hold on the region's energy resources. Robert Karniol, Asia-Pacific editor for *Jane's Defense Weekly*, believes that China and India, as the world's fastest-growing energy consumers, want to secure central Asia's energy resources for their own economies. Iran and Russia, two of the world's largest energy suppliers, want to reduce their dependence on sales to the West.[52]

As discussed in the previous chapter, China has also been greatly expanding its presence in Africa. Since 2000, China's trade with Africa has increased more than fivefold, reaching $55 billion in 2006. Both its foreign direct investments and its foreign aid to Africa have vastly increased during that period. Beijing is particularly interested in countries with oil and other mineral resources and has signed at least forty oil agreements with various African countries. China's oil imports from Africa, which were zero in 1990, now constitute almost a third of China's total oil imports.[53] And China has been cultivating African elites by hosting a China–Africa summit in Beijing and by offering debt forgiveness and duty-free entry to exports from the world's poor countries. The country's pragmatic and soft-power approach seems to be striking a chord in Africa. "We've always known we have a dysfunctional relationship with the West," says South Africa's deputy director of trade and industry. "Now with China we have a relationship as equals. They don't look down on us. They are not condescending."[54] According to the Carnegie Endowment's Joshua Kurlantzick, "China has so quickly created a positive image of itself in Africa that it now rivals the United States, France, and international financial institutions for influence."[55]

Both China's leaders and Chinese citizens appear inclined for China to take on a bigger role in world affairs. In 2004, President Hu Jintao used the term "peaceful rise" to describe the country's foreign policy goals, though the phrase was later altered to "peaceful development" to make it seem less threatening.[56] In 2006, China's central television broadcast a twelve-part documentary series, *Rise of Great Powers*, which partly tracked Paul Kennedy's account in *The Rise and Fall of the Great Powers* of how nations rose to power in the past. This television series seemed to signal an openness to discussion of what it might mean for China to be a major world power. An important article in the scholarly journal *China Journal of International Politics* argued that China had already surpassed Japan, Russia, Britain, France, Germany, and India in its economic, military, and political power, leaving it second only to the United States. "China will enjoy the status of a semi-superpower between the United States and the other major powers," the author predicted.[57] China's leaders frequently proclaim their opposition to "hegemonic" and "unipolar" power politics—code words for U.S. domination. And in May 2003, Presidents Hu Jintao and Vladimir Putin signed a joint declaration calling for a "multipolar" world based on "commonly recognized principles of international law."

In some respects, China's efforts to expand its reach and influence mimic those advocated by Henry Luce for the United States at the beginning of the American Century. China's Ministry of Education has helped establish 140 "Confucius Colleges" around the world with the purpose of promoting the study of Chinese language and culture and creating a more "harmonious world."[58] It has also increased the number of scholarships for foreign students. Foreign students are flocking to China to learn the language. In 2004, more than 110,000 students from 178 countries were enrolled at Chinese universities, a 43 percent increase over 2003. In addition, according to the Chinese news agency Xinhua, more than 30 million people are studying Mandarin Chinese in other countries.[59] The authorities have been allowing and even encouraging its citizens to travel abroad as well. The number of Chinese studying in other countries increased tenfold from 1998 to 2006 to 121,000; the number of Chinese visiting foreign countries increased from 2 million in 1992 to 32 million "person-times" in 2006. China now supplies the largest number of tourists in Asia.[60] Chinese citizens, too, are increasingly imagining their country as a major world power. In 1995, a poll asking Chinese citizens which were "the most prominent countries in the world," only 13 percent chose China. In a similar poll in 2003, 40 percent picked China as "the most prominent country in the world."[61] The Middle Kingdom is reasserting itself.

In addition, most of the rest of the world also seems favorably inclined to the emergence of China as a world power, particularly if it sticks to its soft-power approach. A sixteen-nation poll by the Pew Global Attitudes Survey in 2005 found that in eleven of the countries, a clear majority of the national populations had a "favorable" view of China. And in all but four—the United States, Canada, Poland, and India—a greater number were favorable to China than to the United States (see figure 9.4). Another poll the same year by BBC and Globescan found similar positive attitudes toward China. On average, across all twenty-two countries polled, 48 percent saw China's influence in the world as positive, and only 30 percent saw it as negative.[62]

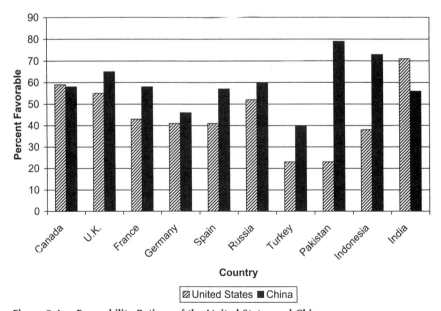

Figure 9.4.   Favorability Ratings of the United States and China
Source: The Pew Global Attitudes Project, "U.S. Image Up Slightly but Still Negative," June 2005, available online at http://www.pewglobal.org.

China is not without its own basket of problems, of course, and some analysts doubt that China can sustain the economic growth and dynamism that would lead it to superpower status. The biggest such problem is the country's continued one-party authoritarian political system. Is it possible to continue to liberalize the economy without liberalizing the political system? The unreliable legal system is a particular obstacle for continued growth of private businesses (especially foreign ones), for example. China has not had any major political disturbances since the Tiananmen Square demonstrations of 1989, but a little political relaxation can lead to demands for much more, as the communist governments in Russia and Eastern Europe discovered two decades ago. Some economists wonder whether China can continue its 10 percent annual economic growth with or without political change. As China expert Ross Terrill observes, "Linear projections of economic growth are subject to the nonlinear realities of politics, culture and human nature."[63]

There are other factors that could throw China's skyrocketing growth off track. As the middle class grows and the country becomes more affluent, wages and prices will increase inside China, and this in turn will make it less attractive as a location for other countries' outsourcing and will gradually cut away at China's low labor-cost advantage. On the other hand, if my projections about U.S. economic decline prove to be true, that will erode China's biggest market and its own trade growth. Another big issue is the demographics of China. The proportion of people aged sixty and older is growing more rapidly than in any other major country, such that by mid-century about a third of the population will be retired. In China, the financial situation for retirees will be even more dire than in the United States and will place huge strains on both the economy and the government.

Despite these caveats, China will certainly reemerge on the world's stage as a major player, if not replacing the United States as the dominant superpower. Its huge and dynamic population, continuing economic growth, impressive international trade prowess, and trillion-dollar foreign currency reserves cannot be ignored. As Thomas Friedman argues in *The World Is Flat*, in an interconnected world of markets and knowledge centers, Americans and Europeans will "have to run at least as fast as the fastest lion . . . and that lion will be China."[64] Oded Shenkar, author of *The Chinese Century*, contends that China's rise is "a watershed event that will change the global landscape and that is on par with the ascent of the United States of America as a global economic, political and military power a century earlier."[65]

Furthermore, China's growing wealth, consumption, and standard of living means that it will place increasing pressures on global energy supplies, and this is likely to bring it head-to-head with the United States, the world's other gobbler of energy. Indeed, China's enormous appetite for petroleum has already put upward pressure on global oil prices. So even apart from direct confrontations with the United States (e.g., over Iran and Iraq), China's growth is already having an impact on the American economy and standard of living.

Multiple Rivals—India, Russia, Iran, and Brazil

The EU and China are the two most imposing challengers to the United States, and each has different advantages in terms of its global power, influence, and appeal. But there are other countries that could emerge as great powers as the U.S. global presence shrinks. These include the so-called BRIC countries (Brazil, Russia, India, and China), which some analysts expect to become among the six biggest economies in the world by 2050.[66] Because the four nicely complement each other economically, with China in manufacturing, India in services, Russia in energy, and Brazil in raw materials, cooperation among the four could make them the most powerful economic bloc in the world by mid-century.

Even without such cooperation, each of the BRIC countries alone will stake a claim to great power status. We have already discussed China. India is also a huge economic dynamo, with a population of more than 1 billion and GDP growth rates of about 6 percent annually from 1980 to 2002 and 7.5 percent per year since then, making it now the world's fourth-largest economy (see figure 9.5). While much of the country remains desperately poor, about 1 percent of the population moves out of poverty each year, and the middle class has quadrupled in size in the past two decades. Some 200 million Indians speak English, and for about 40 million of those, English is their first language, positioning the country well for the global marketplace. The country produces more college graduates each year than either the United States, the EU, or China. Like China, wages in India are very low by world standards, especially for engineers, so India has experienced a boom in information technology, computer software design, biotechnology, and telephone call centers—which is why when you call the Dell computer help center, you get "Bob" with an Indian accent. Although much of the attention to India's rise has been focused on its service industries, the country is increasingly moving into manufacturing. Two-thirds of foreign investments are in manufacturing rather than services, and the growth rate in manufacturing output is about 9 percent a year. India has some advantages over China as a global power: its younger age structure and workforce, its established democratic political traditions, and its modern and efficient financial sector.

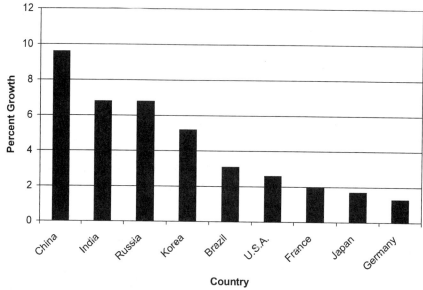

Figure 9.5. Average Annual GDP Growth Rates, 2000–2006
Source: International Monetary Fund data at http://www.imf.org.

India's dynamism has occasioned much speculation in the West about its place in the global power constellation. In his book *Three Billion New Capitalists*, Clyde Prestowitz sees India (as well as China) as a key component in "the great shift of wealth and power to the East." The prestigious U.S. journal *Foreign Affairs* featured "The Rise of India" as its cover feature in the summer of 2006, with the lead article titled "The India Model," suggesting that the country's emphasis on "domestic market more than exports, consumption more than investment, services more than industry, and high-tech more than low-skilled manufacturing" makes it a model for many other countries seeking economic development.[67] The country's testing of a nuclear weapon in 1998 (following a similar test by Pakistan) brought India, for better or for worse, into the elite club of the world's nuclear powers. India's political leaders have worked hard in recent years to improve relations with its neighbors (including Pakistan and China) and to elevate India's global status. Many Indians now speak confidently of the twenty-first century as the "Indian Century."

Russia should also be considered as a (revived) global power. It is true that the country has been greatly diminished from its years at the center of the Soviet Union. The dismemberment of the country in 1991, the reconfiguration of its political system, and its virtual economic collapse posed a very rough transition. But the system has stabilized now, and Russia remains a major force in the global economy and in international politics. It remains by far the largest country in the world, occupying almost twice the territory of the United States. Within those borders, it contains the world's most abundant array of natural resources. It is the world's second-largest producer and exporter of oil, after only Saudi Arabia. After a very rough decade following the collapse of the Soviet Union, Russia's economy is now growing at a very fast clip of more than 6 percent per year, in part because of the increase in world oil prices. It will soon join the World Trade Organization, which will no doubt accelerate its trade and integration into the global economy. Russia remains a potent military power, with the world's fifth-largest army and the world's largest stockpile of nuclear warheads. And both Russia's citizens and its leaders want Russia to play a bigger role on the world stage and to be more respected by other countries. Russia's President (now Premier) Vladimir Putin, in particular, has been highly vocal and critical of U.S. efforts to dominate the globe and its unilateralism, referring not so subtly to a "world of one master, one sovereign."[68] Tensions between the United States and Russia have increased during the Bush administration over the Iraq War, the treatment of Iran, missile defense, and the expansion of NATO. On all these issues, Moscow feels that its views and interests are being ignored or belittled by Washington. The Russian leadership wants a world that is more multilateral, with Russia again one of the players.

Besides these potential global rivals to U.S. influence, there are a multitude of regional powers that will challenge the United States, at least in their own geographic backyards. Already, as we have seen, there have been efforts by some of the global powers, like the EU, China, and India, to become more assertive in their own spheres and to limit U.S. influence in those spheres. Regional powers have already begun doing the same as U.S. power has waned. These regional powers would include South Africa, Brazil, Japan, Indonesia, and, perhaps most important, Iran.

Iran deserves special mention here, simply because it is at the intersection of so many areas and issues of importance to the United States, including oil, Iraq, nuclear technology, and Islamic revival. With 70 million people, Iran is by far the most populous country in the Middle East and a gold mine of energy resources: it has the second-largest reserves of oil in the world, is the fourth-largest producer of oil, and is the fifth-largest producer of natural gas. While many in the United States, including the Bush administration, have demonized Iran's President Mahmoud Ahmadinejad, he does represent a kind of populist, nationalist, Islamic, and anti-American sentiment that is widely admired both inside Iran and in much of the rest of the Islamic world.

He was elected as president in 2005 largely on the basis of his campaign against corruption, privilege, wealth, and inequality within Iran, and these same postures can also be directed against the United States and its global role. Iran is Shiite and Persian, in contrast to the Sunni Arab populations that dominate the Middle East. Even so, opinion polls in the region often show Ahmadinejad as one of the most popular political figures among Arabs at a time when anti-American sentiment there is almost universal.[69] Iran's apparent efforts to acquire nuclear weapons are viewed by Ahmadinejad and his allies "as critical to consolidating Iran's position and helping the country eclipse U.S. influence in the region," according to Ray Takeyh, the author of *Hidden Iran*.[70] As we pointed out in chapter 7, the Iraq War has already dramatically strengthened Iran's dominant role in the region. Saddam Hussein's Iraq was Iran's major rival, and now with the establishment of a largely Shiite government in Iraq, Shiite Iran has gained much political influence within Iraq. Referring to the Iraq War, Vali Nasr, the author of *The Shia Revival*, sums it up: "In short, Iraq has strengthened Iran and weakened the United States."[71]

America's Many Rivals

The EU, China, India, Russia, and growing regional powers all over the world have already begun to step into the vacuum created by the end of the American Century. The most impressive and powerful challenges to U.S. influence are coming from big power blocs that, so far at least, are leveraging global influence through soft power rather than military power. The "European superpower" is based on its affluence and alternative "social model" to the United States. China's rise is due to the enormous weight of its international trade and its astounding economic growth. India is making itself indispensable as the service industry of globalization, with its added reputation as the world's most populous democracy. Russia's future role is a bit more enigmatic, with its combination of soft-power potential, its enormous mineral and energy resources, and its still impressive military capability.

All these powers, though, and many of the regional ones as well offer a different model of economic and political development and a different approach to the rest of the world than does the United States. For most of the American Century, the U.S. model was really the only game in town and, for most countries, by far a more attractive model than the alternative, which was Soviet-style communism. But with the collapse of the Soviet Union and the fracturing of the bipolar world, the global community has become both more heterogeneous and more complex. The world is no longer so susceptible to U.S. domination and influence and no longer so influenced by the distinctive U.S. approach to economics, politics, and society. Peoples and countries everywhere are looking for other examples and models, usually closer to home in terms of their own geography, history, culture, or religion. American exceptionalism is seen more as a disorder than a cure.

So while many other countries will rival, undercut, or replace U.S. influence around the globe, for many of the same reasons it seems unlikely that any one of them will become a global superpower on the scale of the United States during the twentieth century. The appeal of the EU is broad but not universal, and one could say the same thing about China, India, or Iran. Besides, the reach of these powerful entities will themselves be tempered by the increasing globalization of the planet and the expanding role of nonstate actors. These include intergovernmental organizations such as the United Nations, the EU, and the Arab League; nongovernmental organizations such as Human Rights Watch, Greenpeace, and the International Red Cross; and multinational corporations such as Toyota, Shell, and Microsoft. The future of this global environment in the aftermath of the American Century is the subject of the next and final chapter.

Notes

1. T. R. Reid, *The United States of Europe* (New York: Penguin, 2004), 184.
2. Ted Fishman, "The Chinese Century," *New York Times Magazine*, July 4, 2004.
3. T. R. Reid, *The United States of Europe: The New Superpower and the End of American Supremacy* (New York: Penguin, 2005); John McCormick, *The European Superpower* (New York: Palgrave, 2007); Rockwell A. Schnabel with Francis X. Rocca, *The Next Superpower? The Rise of Europe and Its Challenge to the United States* (Lanham, Md.: Rowman & Littlefield, 2005).
4. David S. Mason, *Revolutionary Europe 1789–1989: Liberty, Equality, Solidarity* (Lanham, Md.: Rowman & Littlefield, 2004), 201.
5. Reid, *The United States of Europe*, 199.
6. Graham E. Fuller, "'Old Europe' or 'Old America'?" *New Perspectives Quarterly*, spring 2003, http://www.digitalnpq.org/archive/2003_spring/fuller.html.
7. McCormick, *The European Superpower*, 89.
8. "World Trade Developments," 10, World Trade Organization, http://www.wto.org/english/res_e/statis_e/its2007_c/its07_world_trade_dev_e.pdf. These trends were true even before the 2004 expansion of the EU.
9. McCormick, *The European Superpower*, 190 n. 1.
10. George Will, "Europe's Suicide?" *Jewish World Review*, December 31, 2001, http://www.jewishworldreview.com/cols/will123101.asp.
11. Reid, *The United States of Europe*, 242.
12. Reid, *The United States of Europe*, 242.

13. "Currency Composition of Official Foreign Exchange Reserves," International Monetary Fund, http://www.imf.org/external/np/sta/cofer/eng/cofer.pdf.

14. Kevin Phillips, *American Theocracy* (New York: Viking, 2006), 93–94.

15. Reid, *The United States of Europe*, 243.

16. See, for example, James W. Russell, *Double Standard: Social Policy in Europe and the United States* (Lanham, Md.: Rowman & Littlefield, 2006), 100–113.

17. International Monetary Fund figures calculated in purchasing power parity.

18. R. Veenhoven, *Average Happiness in 95 Nations 1995–2005*, World Database of Happiness, Rank Report 2006-1d, http://worlddatabaseofhappiness.eur.nl.

19. Speech online at http://www.nato.int/docu/speech/2002/s020121a.htm.

20. Reid, *The United States of Europe*, 184.

21. McCormick, *The European Superpower*, 27.

22. Schnabel, *The Next Superpower?* 59.

23. Speech to the UN Security Council on February 14, 2003; available online at http://www.ambafrance-us.org/news/statmnts/2003/villepin021403.asp

24. McCormick, *The European Superpower*, 130

25. Schnabel, *The Next Superpower?* 58.

26. "23 Nation Poll: Who Will Lead the World?" conducted in December 2004 by Globescan and the Program on International Policy Attitudes, available at http://www.worldpublicopinion.org.

27. "Europeans See the World as Americans Do, but Critical of U.S. Foreign Policy," 2002 survey sponsored by the German Marshall Fund and the Chicago Council on Foreign Relations, available at http://www.worldviews.org.

28. Quoted by Reid, *The United States of Europe*, 4.

29. Robert Kagan, *Of Paradise and Power: America and Europe in the New World Order* (New York: Knopf, 2004), 39.

30. Joseph S. Nye, *Soft Power: The Means to Success in World Politics* (New York: Public Affairs, 2004), 79.

31. *New York Times*, July 20, 2007, C3.

32. Fareed Zakaria, "Does the Future Belong to China?" *Newsweek*, May 9, 2005.

33. Oded Shenkar, *The Chinese Century* (Upper Saddle River, N.J.: Wharton School Publishing, 2006).

34. Fishman, "The Chinese Century," 24 ff., and *China Inc: How the Rise of the Next Superpower Challenges America and the World* (New York: Scribner, 2005).

35. In interview in *Johns Hopkins Magazine*, June 2007, 41.

36. Clyde Prestowitz, *Three Billion New Capitalists* (New York: Basic Books, 2005), 59.

37. Prestowitz, *Three Billion New Capitalists*, 74.

38. "There's Peril in the Parallels as China Takes a Top Spot," *New York Times*, October 20, 2007, B3.

39. C. Fred Bergsten et al., *China: The Balance Sheet* (New York: Public Affairs, 2006), 73.

40. Fishman, "The Chinese Century," 27.

41. Bergsten et al., *China*, 78.

42. Zakaria, "Does the Future Belong to China?"

43. Prestowitz, *Three Billion New Capitalists*, 68.

44. "China Threatens 'Nuclear Option' of Dollar Sales," October 8, 2007, *The Telegraph* (London), http://www.telegraph.co.uk.

45. Phillips, *American Theocracy*.

46. Quoted in "China Posts a Surplus Sure to Stir U.S. Alarm," *New York Times*, July 11, 2006, C1.

47. Prestowitz, *Three Billion New Capitalists*, xiii.

48. Todd Conover, "Capitalist Roaders," *New York Times Magazine*, July 2, 2006.

49. Bergsten et al., *China*, 130.

50. Joshua Kurlantzick, "China's Charm: Implications of Chinese Soft Power," Carnegie Endowment for International Peace *Policy Brief*, no. 47 (June 2006).

51. "Chinese Move to Eclipse U.S. Appeal in South Asia," *New York Times*, November 18, 2004, A1.

52. Jehangir Pocha, "Eyes Off the Prize," *In These Times*, February 2007, 38–41.

53. Bergsten and others, *China*, 131.

54. Iqbal Meer-Sharma, quoted in "China's Trade with Africa Carries a Price Tag," *New York Times*, August 21, 2007, A6.

55. Joshua Kurlantzick, "Beijing's Safari," Carnegie Endowment Policy Outlook, November 2006, http://www.CarnegieEndowment.org.

56. Sujian Guo, ed., *China's "Peaceful Rise" in the 21st Century: Domestic and International Conditions* (Burlington, Vt.: Ashgate, 2006), 1–2.

57. Cited in *New York Times*, December 9, 2006, A6.

58. Fan Xiaoyong, "Quanqiu yi jianli 140 suo kongzi xueyuan" (140 Confucius Colleges Have Been Established in Different Parts of the World), *Fazhi Wanbao* 3, no. 26 (2007).

59. "Foreigners Flock to Learn Chinese," BBC News online, January 6, 2006, http://news.bbc.co.uk/1/hi/world/asia-pacific/4594698.stm.

60. Sun Xia, "2006 nian zhongguo chuguo renshu da 3200 wan renci" (The Number of Chinese Visiting Foreign Countries Reached 32 Million Person-Times in 2006), Xinhua News Agency, December 31, 2006.

61. Kurlantzick, "China's Charm," 2.

62. "China Is Seen More Favourably than US or Russia," March 7, 2005, http://www.bbc.co.uk.

63. Ross Terrill, "China Is Not Just Rising, but Also Changing," *New York Times*, September 9, 2006, A27.

64. Thomas L. Friedman, *The World Is Flat: A Brief History of the Twenty-first Century* (New York: Farrar, Straus and Giroux, 2005), 127.

65. Shenkar, *The Chinese Century*, 161.

66. See the 2003 Goldman-Sachs paper "Dreaming with BRICS," http://www2.goldmansachs.com/insight/research/reports/99.pdf.

67. Gurcharan Das, "The Indian Model," *Foreign Affairs*, July/August 2006, 2–16.

68. *New York Times*, May 10, 2007, A6.

69. Karim Sadjadpour, "The Wrong Way to Contain Iran," *International Herald Tribune*, August 3, 2007.

70. Ray Takeyh, "Time for Détente with Iran," *Foreign Affairs*, March/April 2007, 24.

71. "Iran," *Foreign Policy*, March/April 2007, 41.

CHAPTER TEN

~

America and the World after the American Century

For if we should perish, the ruthlessness of the foe would be only the secondary cause of the disaster. The primary cause would be that the
strength of a great nation was directed by eyes too blind to see all the
hazards of the struggle; and the blindness would be induced not by some
accident of history but by hatred and vainglory.

—American theologian Reinhold Niebuhr, 1952[1]

In 1941, the conservative publisher Henry Luce called on the United States
to assume its role as a global power and to save the world from Nazism but
also from poverty and oppression. The same year, the liberal politician and
president Franklin Roosevelt outlined his vision of a world free from fear,
want, and hunger. The critical role played by the United States in the defeat
of Germany and Japan in World War II and its unparalleled strength and
prosperity at the end of the war helped assure the country's success in making the twentieth century an American one. In the second half of that century, the United States had the biggest economy, the most powerful military,
and the richest citizens. English became the world's language and the dollar
the world's currency. The United States led a boom in international trade
that increased by twentyfold. American-style democracy became a model
and aspiration for many countries in the world, and the number of democratic countries expanded from about twenty-five in 1950 to about one hundred in 2000, encompassing over half the world's population. With the collapse of the Soviet Union and European communism and the end of the

Cold War, the United States seemed to stand atop the world as the sole superpower. Many commentators and politicians talked about renewed efforts to reshape the world in America's image.

This triumphalism was sharply tempered by the attacks of September 11 and the utter failure of the U.S. effort to pacify and democratize Afghanistan and Iraq or to stem terrorism. A darker underside to the "American Century" started to come more clearly into focus after the fall of the Berlin Wall and the horrors of September 11. For several decades, American prosperity had been built on borrowed money, growing inequality, and mortgaged futures, and the bill was starting to come due. Furthermore, the very success of U.S. efforts to promote world trade and democratic politics had yielded unintended consequences. Newly affluent and democratic countries around the world were more independent and assertive and no longer needed or wanted the United States as protector or mentor. The perceived arrogance of the United States and its increasingly unilateral approach to world affairs intensified anti-Americanism. Other regions or countries, like the European Union and China, offered economic benefits without the hubris or militarism, so they became attractive alternatives to the United States as economic and political partners. As other countries grew less enamored of the United States and less willing to support it diplomatically, militarily, or economically, the U.S. position in the world weakened, and its domestic decline quickened.

What the United States Has Come To

This book has cataloged a litany of problems for the United States, beginning with the domestic and ending with the international. All these are connected and interact with each other. The most fundamental of all these problems are the economic ones, especially the multiple dimensions of debt, accumulated by both American citizens and the government living beyond their means. But if we dig down to the roots of this problem, one finds an even more basic issue, of American individualism and materialism. In some ways, these have been the cause of both America's success and its failure.

Individualism and acquisitiveness are central to American culture, have been part of Americans' sense of identity, and have been both celebrated and decried in American literature, film, and music. They are part and parcel of "American exceptionalism" for better or for worse. The good side of these characteristics is that they contributed to the settlement, exploration, and development of the United States and were at the core of the enterprise and diligence that built the country into the most affluent and dynamic society in world history. But both individualism and materialism can be carried to excess, a phenomenon that is recognized and censured by virtually every major philosophy and religion in the world. In the United States, which was virtually founded on these principles, they have themselves become almost a religion. And this is the root of the problem. The zeal for the individual and the material has marginalized community and humanity at substantial costs to both the United States and the rest of the world.

As we saw in chapter 1, much of the U.S. economic success of the past twenty years has been built on a foundation of sand. To be sure, the United States continues to have one of the highest standards of living in the world and among the world's most abundant supply and array of consumer goods. The United States is the world's biggest market for consumer goods and the biggest destination for the export of such goods. But it is increasingly obvious that this wealth is illusory, cannot be sustained, or both. It is illusory because much of it has been purchased on borrowed money. It cannot be sustained for several reasons: because other societal needs, like health care, Social Security, and infrastructure repair, can no longer be deferred; because the sources for borrowing are beginning to dry up; and because the planet cannot sustain the ravenous U.S. appetite for goods and resources. As geographer Jared Diamond, author of *Collapse*, warns, "Whether we get there willingly or not, we shall soon have lower consumption rates, because our present rates are unsustainable."[2]

Living on borrowed money has taken many forms in the United States and has led to multiple varieties of government and personal debts, deficits, and unfunded liabilities. The biggest and most obvious of these is the federal government debt, which, as we saw in chapter 1, is close to a historical high, even as a percentage of gross domestic product (GDP). In the past, federal deficits and debts have risen and fallen, eventually recovering with the tide of a rising economy. For numerous reasons, though, such a recovery is unlikely in the present unprecedented combination of circumstances:

- The increased sense of urgency in the United States about the hitherto neglected problems of poverty, education, health care, Medicare, Social Security, and infrastructure repair—all of which will require enormously expensive solutions.
- The high global prices of energy, especially petroleum, which will depress economic growth in the United States and are not likely to go away because of increased global demand for energy, especially from China.

- The increasing weakness of the dollar in international markets, especially under competition from the euro, which will make imported goods more expensive in the United States and further depress the U.S. standard of living.
- The high cost of U.S. defense spending and homeland security, accelerated by the global "war on terror" and the wars in Iraq and Afghanistan.

Even if the U.S. military presence in Iraq and Afghanistan is terminated, defense spending is likely to remain high, and all the remaining problems will persist in any case. Federal deficits seem destined to continue, adding to the growing pile of debt. So far, the United States has been able to live with this debt because other countries have been willing to loan the money to Washington through the purchase of U.S. Treasury notes and other government debt instruments. But this will continue only as long as those countries are confident that the U.S. government can pay back those investments. If they begin to doubt the stability and solidity of the U.S. economy, they will look elsewhere to invest their money, which will block up the "safety valve" that has allowed the United States to sustain deficit spending. Given the many problems the United States is facing, economic and otherwise, and the worsening international reputation of the United States, such a redirection of international investments out of the United States would seem imminent and is indeed already under way.

The federal debt is closely related to and in part caused by the other half of the "twin deficit"—the U.S. trade deficit—which is also at record-high levels both in absolute terms and as a percentage of GDP. The trade deficit will almost certainly diminish, especially if the dollar declines in value, but is unlikely to disappear in the near future. American trade dominance is being challenged by the rapid rise of the enormous trading blocs of the European Union and China, with India and others soon following. The American consumer continues to gobble up huge quantities of imported goods, while U.S. industry is producing very little that can be exported in return. What the United States does offer is financial services and investment instruments, but, as we have seen, these are increasingly resting on shifting and unstable sands, and foreign governments and banks are already beginning to move their currencies and investments out of the dollar and the United States. The only real solution is for the United States to stop importing so much, which will also lead to a reduction in the high and growing standard of living that Americans have come to expect. American expectations and their values will have to change.

Finally, there is the problem of personal debt and lack of personal and re-tirement savings by Americans. As we have seen, the U.S. personal savings rate is now below zero, the first time in history that it has dipped that low. Both personal bankruptcies and housing foreclosures are near record highs and are likely to accelerate with the subprime mortgage crisis, which will force several million Americans out of their homes. Most older Americans have nowhere near enough savings to manage a comfortable retirement.

All these aspects of debt can be traced back, ultimately, to the "excep-tionalism" of Americans that has included, at its core, individualism, mate-rialism, and distrust of government. Americans have come to take for granted the consumer goods, services, and homes that have made the coun-try one of the wealthiest in world history. But much of this wealth was gen-erated at a time of rapid economic growth and productivity, high-quality manufacturing, inexpensive supplies of energy, and global domination. All these are now diminished or gone.

Meanwhile, the U.S. government has not been able to keep up with the growing number of societal needs for health care, retirement, infrastructure repair, and so on, and American citizens have generally opposed the (much) higher taxes that would be required to take care of those needs. As we saw in chapter 2, Americans are much less likely than others in the world to believe that the government should take care of the poor or the needy in society and much more likely to believe that each individual should pull his or her own weight. This notion, grown more widespread and extreme in recent decades, has led to a situation where, compared to other wealthy countries, the United States has more poverty, more inequality, worse health care, more violence, and more people in prison. Much to the puzzlement (and even disgust) of peo-ple in other countries, Americans seem to accept all this with a kind of be-nign neglect. This individualism, combined with materialism, has taken its most extreme form in the proliferation of so-called stand-your-ground or shoot-first laws in the United States. These laws allow crime victims to use deadly force in situations that formerly would have subjected them to prose-cution for murder, including shooting to kill in defense of property.[3] For many looking at the United States from the outside, this is tantamount to placing a value on property ahead of human life and essentially conferring on individ-ual citizens the powers of police, judge, jury, and executioner.

The American citizen's absorption with material gain and the here and now has had impacts far beyond the economic realm. Just as they have not been unable to save for retirement, Americans have been unwilling to con-fer sufficient resources (through taxes) to provide for the broader and longer-term needs of society. Consequently, over the past generation the United

States has witnessed the steady decline of its schools, roads, and infrastructure. An inadequate system of social welfare has stranded millions of people in poverty, many of them without access to health care. The federal government has had to relinquish most welfare programs to the states, many of which are themselves strapped for resources. Economic inequality is the largest it has been in a generation and larger than in any other wealthy country. The two biggest programs in the federal budget, Social Security and Medicare, are being sustained only with borrowed money.

Even the hallowed U.S. political system has been hollowed out by self-interest and money. Most Americans distrust politicians and political leaders, feel they have little influence on politics, and do not even bother with the minimal political commitment of voting. These sentiments are understandable, however, given the powerful role of interest groups in policymaking and of money in elections. Economic inequality has contributed to political inequality, with the poor and marginalized far less likely to vote and participate politically than others. The high-handed behavior of President George W. Bush, often seeming to put himself above both U.S. law and international law, has contributed to the problem but is also symptomatic of a broader decay of a political system originally built on human rights, due process, and checks and balances.

It was this political system and the open and dynamic American economy of the postwar years that attracted emulation and admiration from other countries and peoples around the world. But the United States has lost this edge, both politically and economically, and it is no longer the only model or even the favored model of economic and political development in the eyes of others. The U.S. economic problems, especially its mounting debt, are increasingly a cause of concern among foreign bankers, investors, and government ministries and even in international financial institutions like the International Monetary Fund. The U.S. economy is no longer seen as the world's engine of economic growth, and the U.S. business model is also losing popularity. Even the U.S. political system, with its exaggerated role of money, its problematic presidential elections, and its short-term (two-year) perspectives, is now often viewed by others with disdain rather than admiration. So one major element of U.S. "soft-power" influence in the world, the attractiveness of its own national example, has steadily eroded. The hope expressed in the 1940s by both the conservative Henry Luce and the liberal Franklin Roosevelt, that the U.S. experiment could be replicated around the globe, no longer seems feasible or even desirable.

In the international arena, American exceptionalism, individualism, and materialism have taken the form of unilateralism. The country that was at the center of the postwar effort to build a world community based on coop-eration and law is now missing in action on the most important international agreements of the day. The United States has refused to sign treaties ad-dressing climate change, genocide, laws of the sea, the elimination of land mines, the rights of women and of children, and many others—most of which have been ratified by all the other major powers in the world. In every case, the United States claims some special, exceptional status that prevents it from adhering to the treaty. But from the point of view of people outside the United States, each one is another example of Americans putting their own narrow (usually economic) interests ahead of those of the global community.

American unilateralism and disregard for international law moved to a whole new level under the presidency of George W. Bush, who bypassed the United Nations with the invasion of Iraq. Bush also claimed exemption from international human rights law in U.S. conduct of the war on terror and in the treatment of prisoners of war and the employment of torture. Around the world, Bush's policies occasioned large-scale protests and widespread disgust. But these negative international feelings were increasingly directed not only at the Bush administration or the U.S. government but at the United States and its citizens as well. These policies were increasingly seen as symptomatic of broader problems within the United States. The muscular and activist for-eign policies of the Bush administration, which were meant to shore up America's flagging international reputation and influence, had exactly the opposite effect. America's soft power was in serious decline, both because of its own domestic problems and because of its decreasing ability to influence other countries on the basis of its example or its diplomacy.

The last remaining component of U.S. power, the "hard power" of its im-pressive military, was also proving to be ineffectual in accomplishing U.S. goals abroad. A generation earlier, the United States had been unable to achieve military victory in Vietnam, and its military adventure in Iraq proved to be even more counterproductive. Rather than eliminating terror-ism and establishing democracy in Iraq, after five years the world's preemi-nent military power was stalemated in a small, poor country with a haphaz-ard insurgency. By 2007, more than 3,000 Americans had died there, along with tens of thousands of Iraqis. The country was torn by civil war and sec-tarian violence, and the big cities were without electricity most of the day. The country had become a breeding ground and training camp for global ter-rorism, and the incidence of terrorism worldwide multiplied sharply after the U.S. invasion. The war intensified anti-Americanism in the Arab world and beyond.

Indeed, it is increasingly apparent that military power is not very effective at solving most of the world's biggest international problems by any country. During World War II and the Cold War, the major goal of the United States was to defeat or deter enemies with superior military force. Against Nazi Germany and the Soviet Union, that mission was accomplished. But the major threats to global peace and stability since that time are different: ethnic and religious militancy, terrorism, global warming, poverty, hunger, and epidemic diseases. These are not primarily military threats, and they cannot be solved by the application of military force. The United States discovered the limits of military power in Vietnam, Somalia, and Haiti, among others, and in almost every case of U.S. military intervention in the postwar period, U.S. goals were not ultimately achieved. The second-mightiest military power during the American Century, the Soviet Union, also found the military instrument to be increasingly ineffectual. Moscow was able to use the military to crush democratic or anticommunist movements in Hungary in 1956 and Czechoslovakia in 1968 but by the 1980s was (wisely) unwilling to use force to put down the popular and peaceful "velvet" revolutions that swept through Eastern Europe and brought communism to its knees. The Kremlin also decided that the decade-long war against the mujahideen in Afghanistan was unwinnable and began withdrawing its troops from that country in 1989. In all these cases—Vietnam, eastern Europe, Afghanistan, and now Iraq—the major power was trying to accomplish a goal that required substantial commitment and support from the local populations. When that is not forthcoming, military power alone cannot work. As General Rupert Smith points out in his book *The Utility of Force*, "No act of force will ever be decisive: winning the trial of strength will not deliver the will of the people, and at base that is the only true aim of any use of force in our modern conflicts."[4] Ironically, the Cold War, which was sustained by huge buildups in military weaponry, including tens of thousands of nuclear weapons, turned out as proof of the ineffectiveness of military power. The preeminent historian of the Cold War, John Lewis Gaddis, writes that one of the key lessons of that period was that "military strength, a defining characteristic of 'power' itself for the past five centuries, ceased to be that."[5]

So this was the situation in the early years of the new millennium: the United States had overwhelming military power, but that power was useless; it had squandered its soft power by neglecting the home front and acting unilaterally and with arrogance in the international arena; and the world itself had changed in ways that made the United States less influential and powerful. The nature of the world's most pressing problems meant that they could not be solved either by brute force or by one big superpower acting alone.

They required international, cooperative, and multilateral solutions. The United States was not particularly inclined to pursue such strategies, but even if it were, other countries were less willing to accept U.S. leadership. Other countries and regions had matured or emerged, in the European Union, China, India, and elsewhere, and most of them were more amenable to cooperative and multilateral approaches to international relations. They were in a better position than the United States to assume regional or global leadership and to take up the slack of the twentieth-century superpowers.

Given all the problems facing the United States, where is the country headed? At a minimum, the United States will suffer declines in wealth, standard of living, and global influence. But the picture painted in this book, of a bankrupt nation in domestic decline, courting disaster with its foreign policy, portends a far worse fate. Of course, nobody can predict the future, and some of the world's most intelligent people have been totally blindsided by world-changing events like Pearl Harbor, the sudden collapse of communism, and the terrorist attacks of September 11. Throughout this book, I have used authoritative evidence to describe and explain what is happening to the United States and its place in the world. But even the best evidence in the world is not much help in predicting the future. One can make a stab at prediction by extrapolating trends, but even so, that can produce only educated guesses about potential outcomes. Here, I define the range of possible developments for the United States by suggesting the worst case and the best case. Probably the reality will be somewhere in between.

The Worst Case

For the United States, the worst case could be unleashed by another major terrorist attack on U.S. territory. Some such attack seems almost inevitable, and some potential scenarios could bring unimaginable horror. As we saw in chapter 7 on the Iraq War, that war has provided both a training ground for terrorists and a stimulus to a huge increase in global terrorist activity and attacks. One goal of the Bush administration in launching this war was to weaken the terrorists and keep them away from the United States itself, but the consequences have been exactly the opposite. Terrorism has been strengthened, while the United States itself has remained extremely vulnerable, especially because of weak port security, the accessibility of nuclear materials in the former Soviet Union, and the vulnerability of industrial chemicals in the United States. Osama bin Laden is still at large, and we know that in 2003 he received religious sanction from a radical Saudi cleric to kill up to 10 million Americans with a nuclear or biological weapon. Al-Qaeda has significantly strengthened over the past two years, according to U.S. intelligence agencies.[6] Vice Admiral John Redd, chief of the U.S. National Counterterrorism Center, asserts that "we have very strong indicators that Al Qaeda is planning to attack the West and is likely to attack, and we are pretty sure about that." Hank Crumpton, recently retired as the State Department's coordinator of counterterrorism, agrees: "It's bad; it's going to come."[7]

The very worst case would be the detonation of a nuclear device in a densely populated urban area, which could potentially kill hundreds of thousands of American citizens or more. But even a much less deadly attack could have a devastating impact on the country. The September 11 attacks provoked a stock market collapse and contributed to a deepened and lengthened economic recession. Of course, before September 2001, the economy was already terribly fragile and vulnerable and deeply in debt. Afterward, it was even more so, and another attack could be a final blow that would bring down this U.S. economic house of cards. Fearful investors, both here and abroad, would withdraw funds from U.S. stocks and financial institutions and from holdings of the dollar.

Such a "run on the bank" would precipitate a more general financial and economic collapse in the United States. Bankruptcies and mortgage foreclosures, already at record levels before this new attack, would skyrocket, and millions of people would be forced out of their homes and into poverty. The U.S. government, no longer able to depend on foreigners to subsidize deficit spending, would have to cut government programs, including spending on Social Security, Medicare, education, health, and welfare—programs that are already strapped or in the red. This would lead to broader and deeper poverty in the United States and sharpen social and political tensions.

Perhaps what is most worrying of all about this scenario is the political consequences of such a human and economic catastrophe. When people are frightened or insecure, they are more concerned about order and security than about human rights and freedom. There was already a worrisome strain of authoritarianism in the American political culture, and this was revealed in the aftermath of September 11. In the fear and rage following the collapse of the twin towers, Americans accepted, almost without blinking, governmental restrictions on their movement, activities, and privacy and even on the bedrock democratic principle of habeas corpus. The U.S. Congress passed, almost without debate, the USA Patriot Act with its questionable limits on civil rights and a war authorization bill that gave the president powers as commander in chief that were almost unlimited in scope and in time. The mass media meekly accepted the administration's assertions about weapons of mass destruction in Iraq and its justifications for the war. Academics were afraid to speak out. Another terrorist attack, in combination with imminent economic collapse, would almost surely lead to an even stronger assertion of executive authority, and who would be there to oppose this? A beleaguered government in a crisis of such magnitude might even be tempted to suspend the Constitution or to invoke martial law. The long U.S. experiment with democracy would be at an end.

This whole scenario is depressing as well as frightening, largely because the possibility seems so real. But it is not inevitable, so let's turn to a rosier, best-case scenario.

The Best Case

A best-case scenario for the future of the United States would have to begin with new political leadership. The George W. Bush administration has been a catastrophe for the economic and social health of the country and for America's standing in the world. Congress has not been much better. But new leadership will not reverse or solve the problems of American decline. As pointed out time and again in this book, the problems the country is facing are systemic and deep seated and will not disappear even with radical shifts in direction or policy. The Bush administration has put the final nail in the coffin of the American Century but is not responsible for the underlying problems that have been building for several generations.

The first thing a new president could do, however, would be to mend American relations with the rest of the world and to temper the unilateralism, hubris, and militarism that have made it so difficult for the United States to work with other countries in solving pressing global issues. This is particularly urgent precisely because the United States is in decline. As historians like Paul Kennedy and Niall Ferguson have pointed out, periods of major power decline are inherently unstable and dangerous for the whole world. Thus, it is all the more imperative now, for the world's sake, that the United States have at its helm a leader who recognizes and accepts a more limited global role for the United States and who is willing to engage other countries from a position of equality rather than domination and with the goal of cooperation rather than imposition. A quarter of a century ago, in *The Rise and Fall of the Great Powers*, Paul Kennedy suggested that the United States would "a long time into the future" eventually decline to its "natural" share of the world's wealth and power. Given the country's large size, population, and natural resources, this should be "perhaps 16 or 18 percent of the world's wealth and power"[8] rather than the 30 to 40 percent held by the

United States from the beginning to the end of the American Century. The United States is now moving toward that more "natural" position in the world. It will be a substantial test of U.S. leadership to manage that decline.

Accepting a reduced and more cooperative role in the world will require wisdom and statesmanship but will actually find considerable support among U.S. citizens. Recent polls show that only about 8 percent of Americans believed that the United States should be the preeminent world leader in solving international problems. More than 70 percent are opposed to the United States playing the role of world policeman. The overwhelming majority believe that the United States should do its share in efforts to solve international problems together with other countries. Solid majorities of Americans believe that the United Nations should be significantly more powerful in world affairs, and majorities favor U.S. ratification of the treaty on the International Criminal Court, the Kyoto treaty on climate change, the Comprehensive Nuclear Test Ban Treaty, and the convention banning land mines.[9] Other surveys by the Pew Global Attitudes project have shown a similar preference by Americans for the country to play a less dominant and more cooperative role in world affairs. In every Pew survey since 1993, no more than 12 percent of Americans want the United States to be "the single world leader."[10] A new leadership in Washington could capitalize on and channel such sentiments in guiding the United States toward this new global position.

Maybe an even more difficult task for any U.S. leader will be to preside over and supervise a decline in the U.S. standard of living. Such a decline seems inevitable, given that both the U.S. government and the American citizen have been living well beyond their means for several decades. As we have seen, the admirable U.S. standard of living, the tendency to buy and consume more than Americans produce and sell, and the extravagant spending of the federal government have all essentially been underwritten by foreigners. But this is already changing and will mean that government and citizens alike will have to start living within their means. For most Americans, this will mean declining incomes, reduced consumption, boosted savings, and deferred gratification. These will be wrenching changes for most Americans and not the kind that politicians like to promote. The last American president to call on his constituents to live more frugally and tighten their belts—Jimmy Carter—was ridiculed for his efforts and lasted only one term in office.

A reduced standard of living for American citizens also has the potential to "autocorrect" many of the country's current problems. Less consumption, for example, will mean less of a burden on the world's resources, and fewer carbon emissions that contribute to global warming. Higher gas prices, in combination with diminished incomes, will create greater incentives to produce energy-efficient cars and technologies, helping to improve the environment. A declining dollar will help boost U.S. exports, alleviating the balance-of-trade deficit. So some of America's problems can be mitigated somewhat—but at the difficult cost of reduced affluence.

In the best-case scenario, a less militaristic, unilateralist, and interventionist international role for the United States will allow a reduction in U.S. military spending, which should free up substantial resources to begin repairing the badly damaged physical and social infrastructure of the United States. More attention to education, for example, would go a long way toward solving many of the country's domestic problems. Better schools and broader access to quality education would help reduce the shameful poverty and inequality in the United States. It would stimulate political participation, including voting, especially from minorities. Broader political participation could serve to reinvigorate the political system and relieve the stranglehold of money on politics. Even more important, perhaps, better education would make American citizens more informed about their own country and its problems and about other countries and theirs. It could make Americans more critical and intellectually discriminating and less susceptible to propaganda, mendacity, and fundamentalism of all stripes.

A revitalized political system could bring the public back into discussions of important domestic and global issues and help restore a sense of common purpose and community, so long missing in an America divided and contentious, with a political system monopolized by special interests and big money. The United States could try, once again, to achieve the goals of equality, security, and civil liberties articulated by the founding fathers in the eighteenth century, the global "good Samaritanism" advocated by Henry Luce in 1941, and the social justice and compassion called for by Franklin Roosevelt, who in 1932 proclaimed, "In these days of difficulty, we Americans everywhere must and shall choose the path of social justice, the path of faith, the path of hope and the path of love toward our fellow men."[11] These big issues, so long absent in U.S. political discourse, desperately need to be brought back into the political arena.

This optimistic scenario, however, also requires a kind of psychological shift by American citizens. In 1941, Americans were not as affluent, confident, and self-assured as they are now. Indeed, the appeals of both Luce and Roosevelt were for Americans to become more assertive and active in world affairs. But over the course of the American Century, the pendulum swung far in the opposite direction, to the point where many Americans and even their president assumed a kind of divine mission for the United States to lead, guide, and even govern the world. American exceptionalism morphed into excesses of individualism, ethnocentrism, arrogance, and a sense of entitlement. At the beginning of the American Century, the preeminent American theologian, Reinhold Niebuhr, cautioned against such excessive self-confidence and worried that U.S. idealism could degenerate into fanaticism. What the world needs now, even more than in Niebuhr's time, is an America willing to recognize its own shortcomings, to listen to the voice and ideals of others, and to adjust its own interests and needs to those of the broader global community. As Niebuhr argued, open-mindedness is not "a virtue of people who don't believe anything. It is a virtue of people who know . . . that their beliefs are not absolutely true."[12] Now, more than ever, the world needs a more humble American.

The World after the American Century

For the United States, the end of U.S. global hegemony will cause many problems but also open new opportunities. The same could be said for the rest of the world. The decline of a major world power will be destabilizing for the international system—indeed it already is so. But it also raises the possibilities of new forms of international interaction and new ways to address global problems. The scale and scope of those problems and the fact that many of them have gotten worse over the past few decades suggest how insufficient were both the bipolar international system of the Cold War era and the unipolar one after that. The bipolar balance of power between the United States and the Soviet Union did manage to avoid a thermonuclear war, which some scientists thought could lead to extinction of all life on the planet—no small accomplishment. On the other hand, during the Cold War, the world experienced growing poverty and inequality, continued outbreaks of national and ethnic conflict, increasing strains on the environment, and a growing militarization of the planet. The period of U.S. dominance since the end of the Cold War has not seen any improvement in any of those problems while adding new ones: increased intensity and scope of terrorism and growing tension and conflict in the Middle East.

There has been much debate among scholars and journalists about what the world might look like without the United States as a superpower (though there are many who believe that the United States will continue in that role). One option is the return to a "multipolar" world, where the United States is simply one major power among many others, including China, the European Union, Russia, and possibly Japan, India, Brazil, South Africa,

Iran, or others. A variant of this theme envisions a global "concert of democracies" that has the United States allied with other liberal democracies "to institutionalize and ratify the 'democratic peace,'"[13] though to me this does not seem much different from the old arrangements. The British historian Niall Ferguson worries that the disappearance of the United States as a global hegemon will lead not to a multipolar world but instead to "apolarity"—a global vacuum of power creating "a new Dark Age" that will be far worse, in his view, than "the good old balance of power."[14] This vision could stand in as the global counterpart to our domestic worst-case scenario discussed previously.

All these predictions are based on a view of the world in which power continues as the primary medium of exchange and where the nation-state is the main repository of power. But the world has changed a lot in the past few decades and in ways that suggest that the nation-state may no longer be the central player in the global system. Globalization has eroded national boundaries while creating new problems that transcend national boundaries and that are not susceptible to purely national solutions. Global warming, climate change, air and water pollution, energy and resource shortages, global poverty and hunger, epidemic diseases, nuclear proliferation, terrorism—none of these originate in any one country, and none of them can be solved by even the most wealthy and powerful nation-states.

In fact, the United States has been reduced as a superpower by a one-two body blow of these global forces. The globalization of trade and finance allowed the United States to live beyond its means by accumulating enormous debts to other countries. The tragedies of September 11 and the Iraq quagmire are a function of several aspects of globalization: the spread of transnational forces, including terrorist ones; the global reach of technology (including airplanes and cell phones); and the increased permeability of national borders.

If the primary purpose of the nation-state is to provide for people's well-being and happiness, it is increasingly inadequate to the task. People are recognizing this and expressing discontent with national governments all over the world, including in most democratic countries. Global surveys conducted between 1997 and 2002 found that most people felt their countries were not governed by the will of the people, and they expressed little trust in their parliaments, political parties, and governments. In most countries, not just in the United States, a majority of the population feels that their government "was run by a few big interests looking out for themselves." There is a kind of global crisis of political legitimacy that is expressed as distrust in national governments. University of Southern California professor Manuel Castells, author of *The Network Society*, contends that this crisis of legitimacy is a result of "the increasing inability of the political system anchored in the nation-state to represent citizens in the effective practice of global governance and the ascendance of global governance as an increasingly essential component of national and local government."[15] The nation-state is losing out in effectiveness and popularity to other forms of governance, including grassroots organizations, nongovernmental organizations (NGOs), transnational corporations and movements, and intergovernmental organizations (IGOs). Furthermore, "transnational collective action" is challenging even these institutions as well as the nation-state.[16]

Addressing all these developments is far beyond the scope of this book, which focuses on only one aspect of the shift in global power—the decline of the United States. But U.S. decline is both a consequence and a cause of these broader global changes. Just as American citizens need to recognize the problems and weaknesses of U.S. society, they must begin to face and understand these global transformations as well. They are already affecting American citizens, so understanding the broader picture will help American citizens in making the difficult transition away from global superpower. Recognition and understanding of these trends, both in the United States and globally, are the first step toward dealing with them and adjusting to them.

In his prescient and influential book *Jihad vs. McWorld*, published in 1995, Benjamin Barber saw the power of the nation-state being pulled apart from two different directions: from below by the forces of ethnic and religious nationalism ("jihad") and from above by the growing power of multinational corporations ("McWorld").[17] Barber was on to something, and in the years since then, the world has had to come face-to-face with both processes. Americans, especially, have been shocked and hurt both by real jihad, on September 11, and by globalization, taking the form of layoffs, outsourcing, and declining wages. Religious fundamentalism and transnational terrorism pose serious threats to the United States and to peace and stability across the globe. Many multinational corporations have annual proceeds that exceed the gross national products of small countries and have political and economic influence that often dwarfs that of the countries in which they operate.

But transnational terrorism and multinational corporations are only two elements of a much broader pattern of change in global governance.[18] Nation-states, which have dominated international politics for several centuries, face increasing competition in power, influence, and popularity from "nonstate actors," including tens of thousands of NGOs and IGOs. Examples of IGOs include both global organizations like the United Nations and its many affiliates and regional organizations like the European Union and the Shanghai Cooperation Organization. As we have seen, both varieties are posing challenges to the dominant role of the United States but also to the power of other nation-states. The European Union has required member states to relinquish a considerable element of national sovereignty. And it has increasingly fostered, especially among young people, a sense of European rather than national identity.

The growth of NGOs has been even more rapid and impressive both within countries and across national borders, reflecting the tendency of people to join together in finding solutions to problems outside of government. There are as many as a half million NGOs in the United States alone. Many national NGOs are very local and particularistic, like U.S. neighborhood associations that work on community development and beautification, legal assistance organizations that provide services to the poor, or "peace communities" in Latin America that try to foster peace, community, and stability in their villages to insulate themselves from surrounding violence induced by governments, insurgents, or criminals.[19]

Other NGOs have broader goals, such as those regarding human rights, the environment, or social justice, that often transcend borders. When an NGO has programs or affiliates in multiple countries, it is referred to as an international NGO (INGO), and these have become especially prolific, growing from fewer than 400 a century ago to more than 25,000 today. Some of these have become important actors in international politics, often challenging governments or sparking international negotiations that have led to consequential treaties. The International Campaign to Ban Landmines, an NGO coalition, was the prime mover behind the adoption of the Mine Ban Treaty of 1997, for which the organization won the Nobel Peace Prize. Environmental NGOs were also instrumental in the development and passage of international protocols on the ozone layer and on climate change.

These INGOs are part of a global movement that is challenging the authority of national governments but also bringing together people from different countries to work on issues that affect all people and that transcend national boundaries. Often their work is sustained by young people and made possible by the Internet and the increasing ease of international travel. Such interactions inevitably reduce ethnocentrism and enhance friendships among citizens in different countries, even if their governments are not so friendly with each other. Some observers refer to this phenomenon as the emergence of a "global civil society." This trend, too, is undermining the power, legitimacy, and authority of the nation-state.

The end of the American Century will not be easy for Americans and will disrupt the rest of the world too. Americans will have to live with less and adjust to a reduced role in the world. But a decline in U.S. materialism, consumption, and power could open up new opportunities for global cooperation and for a more peaceful and sustainable world. If Americans are at the same time benevolent, as Luce and Roosevelt asked them to be, and more humble, as Niebuhr suggested, the United States could continue to play an important role in the world and make it better. So, in the end, the news is not all that bad. Because even if the United States is not yet working out according to the vision of Roosevelt or Luce, there are millions of American citizens doing good works in charities, voluntary associations, and NGOs, and they are often interacting with similar people in other countries. One can take heart from the sentiments expressed by the American novelist and poet Alice Walker:

> When it is all too much, when the news is so bad meditation itself feels useless, and a single life feels too small a stone to offer on the altar of peace, find a human sunrise. Find those people who are committed to changing our scary reality. Human sunrises are happening all over the earth, at every moment. People gathering, people working to change the intolerable, people coming in their robes and sandals or in their rags and bare feet, and they are singing, or not, and they are chanting, or not. But they are working to bring peace, light, compassion to the infinitely frightening downhill side of human life.[20]

The United States may be at the end of its era of great power, and the nation-state may also be running out of steam. But as another American novelist, William Faulkner, once said in a much earlier commencement address, "What's wrong with this world is, it's not finished yet."[21]

Notes

1. Reinhold Niebuhr, *The Irony of American History* (New York: Scribner's, 1952), 174.

2. Jared Diamond, "What's Your Consumption Factor?" *New York Times*, January 2, 2008, A19; Jared Diamond, *Collapse: How Societies Choose to Fail or Succeed* (New York: Viking, 2005).

3. "15 States Expand Victims' Rights on Self-Defense," *New York Times*, August 7, 2006, A1.

4. General Rupert Smith, *The Utility of Force: The Art of War in the Modern World* (New York: Knopf, 2007); cited in review in the *New York Times*, January 18, 2007.

5. John Lewis Gaddis, *The Cold War: A New History* (New York: Penguin, 2005), 263.

6. From the 2007 U.S. National Intelligence Estimate, reported in "Bush Advisers See a Failed Strategy against Al Qaeda," *New York Times*, July 18, 2007, A1.

7. Quoted in *Newsweek*, September 3, 2007, 25 and 33.

8. Paul Kennedy, *The Rise and Fall of the Great Powers* (New York: Random House, 1987), 533–34.

9. Zia Mian, "A New American Century?" *Foreign Policy in Focus*, May 4, 2005.

10. Andrew Kohut and Bruce Stokes, *America against the World* (New York: Times Books, 2006), 204.

11. Campaign Address, Detroit, Michigan, October 2, 1932.

12. Cited in Peter Beinart, "The Rehabilitation of the Cold-War Liberal," *New York Times Magazine*, April 30, 2006, 42.

13. John Ikenberry and Anne Marie Slaughter, "Forging a World of Liberty under Law: U.S. National Security in the 21st Century," Final Paper of the Princeton Project on National Security, Princeton University, 2006.

14. Niall Ferguson, "A World without Power," *Foreign Policy*, July/August 2004, 32–39.

15. Manuel Castells, "Global Governance and Global Politics," *PS: Political Science and Politics*, January 2005, 10.

16. Donatella della Porta and Sidney Tarrow, eds., *Transnational Protest and Global Activism* (Lanham, Md.: Rowman & Littlefield, 2005), 2.

17. Benjamin Barber, *Jihad vs. McWorld* (New York: Times Books, 1995).

18. A landmark study addressing these phenomena is Robert O. Keohane and Joseph S. Nye, *Power and Interdependence* (New York: Longman, 2001).

19. See, for example, Dana Mason, *Living Peace in the Midst of War: The Experience of the Colombian Peace Communities*, Bologna Center M.A.I.A. thesis, Johns Hopkins School of Advanced International Studies, 2003.

20. In a commencement address to Naropa University, *New York Times*, June 10, 2007, 20.

21. In his address to the graduating class at Pine Manor Junior College, Wellesley, Massachusetts, June 8, 1953; this quotation and these sentiments appear in a convocation address delivered by Dean Lynn Franken at Beloit College in August 2005.

Bibliography

"15 States Expand Victims' Rights on Self-Defense." *New York Times*, August 7, 2006, A1.

The "2006 Environmental Performance Index." Produced jointly by Yale and Columbia universities, *New York Times*, January 23, 2006, A3.

Abramowitz, Michael. "Bush's Unpopularity in Europe Hangs over Summit." *Washington Post*, June 21, 2006, A15.

Adler, Jerry. "What the World Thinks of America." *Newsweek*, July 11, 1983, 45.

Allison, Kevin. "World Turning Its Back on Brand America." *Financial Times* (London), July 31, 2005.

American Electronics Association. *Losing the Competitive Advantage? The Challenge for Science and Technology in the United States*. Washington, D.C.: American Electronics Association, 2005.

American Political Science Association. *American Democracy in an Age of Rising Inequality*. Washington, D.C.: American Political Science Association, 2004.

Amnesty International USA. "Death Penalty Fact Sheets." http://www.amnestyusa.org/abolish/juveniles.html

Andrews, Edmund. "Trade Deficit Hits Record, Threatening U.S. Growth," *New York Times*, December 15, 2005, C3.

Andrulis, Dennis, Lisa Duchon, and Hailey Reid. *Before and after Welfare Reform*. State University of New York Downstate Medical Center, July 2003. Online.

Anelauskas, Valdas. *Discovering America As It Is*. Atlanta: Clarity, 1999.

Anonymous (Michael Scheur). *Imperial Hubris: Why the West Is Losing the War on Terrorism*. Washington, D.C.: Brassey's, 2004.

"Arab Attitudes toward Political and Social Issues, Foreign Policy and the Media." 2005 poll conducted by Professor Shibley Telhami, University of Maryland, and Zogby International. http://www.bsos.umd.edu/sadat/pub/arab-attitudes-2005.htm

Bagdikian, Ben. *The New Media Monopoly*. Boston: Beacon Press, 2004.

Baker, James A. III, and Lee H. Hamilton, cochairs. *The Iraq Study Group Report*. New York: Vintage, 2006.

Balch, Stephen H., and Rita Zurcher. "The Dissolution of General Higher Education: 1914–1993." Report from the National Association of Scholars. http://www.nas.org/reports/disogened/disogened_full.pdf

Barber, Benjamin. *Jihad vs. McWorld*. New York: Times Books, 1995.

Barry, Patricia. "Coverage for All." *AARP Bulletin*, July–August 2006, 8.

Barton, Paul, and Archie LaPointe. *Learning by Degrees*. Princeton, N.J.: Educational Testing Service, 1995.

Beinart, Peter. "The Rehabilitation of the Cold-War Liberal." *New York Times Magazine*, April 30, 2006.

Benjamin, Daniel, and Steven Simon. *The Next Attack*. New York: Times Books, 2005.

Bergsten, C. Fred, et al. *China: The Balance Sheet*. New York: Public Affairs, 2006.

Bernasek, Anna. "Income Inequality, and Its Cost." *New York Times*, June 25, 2006, B4.

———. "The State of Research Isn't All That Grand." *New York Times*, September 3, 2006, Business section, 3.

Blomquist, Kerry. "Help Them Live without Fear." *Indianapolis Star*, December 30, 2007.

Boehlert, Eric. *Lapdogs: How the Press Rolled over for Bush*. New York: Free Press, 2006.

Broken Engagement: America's Civic Health Index. Report of the National Conference on Citizenship. Washington, D.C.: National Conference on Citizenship, 2006.

Brooks, Stephen. *As Others See Us*. Guelph, Ontario: Broadview, 2006.

Brzezinski, Zbigniew. *Second Chance: Three Presidents and the Crisis of American Superpower*. New York: Basic Books, 2007.

Bureau of Labor Education. University of Maine. "The U.S. Health Care System: Best in the World, or Just the Most Expensive?" 2001. http://dll.umaine.edu/ble/U.S.%20HCweb.pdf

"Bush Advisers See a Failed Strategy against Al Qaeda." *New York Times*, July 18, 2007, A1.

Byrd, Robert C. *Losing America: Confronting a Reckless and Arrogant Presidency*. New York: Norton, 2004.

Clarke, Richard. *Against All Enemies*. New York: Free Press, 2004.

Camp, Nina, Michael O'Hanlon, and Amy Unikewicz. "The State of Iraq: An Update." *New York Times*, December 20, 2006.

Carnegie Task Force on Meeting the Needs of Young Children. *Starting Points: Meeting the Needs of Our Youngest Children.* New York: Carnegie Corporation, 1994.

Caryl, Christian. "Iraq's Young Blood." *Newsweek*, January 22, 2007, 25–32.

Castells, Manuel. "Global Governance and Global Politics." *PS: Political Science and Politics*, January 2005.

"Catholics, Protestants, Urge New Iraq Policy." *The Christian Century*, June 1, 2004.

Center for Responsive Politics. http://www.opensecrets.com

"China Is Seen More Favourably than US or Russia." March 7, 2005. http://www.bbc.co.uk

"China Posts a Surplus Sure to Stir U.S. Alarm." *New York Times*, July 11, 2006, C1.

"Chinese Move to Eclipse U.S. Appeal in South Asia." *New York Times*, November 18, 2004, A1.

"Chirac Tells Bush to Keep His Nose Out." *Daily Telegraph* (London), June 29, 2004.

Climate Action Network. http://www.climnet.org

Congressional Research Service. *CRS Report for Congress: The Cost of Iraq, Afghanistan, and Other Global War on Terror Operations since 9/11.* Washington, D.C.: U.S. Government Printing Office, November 2007.

Conover, Todd. "Capitalist Roaders." *New York Times Magazine*, July 2, 2006.

Crawford, Craig. *Attack the Messenger: How Politicians Turn You against the Media.* Boulder, Colo.: Rowman & Littlefield, 2005.

Cultural Diplomacy: The Linchpin of Public Diplomacy. Report of the Advisory Committee on Cultural Diplomacy, U.S. Department of State, September 2005.

Danner, Mark. *Torture and Truth: America, Abu Ghraib, and the War on Terror.* New York: New York Review of Books, 2004.

— —. "Taking Stock of the Forever War." *New York Times Magazine*, September 11, 2005, 44–87.

———. "Iraq: The War of the Imagination." *New York Review of Books*, December 21, 2006.

Das, Gurcharan. "The India Model." *Foreign Affairs*, July/August 2006, 2–16.

Dash, Eric. "Off to the Races Again, Leaving Many Behind." *New York Times*, April 9, 2006, sec. 3, p. 1.

Davis, Karen, et al. *Mirror, Mirror on the Wall: An International Update on the Comparative Performance of American Health Care.* 2007. http://www.commonwealthfund.org

Declining by Degrees: Higher Education at Risk. PBS Home Video, 2005.

Della Porta, Donatella, and Sidney Tarrow, eds. *Transnational Protest and Global Activism.* Lanham, Md.: Rowman & Littlefield, 2005.

Delli Carpini, Michael X., and Scott Keeter. *What Americans Know about Politics and Why It Matters.* New Haven, Conn.: Yale University Press, 1989.

Diamond, Jared. *Collapse: How Societies Choose to Fail or Succeed.* New York: Viking, 2005.

———. "What's Your Consumption Factor?" *New York Times*, January 2, 2008, A19

"Diplomas Count." *Education Week*, June 22, 2006.

Donelan, Karen, et al. "Whatever Happened to the Health Insurance Crisis in the United States?" *Journal of the American Medical Association* 276, no. 16 (1996): 1346–50.

"Dreaming with BRICS." Report produced by Goldman-Sachs. 2003. http://www2 .goldmansachs.com/insight/research/reports/99.pdf

Economic Policy Institute. *The State of Working America 2004/2005.* http://www .epi.org

Ehrenreich, Barbara. *Nickel and Dimed: On (Not) Getting By in America.* New York: Metropolitan, 2001.

Elkus, Adam. "Surging Right into bin Laden's Hands." *Foreign Policy in Focus*, February 2, 2007. http://www.fpif.org

Eurobarometer surveys at the EU website. http://ec.europa.eu/public_opinion

"Europeans See the World as Americans Do, but Critical of U.S. Foreign Policy." 2002 survey sponsored by the German Marshall Fund and the Chicago Council on Foreign Relations. http://www.worldviews.org

Faulkner, William. "Address to the Graduating Class Pine Manor Junior College," Wellesley, Massachusetts, June 1953.

Federal Bureau of Investigation. *Crime in the United States 2004: Uniform Crime Reports.* Washington, D.C.: Federal Bureau of Investigation, 2005

Fein, Oliver. "The Influence of Social Class on Health Status: American and British Research on Health Inequalities." *Journal of General Internal Medicine* 10, no. 10 (1995): 577–86.

Ferguson, Niall. *Colossus: The Price of America's Empire.* New York: Penguin, 2004.

———. "A World without Power." *Foreign Policy*, July/August 2004, 32–39.

Fishman, Ted C. "The Chinese Century." *New York Times Magazine*, July 4, 2004, 24 ff.

———. *China Inc: How the Rise of the Next Superpower Challenges America and the World.* New York: Scribner, 2005.

Flannery, Tim. *The Weather Makers.* New York: Atlantic Monthly Press, 2006.

Forster, Michael, and Marco Mira d'Ercole. *Income Distribution and Poverty in OECD Countries in the Second Half of the 1990s.* OECD Working Paper no. 22, March 2005. http://www.oecd.org/dataoecd/48/9/34483698.pdf

"Fraying Nation, Divided Opinions." *Washington Post*, May 13, 2007, B2.

Freedom House data. http://www.freedomhouse.org

Friedman, Thomas L. *The World Is Flat: A Brief History of the Twenty-first Century.* New York: Farrar, Straus and Giroux, 2005.

Fukuyama, Francis. "The End of History?" *The National Interest*, summer 1989.

Fuller, Graham E. "'Old Europe' or 'Old America'?" *New Perspectives Quarterly*, spring 2003. http://www.digitalnpq.org/archive/2003_spring/fuller.html

Gaddis, John Lewis. *The Cold War: A New History.* New York: Penguin, 2005.

Galbraith, Peter. *The End of Iraq.* New York: Simon and Schuster, 2006.

Galston, William. "Political Knowledge, Political Engagement, and Civic Education." *Annual Review of Political Science*, June 2001.

"Gangs of Iraq." *America at a Crossroads.* PBS, aired April 17, 2007.

Gettleman, Jeffrey. "Across Africa, a Sense that U.S. Power Isn't So Super." *New York Times*, December 24, 2006, sec. 4, p. 1.

Greenhouse, Steven. "Many Participants in Workfare Take the Place of City Workers." *New York Times*, April 13, 1998, A1.

Guo, Sujian, ed. *China's "Peaceful Rise" in the 21st Century: Domestic and International Conditions*. Burlington, Vt.: Ashgate, 2006.

Hamilton, Lee. "Deficit Keeps America Living on Borrowed Time." *Indianapolis Star*, April 10, 2006, A8.

Hammond, Andrew. *What the Arabs Think of America*. Westport, Conn.: Greenwood, 2007.

Harris polls at Harris Interactive. http://www.harrisinteractive.com

Hirsch, Seymour M. "Torture at Abu Ghraib." *New Yorker*, May 10, 2004.

"Hot Politics." PBS *Frontline*, April 29, 2007.

Ikenberry, G. John, ed. *America Unrivalled: The Future of the Balance of Power*. Ithaca, N.Y.: Cornell University Press, 2002.

Ikenberry, John, and Anne Marie Slaughter. "Forging a World of Liberty under Law: U.S. National Security in the 21st Century." Final Paper of the Princeton Project on National Security, Princeton University, 2006.

"In New Congress, Pork May Linger." *New York Times*, November 26, 2006, 1, 22.

Institute for Labor Research. http://www.laborresearch.org

Institute for Taxation and Monetary Policy. http://www.ctj.org/pdf/gwbdata.pdf

International Institute for Democracy and Electoral Assistance. http://www.idea.int/vt/survey/voter_turnout_pop2-2.cfm

International Monetary Fund. "Currency Composition of Official Foreign Exchange Reserves." http://www.imf.org/external/np/sta/cofer/eng/cofer.pdf

International Social Justice Project. *ISJP Codebook*. Edited by Duane Alwin. Ann Arbor, Mich.: Institute for Social Research, 1991.

"Iran." *Foreign Policy*, March/April 2007, 41.

Iraq Index. Washington, D.C.: Brookings Institution, 2008. http://www.brookings.edu/saban/~/media/Files/Centers/Saban/Iraq%20Index/index.pdf

Ivry, Bob. "Foreclosures May Hit 1.5. Million in U.S. Housing Bust." March 12, 2007. http://www.bloomberg.com

Johnson, Chalmers. "The Arithmetic of America's Military Bases Abroad." *History News Network*. January 19, 2004. http://hnn.us/articles/3097.html

———. *The Sorrows of Empire: Militarism, Secrecy and the End of the Republic*. New York: Metropolitan Books, 2004.

Kagan, Robert. *Of Paradise and Power: America and Europe in the New World Order*. New York: Knopf, 2004.

Keillor, Garrison. "Mark Their Names." *International Herald Tribune*, October 2, 2006.

Kennan, George. "The Sources of Soviet Conduct." *Foreign Affairs* (1947).

Kennedy, Paul. *The Rise and Fall of the Great Powers*. New York: Random House, 1987.

————. "The Eagle Has Landed." *Financial Times* (London), February 2, 2002.

Keohane, Robert O., and Joseph S. Nye. *Power and Interdependence*. New York: Longman, 2001.

Kinzer, Stephen. *Overthrow: America's Century of Regime Change from Hawaii to Iraq*. New York: Times Books, 2006.

Kohut, Andrew. "America's Image in the World." Findings from the Pew Global Attitudes Project." Testimony before the Committee on Foreign Affairs of the U.S. House of Representatives, March 14, 2007.

Kohut, Andrew, and Bruce Stokes. *America against the World: How We Are Different and Why We Are Disliked*. New York: Times Books, 2006.

Kozol, Jonathan. *Illiterate America*. New York: Doubleday, 1985.

Krieger, Zvika. "Iraq's Universities Near Collapse." *Chronicle of Higher Education*, May 18, 2007, A35–A39.

Krugman, Paul. "The Medical Money Pit." *New York Times*, April 15, 2005, A19.

Kurlantzick, Joshua. "China's Charm: Implications of Chinese Soft Power." Carnegie Endowment for International Peace *Policy Brief*, no. 47, June 2006. http://www.carnegieendowment.org

————. "Beijing's Safari." Carnegie Endowment for International Peace *Policy Outlook* (China Program). November 2006. http:// www.carnegiewendowment.org

Lane, Charles. "5-4 Supreme Court Abolishes Juvenile Executions." *Washington Post*, March 2, 2005, A1.

Leopold, Evelyn. "Annan Challenges U.S. Doctrine of Preventive Action." Reuters, September 23, 2003.

"Life in Iraq." http://news.bbc.co.uk/2/shared/spl/hi/in_depth/post_saddam_iraq/html/2.stm

Lipset, Seymour Martin. *American Exceptionalism: A Double-Edged Sword*. New York: Norton, 1996.

"Lorry Bomb Kills Children in School." *Times* (London), April 3, 2007.

Lowenstein, Roger. "The Inequality Conundrum," *New York Times Magazine*, June 10, 2007, 12.

Luce, Henry R. "The American Century." *Life*, February 17, 1941.

Majendie, Paul. "Iraqi Prison Photos Mar U.S. Image." Reuters, April 30, 2004.

Maliniak, Daniel, et al. *The View from the Ivory Tower: TRIP Survey of International Relations Faculty in the United States and Canada*. Williamsburg, Va.: College of William and Mary, 2007.

Mallaby, Sebastian. "Tax Cuts Don't Raise Revenue." *Hartford Courant*, June 21, 2006.

Mandelbaum, Michael. *The Case for Goliath: How America Acts As the World's Government in the 21st Century*. New York: Public Affairs, 2005.

Mann, Thomas E., and Norman J. Ornstein. *The Broken Branch: How Congress Is Failing America and How to Get It Back on Track*. New York: Oxford University Press, 2006.

Markovitz, Andrei. "Western Europe's America Problem." *Chronicle of Higher Education*, January 19, 2007, B6.

Mason, Dana. *Living Peace in the Midst of War: The Experience of the Colombian Peace Communities*. A Bologna Center M.A.I.A. thesis, Johns Hopkins School of Advanced International Studies, 2003.

Mason, David S. *Revolutionary Europe 1789–1989: Liberty, Equality, Solidarity*. Lanham, Md.: Rowman & Littlefield, 2004.

Mason, David S., and James R. Kluegel. *Marketing Democracy: Changing Opinion about Equality and Politics in East Central Europe*. Lanham, Md.: Rowman & Littlefield, 2000.

Mazur, Allen. "Believers and Disbelievers in Evolution." *Politics and the Life Sciences* 23, no. 2 (2005): 55 ff.

Mazzetti, Mark. "Analysis Is Bleak on Iraq's Future." *New York Times*, February 3, 2007.

McCormick, John. *The European Superpower*. New York: Palgrave, 2007.

McEvoy-Levy, Siobhan. *American Exceptionalism and US Foreign Policy*. New York: Palgrave, 2001.

Medalia, Jonathan. *Terrorist Nuclear Attacks on Seaports: Threat and Response*. Congressional Research Service report to Congress, January 2005. http://www.fas.org/irp/crs/RS21293.pdf

Mian, Zia. "A New American Century?" *Foreign Policy in Focus*, May 4, 2005.

"Millions Join Global Anti-war Protests." BBC Online. February 17, 2003. http://news.bbc.co.uk/1/hi/world/europe/2765215.stm#map

Mooney, Chris. *The Republican War on Science*. New York: Basic Books, 2005.

Moyers, Bill. "A Time for Heresy." http://www.tompaine.com/print/a_time_for_heresy.php.

Muhleisen, Martin, and Christopher Towe, eds. *U.S. Fiscal Policies and Priorities for Long-Run Sustainability*. International Monetary Fund. 2004. http://www.imf.org

"NASA's Goals Delete Mention of Home Planet." *New York Times*, July 22, 2006, A1.

A Nation at Risk: The Imperative for Educational Reform. Report by the National Commission on Excellence in Education. Washington, D.C.: National Commission on Excellence in Education, 1983.

National Academy of Sciences. Institute of Medicine. *America's Children: Health Insurance and Access to Care*. Washington, D.C.: National Academy Press, 1998.

National Association of Scholars. *Today's College Students and Yesteryear's High School Grads: A Comparison of General Cultural Knowledge*. 2002. http://www.nas.org/reports.html

National Center for Education Statistics. *National Assessment of Adult Literacy* (conducted in 1992 and 2003). http://nces.ed.gov/NAAL/PDF/2006470.PDF

National Center for Public Policy and Education. *Measuring Up 2006: The National Report Card on Higher Education*. 2006. http://measuringup.highereducation.org/_docs/2006/NationalReport_2006.pdf

National Coalition on Health Care. "Health Insurance Cost." http://www.nchc .org/facts/cost.shtml

National Election Studies. http://www.electionstudies.org/nesguide/gd-index.htm#5

National Endowment for the Arts. *To Read or Not to Read*. Research Report no. 47, November 2007. http://www.nea.gov/research/ToRead.pdf

National Geographic Education Foundation. *National Geographic—Roper 2002 Global Geographic Literacy Survey*. November 2002. http://www.nationalgeographic .com

———. *National Geographic—Roper Public Affairs 2006 Geographic Literacy Study*. May 2006. http://www.nationalgeographic.com

National Priorities Project. "Cost of Iraq War Calculator." http://costofwar.com/ numbers.html

National Science Foundation. "Science and Technology Indicators 2006." http:// www.nsf.gov/statistics/seind06/pdf_v2.htm#c2

Natural Resources Defense Council. "Consequences of Global Warming." http:// www.nrdc.org/globalWarming/fcons.asp

Newport, Frank. "Americans Still Think Iraq Had Weapons of Mass Destruction before War." Gallup News Service, June 16, 2003. http://www.gallup.com

———. "Third of Americans Say Evidence Has Supported Darwin's Evolution Theory." Gallup Poll News Service. November 2004. http://poll.gallup.com

Niebuhr, Reinhold. *The Irony of American History*. New York: Scribner's, 1952.

"Niger Uranium Rumors Wouldn't Die." *Los Angeles Times*, February 17, 2006.

Nye, Joseph S., Jr. *Bound to Lead: The Changing Nature of American Power*. New York: Basic Books, 1990.

———. *The Paradox of American Power*. New York: Oxford University Press, 2002.

———. *Soft Power: The Means to Succeed in World Politics*. New York: Public Affairs, 2004.

Oreskes, Naomi. "The Scientific Consensus on Climate Change." *Science* 306, no. 5702 (2004): 1686.

Organization for Economic Cooperation and Development. http://www.oecd.org

Parenti, Michael. *Democracy for the Few*. 8th ed. Boston: Thomson-Wadsworth, 2008.

Parrott, Sharon. *How Much Do We Spend on "Welfare?"* Washington, D.C.: Center on Budget and Policy Priorities, March 1995.

"Pentagon Approved Tougher Interrogation." *Washington Post*, May 9, 2004.

Peterson, Peter G. *Running on Empty*. New York: Picador, 2005.

Pew Center for the People and the Press. "Public Knowledge of Current Affairs Little Changed by News and Information Revolutions" Report released April 15, 2007. http://people-press.org/reports/display.php3?ReportID=319

Pew Global Attitudes Project. "U.S. Image Up Slightly but Still Negative." June 2005. http://www.pewglobal.org

———. "Bucking the Global Trend, U.S. Popularity Soared in India in '05." 2005. http://www.pewglobal.org

——. *Global Unease with Major World Powers*. Washington, D.C.: Pew Research Center, 2007. http://www.pewglobal.org

Pew Research Center. "A Year after the Iraq War." 2004. http://people-press.org/reports/display.php3?PageID=796

——. "Global Opinion: The Spread of Anti-Americanism." Chapter 7 of *Trends 2005* produced by the Pew Research Center, released January 2005. http://pewglobal.org/commentary/display.php?AnalysisID=104

Phillips, Kevin. *American Theocracy: The Peril and Politics of Radical Religion, Oil and Borrowed Money in the 21st Century*. New York: Viking, 2006.

Pocha, Jehangir. "Eyes Off the Prize." In *These Times*, February 2007, 38–41.

Porter Eduardo. "Step by Step." *New York Times*, April 12, 2005, E1.

"President Claims Power to Disregard 750 Statutes." *Indianapolis Star*, April 20, 2006, A1.

Prestowitz, Clyde. *Three Billion New Capitalists*. New York: Basic Books, 2005.

Priest, Dana, and Glenn Kessler. "Iraq, 9/11 Still Linked by Cheney." *Washington Post*, September 29, 2003.

Program on International Policy Attitudes at the University of Maryland. "In 20 of 23 Countries Polled, Citizens Want Europe to Be More Influential than US." http://worldpublicopinion.org/pipa/articles/home_page

Program on International Policy Attitudes at the University of Maryland and Globescan. "23 Nation Poll: Who Will Lead the World?" Conducted in December 2004. http://www.worldpublicopinion.org

Rebuilding America's Defenses: Strategy, Forces and Resources for a New Century. Report of the Project for the New American Century, September 2000.

Reid, T. R. *The United States of Europe: The New Superpower and the End of American Supremacy*. New York: Penguin, 2005.

"Report: Iraq War Costs Could Top $2 Trillion." *Christian Science Monitor*, January 10, 2006.

Reynie, Dominique. *La Fracture occidentale: Naissance d'une opinion européenne*. Paris: Editions de La Table Ronde, 2004.

Rice, Condoleezza. "Campaign 2000: Promoting the National Interest." *Foreign Affairs*, January/February 2000.

Ricks, Thomas E. *Fiasco: The American Military Adventure in Iraq*. New York: Penguin, 2006.

Rieff, David. "A New Castro?" *New York Times Magazine*, January 28, 2007, 16.

Roberts, Dan. "Is the World Falling Out of Love with US Brands?" *Financial Times* (London), January 5, 2005.

Romano, Lois. "Literacy of College Graduates Is on Decline." *Washington Post*, December 25, 2005, A12.

Rosen, Jeffrey. "Conscience of a Conservative." *New York Times Magazine*, September 9, 2007.

Russell, James W. *Double Standard: Social Policy in Europe and the United States*. Lanham, Md.: Rowman & Littlefield, 2006.

Saad, Lydia. "Americans Still Not Highly Concerned about Global Warming." Gallup Poll News Service, April 7, 2006. http://www.gallup.com

Sadjadpour, Karim. "The Wrong Way to Contain Iran." *International Herald Tribune*, August 3, 2007.

Sands, Philippe. *Lawless World: America and the Making and Breaking of Global Rules from FDR's Atlantic Charter to George W. Bush's Illegal War.* New York: Viking, 2005.

Savage, Charlie. *Takeover: The Return of the Imperial Presidency and the Subversion of American Democracy.* New York: Little, Brown, 2007.

Schemo, Diana. "At 2-Year Colleges, Students Eager but Unready." *New York Times*, September 2, 2006, A1.

Schlesinger, Arthur, Jr. "Good Foreign Policy a Casualty of War." *Los Angeles Times*, March 23, 2003.

Schnabel, Rockwell A., with Francis X. Rocca. *The Next Superpower? The Rise of Europe and Its Challenge to the United States.* Lanham, Md.: Rowman & Littlefield, 2005.

Schwarz, John E., and Thomas J. Volgy. *The Forgotten Americans.* New York: Norton, 1992.

Scowcroft, Brent. "Don't Attack Saddam." *Wall Street Journal*, August 15, 2002.

Sengupta, Somini, and Salman Masood. "Guantanamo Comes to Define U.S. to Muslims." *New York Times*, May 21, 2005.

Shenkar, Oded. *The Chinese Century.* Upper Saddle River, N.J.: Wharton School Publishing, 2006.

Shenon, Philip. "Senators Clash with Nominee about Torture." *New York Times*, October 19, 2007, A1.

"Shoot First—No Questions Asked. " *New York Times*, August 14, 2006, A24 (editorial).

Silkenat, James R., and Mark R. Shulman, eds. *The Imperial Presidency and the Consequences of 9/11.* Westport, Conn.: Praeger, 2007.

Smeeding, Timothy M. *Financial Poverty in Developed Countries: The Evidence from LIS.* Working Paper no. 155, Final Report to the UNDP, April 1997. http://www.lisproject.org

Smith, General Rupert. *The Utility of Force: The Art of War in the Modern World.* New York: Knopf, 2007.

Smith, Tom. *Public Attitudes towards the Regulation of Firearms.* March 2007. http://www-news.uchicago.edu/releases/07/pdf/070410.guns.norc.pdf

Starting Points: Meeting the Needs of Our Youngest Children. Report of the Carnegie Task Force on Meeting the Needs of Young Children. New York: Carnegie Task Force on Meeting the Needs of Young Children, 1994.

"The State of Iraq: An Update," *New York Times*, December 20, 2006.

Stein, Jeff. "Democrats' New Intelligence Chairman Needs a Crash Course on al Qaeda." December 8, 2006. http://www.cq.com

Sullivan, Kevin. "Views on U.S. Drop Sharply in Worldwide Opinion Poll." *Washington Post*, January 23, 2007, A14.

Suskind, Ron. "Faith, Certainty and the Presidency of George W. Bush." *New York Times Magazine*, October 17, 2004.

———. *The One Percent Doctrine*. New York: Simon & Schuster, 2006.

Sweig, Julia. *Friendly Fire: Losing Friends and Making Enemies in the Anti-American Century*. New York: Public Affairs, 2006.

Takeyh, Ray. "Time for Détente with Iran." *Foreign Affairs*, March/April 2007, 24.

"Taxpayers Are Angry. They're Expensive, Too." *New York Times*, November 20, 1994.

Terrill, Ross. "China Is Not Just Rising, but Also Changing." *New York Times*, September 9, 2006, A27.

Terrorism Knowledge Base: http://tkb.org/chwiz4.jsp

Thurow, Lester. "The Rich: Why Their World Might Crumble." *New York Times*, November 19, 1995.

———. "Geared for Slow Growth." *Minneapolis Star Tribune*, April 21, 1996, A27.

Tocqueville, Alexis de. *Democracy in America*. Edited by Richard Heffner. New York: Signet, 2001.

Todd, Emmanuel. *After the Empire: The Breakdown of the American Order*. New York: Columbia University Press, 2003.

Transparency International: http://www.transparency.org

"Twilight for the Enlightenment?" *Science* 308 (April 2005): 165.

Union of Concerned Scientists. "Restoring Scientific Integrity in Policymaking." http://www.ucsusa.org/scientific_integrity/interference/scientists-signon-statement.html

United Nations Development Program. *Human Development Report 2006*. New York: United Nations, 2006.

United Nations Environmental Program. *Planet in Peril*. Arendal, Norway: United Nations, 2006.

UNICEF. *Child Poverty in Rich Nations*. Florence: UNICEF, 2000. http://www.unicef-icdc.org/publications/pdf/repcard1e.pdf

———. *Child Poverty in Rich Countries in 2005*. http://www.unicef.org/brazil/repcard6e.pdf

U.S. Census Bureau. http://www.census.gov.

———. *Income, Poverty and Health Insurance Coverage in the United States: 2006*. Washington, D.C.: U.S. Government Printing Office, 2007. http://www.census.gov

———. "Historical Poverty Tables." http://www.census.gov/hhes/www/poverty/histpov/hstpov2.html

———. *Current Population Survey, Annual Social and Economic Supplements*. http://www.census.gov/hhes/www/income/histinc/f04.html

U.S. Department of Defense. *Measuring Stability and Security in Iraq*. Report to Congress. Washington, D.C., September 2007.

U.S. Department of Justice. "Prison Statistics." December 2006. http://www.ojp
.usdoj.gov/bjs/prisons.htm

U.S. Department of Justice. Bureau of Justice Statistics. "Intimate Partner Violence
in the United States." 2007. http://www.ojp.usdoj.gov/bjs/pub/pdf/ipvus.pdf

"U.S. Rejects Taliban Offer to Try bin Laden." October 7, 2001. http://www.cnn.com

U.S. Senate Judiciary Committee. Children, Violence and the Media. September 1999.
http://judiciary.senate.gov/oldsite/mediavio.htm

Veenhoven, R. Average Happiness in 95 Nations 1995–2005. World Database of Happiness, Rank Report 2006-1d. http://www.worlddatabaseofhappiness.eur.nl

Verba, Sidney, Kay Lehman Schlozman, and Henry E. Brady. Voice and Equality.
Cambridge, Mass.: Harvard University Press, 1995.

Walker, Alice. Excerpts from a commencement address to Naropa University. New
York Times, June 10, 2007, 20.

Walmsley, Roy. World Prison Population List. 6th ed. http://www.kcl.ac.uk/depsta/
rel/icps/world-prison-population-list-2005.pdf

Walt, Stephen. Taming American Power: The Global Response to U.S. Primacy. New
York: Norton, 2005.

"Warriors." America at a Crossroads. PBS, aired April 16, 2007.

Weisman, Jonathan. "Projected Iraq War Costs Soar." Washington Post, April 27,
2006, A16.

White House: http://www.whitehouse.gov

Will, George. "Europe's Suicide?" December 31, 2001. http://www.jewishworldreview
.com/cols/will123101.asp

Woodward, Bob. Bush at War. New York: Simon and Schuster, 2002.

———. State of Denial. New York: Simon and Schuster, 2006.

Woolhandler, Steffie, and David Himmelstein. "Costs of Care and Administration at
For-Profit and Other Hospitals in the United States." New England Journal of Medicine 336 (March 13, 1997): 769–74.

World Bank. World Development Report 2006: Equity and Development. New York: Oxford University Press, 2005.

World Health Organization. World Report on Violence and Health. Geneva: World
Health Organization, 2002.

"World Polls: U.S. Reputation Falls." October 15, 2004. http://www.cbsnews.com/
stories/2004/10/15/world/printable649513.shtml

"World Public Says Iraq War Has Increased Global Terrorist Threat."
http://www.worldopinion.org/incl/printable_version.php?pnt=172

World Trade Organization. "World Trade Developments." http://www.wto.org/
english/res_e/statis_e/its2007_e/its07_world_trade_dev_e.pdf.

"World's Best Medical Care?" New York Times, August 12, 2007 (editorial).

Xiaoyong, Fan. "Quanqiu yi jianli 140 suo kongzi xueyuan" (140 Confucius Colleges
Have Been Established in Different Parts of the World). Fazhi Wanbao 3, no. 26
(2007).

Yankelovich, Daniel. "The Tipping Points." *Foreign Affairs*, May/June 2006.
Young, Jeffrey. "Homework, What Homework?" *Chronicle of Higher Education*, December 6, 2002.
Zakaria, Fareed. "Does the Future Belong to China?" *Newsweek*, May 9, 2005.
———. "The Enemy Within." *New York Times Book Review*, December 17, 2006, 10.
———. "America the Unwelcoming." *Newsweek*, November 26, 2007, 42.

Index

About the Author

David S. Mason is professor of political science at Butler University, where he teaches international and comparative politics and directs and teaches in the university's core curriculum course "Change and Tradition," which addresses major world civilizations at times of transformative change. For many years, he was the director of an international collaborative research effort—the International Social Justice Project—exploring global attitudes on social justice. He has published widely on international politics, European politics and history, revolutions, and public opinion. His recent books include *Social Justice and Political Change: Public Opinion in Capitalist and Post-Communist States* (coedited with James Kluegel and Bernd Wegener) and *Revolutionary Europe, 1789–1989: Liberty, Equality, Solidarity.*

He received his B.A. from Cornell University, his M.A. from the Johns Hopkins School of Advanced International Studies in Bologna, Italy, and Washington, D.C., and his Ph.D. in political science, with a certificate in Russian and East European studies, from Indiana University.